HISTORY'S ASSASSINS

MOTIVES FOR MURDER

DON MANN AND **JEFF EMDE**

Skyhorse Publishing

Skyhorse Publishing books may be purchased in bulk at special discounts for sales promotion, corporate gifts, fund-raising, or educational purposes. Special editions can also be created to specifications. For details, contact the Special Sales Department, Skyhorse Publishing, 307 West 36th Street, 11th Floor, New York, NY 10018 or info@skyhorsepublishing.com.

Skyhorse® and Skyhorse Publishing® are registered trademarks of Skyhorse Publishing, Inc.®, a Delaware corporation.

Visit our website at www.skyhorsepublishing.com.

10 9 8 7 6 5 4 3 2 1

Library of Congress Cataloging-in-Publication Data is available on file.

Cover design by Bar-MD
Cover Image © Jakub Krechowicz / Adobe Stock

Print ISBN: 978-1-5107-6801-7
Ebook ISBN: 978-1-5107-7172-7

Printed in China

Table of Contents

Prologue

Assassination is defined as murder by sudden or secret attack, often for political reasons. What separates assassination from simple murder is the prominence of the victim—a king, politician, or celebrity—and political aspect of the motive. Though the first assassination is lost to history, it likely came shortly after politics was invented. Virtually every ancient and modern culture has experienced it. When it comes to the study of assassinations, historically the focus has been on the victim, and rightfully so. It is their lives that are being ended prematurely, and they are ones with the notoriety. Oftentimes the assassin is but a footnote. In this book, we intend to look equally at both the assassins and their victims.

It is not our purpose to glorify or demonize the assassins but rather to put their actions into perspective. We seek only to shed light on these persons, their backgrounds, and why they thought killing was the best way to achieve their political objectives. For this reason, we chose not to include assassins who acted out of personal malice or vendetta or had apparent mental illness, or assassins for which insufficient historical records exist to reasonably discern their motives.

In most of the cases detailed in this book, the assassinations were the product of political conspiracies with clear political motives. As such, we examined the aftermath of these acts—the short-term and long-term effect of the assassinations—and asked, "Did they achieve the overall political goals of the assassins?" In most cases, we learned they did not. They resulted in more harm than good for the conspirators and their causes. The assassinations detailed in this book are all true, as are the players. Dialogue and some minor characters were fictionalized to make the story more entertaining, but direct quotes, when available, were used, and all events and dates are factual. We hope you find it enlightening.

Chapter 1

Brutus, the Senate, and Caesar
—Nobody Likes a Tyrant

It was late 50 BCE and a year since Gaius Julius Caesar defeated the last organized Gallic force at Uxellodunum. After the battle, he had the hands cut off of every surviving Gallic soldier and then released them as an example of what happened to those who dared challenge Roman rule. Not surprisingly, local resistance was low.

Gaius Julius Caesar

He sat quietly in his tent in southern Gaul, reading and rereading the scroll delivered by courier that morning. It was from the Senate. It ordered him to disband his legions and return to Rome. This was not unexpected news. Provincial governors traditionally served for only one year. Caesar had been serving as governor of Gaul (modern-day France) for over eight years, ever since his one-year term as Consul of Rome expired in 58 BCE.

Caesar had to get special legislation passed—the *lex Vatinia*—granting him governorship of Cisalpine Gaul (northern Italy) and Illyricum (southeastern Europe). While a governor, he was immune from prosecution for crimes committed during his consulship, and he desired this

1

more than the position itself. Fate intervened on his behalf when the governor of Transalpine Gaul (southern France) died and the Senate gave him control of that region as well. Transalpine Gaul came with four Roman legions, each with 4,200 infantry and 300 cavalry. Caesar raised two additional legions on his own, and with these troops he conquered all of Gaul. That made him popular, powerful, and extremely wealthy. He wanted to use his status to run again for Consul of Rome and continue his immunity.

The order came from the Senate, but Caesar had no illusions; the order really came from Gnaeus Pompeius Magnus, Pompey the Great. Pompey was Caesar's former political ally when they, along with Marcus Licinius Crassus, formed the First Triumvirate. It was an unofficial partnership through which they wielded great influence. Pompey was also Caesar's son-in-law, married to his only daughter, Julia. When Julia died in childbirth in 54 BCE, Caesar offered Pompey his great niece Octavia as a new wife to reaffirm their alliance, but Pompey declined. Instead, he

Gnaeus Pompeius Magnus, Pompey the Great

married the daughter of one of Caesar's rivals, a sure sign their old partnership was dead.

Julius Caesar was in a quandary. He needed to run for consul, but if he returned to Rome as a private citizen, his immunity would be void. He feared his political rivals would prosecute him for old crimes, real and imagined. Caesar dragged his feet. If he disbanded his legions, he'd be at the mercy of his rivals. In response to his delay, Pompey accused him of insubordination and treason. As Caesar considered his limited options, a

Marcus Antonius

brash soldier abruptly entered the tent. It was his best general, Marcus Antonius, Mark Antony.

"Caesar, what are your orders? The men are getting antsy."

Caesar smirked. "That's a good question to which I have no answer." He handed the scroll to Antony. "This arrived this morning. I've been ordered by the Senate to disband my legions and return to Rome."

"Senate? Bah, you mean that blustering ass Pompey."

"Undoubtedly. He might as well have signed it himself."

Antony read the scroll. "What's this 'You are explicitly forbidden from taking your legions across the Rubicon' nonsense?"

"Since it is the official boundary of Illyricum, if I were to cross it in force, I'd be invading Rome. That would make me an insurrectionist and a traitor. It would be tantamount to a declaration of war."

"Pompey is an old, fat blowhard. He's bluffing."

Caesar cautioned jokingly, "Careful my friend—Pompey and I are the same age."

"Okay, Pompey is a fat blowhard. I say I go to Rome and shove this scroll up his arse."

Caesar smiled. "Not a pretty picture."

Antony grinned. "Since I was just elected one of the plebian tribunes for next year, I can travel there without issue. Or better yet, we could march on Rome itself. There are no troops between us and them. It'd be easy."

"Well, I don't know about that, but this is a decision not to be made lightly. Pompey may be soft from living on his estates, but he's a fine general. You underestimate him at your peril."

"So says you. I've never seen 'Pompey the general'; I've only seen 'Pompey the fat senator.' And it's not a pretty sight. Your niece Octavia should make sacrifice to the gods every day for not having to marry that pig."

Caesar chuckled. "He'd have you crucified if he heard you talk like that."

"Well, I wouldn't have to worry about him driving in the spikes. I doubt he could even lift a hammer, let alone swing one."

"All hypothetical, my young friend. I don't plan to put him in a position to do anything of the sort. The law is clear. As governor, I'm a promagistrate and only have *imperium*, the right to command troops, in the provinces. Under Roman law, only a consul or a praetor has *imperium* within Italy. If I enter Italy at the head of my legions, I forfeit my *imperium* and can no longer legally command my troops."

Antony snorted, "That's such hypocrisy. Pompey is officially the governor of Spain, is he not? But that law does not apply to him since the lazy bastard is running Spain from Rome. He's already doing what he condemns you for even contemplating. Just give the order. The legions would follow you to the gates of hell itself if you asked them."

"That would make all of us criminals and subject to execution."

Antony grinned. "They can only execute you if you lose. And we wouldn't lose."

"We? I can't ask you to join me in such an endeavor."

"You didn't ask—I volunteered. I'd pay for the chance to stick it to those pompous goats in the Senate." Antony leaned in. "So, general, what are your orders?"

Caesar took a deep breath. "I will not disband my legions. But I don't want to march near Italy with all my army. That would be too provocative. We'll leave four legions here with Gaius Trebonius to secure Belgic Gaul and move the rest to Illyricum. I don't want them so close as to be seen as a provocation, but close enough to be available if we need them. Pompey's legions are in Spain, too far away to be an immediate threat. I'll move south, but with only one legion."

"Who will you take?"

"There is but one choice. My most loyal troops. The Legio XIII Gemina. The Thirteenth Legion."

Caesar's troops broke camp and began moving east. It took a few weeks to cover the distance, but his troops were all disciplined veterans and accustomed to long marches. When they reached Italy, the Thirteenth Legion continued south along the eastern side of the peninsula to avoid the swollen Arno River. In early January 49 BCE, they reached Ravenna,

a town just north of the Rubicon River. To call it a river was being generous. It was only knee deep and a few meters across, but it was the official
boundary between Cisalpine Gaul and Italy proper.

Approaching the stream at the head of his column, Caesar halted and
dismounted his horse. Antony approached and asked, "Well?"

Caesar gazed at the muddy waters. "On the north side of this humble
stream, we are in Cisalpine Gaul where I am still the governor. This is the
limit of my lawful authority. Beyond it lies Italy and Rome. If I cross this,
we are traitors and criminals."

Caesar was wavering. Antony asked, "Your orders, sir?"

Caesar handed Antony a scroll. "Take this to Pompey and the Senate.
It is my last, best offer. I want to avoid bloodshed, but I will do what I
must to defend my rights."

* * *

Marcus Junius Brutus was in his estate going
over paperwork when a servant entered. "Excuse
me, dominus. You have a visitor."

"Who is it?"

"It is your brother-in-law, Senator Cassius."

"Show him in and then leave us."

"Yes, dominus." The little man scurried
away and returned a moment later with Gaius
Cassius Longinus in tow.

"Cassius, what brings you to my home? I
assume my sister isn't mistreating you."

Cassius laughed, "No. Of course not. I bring
news regarding Caesar."

Marcus Junius Brutus

"Oh?"

"*Tribune* Mark Antony has called a meeting of the Senate." His voice
dripped with sarcasm. "He wants to resolve the conflict between Caesar
and Pompey."

Brutus replied, "Well, then we shall hear him out. I would like to resolve this peacefully."

Later that day, the senators of Rome dutifully gathered to receive Caesar's offer. Antony addressed the crowd, "Senators of Rome, I extend you greetings from my commander, General Gaius Julius Caesar. He wishes to resolve the problems straining the relationship with his oldest and dearest friend, the great Pompey Magnus."

Cato, an irascible, old senator famous for his wit and his bile, asked sarcastically, "And what does the great Caesar offer to us humble denizens of the Senate?"

"Caesar and Pompey are both provincial governors with many legions at their disposal. Caesar proposes that both give up their commands and return to life as private citizens. A mutual de-escalation of tensions, if you will."

Many of the senators nodded in agree-   *Cato the Younger*
ment, but Cato and both of the current consuls, Claudius Marcellus and Cornelius Lentulus, loudly disagreed. Lentulus roared, "Preposterous! He is offering us something that he is required by law to do anyway! That's like paying a thief not to steal your goat."

Antony raised his hand to quiet the crowd. "All right, all right. An optional proposal. Caesar will retain two of his eight legions and remain the governor of Illyricum if he is allowed to stand for consulship *in absentia.*"

Pompey had been quiet up to this point. "He only wants to avoid prosecution for his crimes, but I would find such an arrangement acceptable."

Lentulus shouted, "As consul, I do not accept." Cato nodded in agreement. "How dare you dictate terms to us! You insult this august body by your very presence. Tribune or not, I want you out!"

Antony stood firm. "As you so correctly point out, I *am* a tribune of Rome, a position with considerable rights and privileges of its own."

Lentulus motioned to the guards and shouted, "Put this man out!" The guards roughly hustled Antony to the door and tossed him out onto the steps. Fearing they would kill him, Antony fled.

Brutus whispered to Cassius, "Well, that could have gone better. I admire Cato, but he can be a little too fixed in his ways. Caesar's offer was quite reasonable."

Cassius sighed, "Brutus, I know you have a soft spot for Caesar and he for you. I understand that he and your mother, Servilia, have been . . . close for a long time. However, what Caesar is proposing is dangerous. We cannot let one man dictate to the Senate what will and will not be done."

"Yes, I agree. I just wanted to avoid any unnecessary bloodshed. I'm not sure that's possible now."

Cassius replied, "Caesar's political power comes from the Populares, the common rabble. With the fortune he amassed in Gaul, he could easily bribe enough of them to get elected Consul of Rome. We are the Optimates, the elites of Roman society. It is our responsibility to stand up for the traditions of the Republic. Were it left to the common folk, they'd keep chickens in the Senate chambers."

* * *

On January 7, the Senate met again with Cato taking charge. Pompey's silence was interpreted as tacit support. At Cato's urging, the Senate passed a *senatus consultum ulitmum*, a final decree of the Senate, which stripped Caesar of his command and ordered him to come to Rome to be tried for war crimes. If he did not immediately disperse his army, Caesar would be proclaimed a traitor and a public enemy.

* * *

On January 10, Mark Antony rode back into Caesar's camp in Ravenna. He was cold, tired, and dirty.

"Where is he?"

The sentry saluted and then pointed him to a cluster of tents near the top of a low hill. Antony strode up the hill and into Caesar's tent.

Caesar sat up with a start. "Will you ever learn to announce yourself before entering? Heaven forbid I should be indisposed." Antony's only response was an expression of irritation and contempt. "Well, what news have you?"

"They rejected your offer. On top of that, I barely escaped with my hide! I traveled northeast for a ways just to make sure I wasn't being pursued."

"I know. Word arrived from Rome this morning. The Senate, meaning Cato and Pompey, has stripped me of my command and ordered me back to Rome to stand trial."

"Trial? For what?"

Caesar chuckled. "War crimes."

"Since when is winning a war considered a crime? We need to crush these fools."

Caesar sighed. "I must agree with you. I'll not have Cato and Pompey deny me what is mine by right. Do you think the men will follow me? They risk condemning themselves if they do."

"They'll follow you, general. They owe their lives—past, present, and future—to you. If you don't prevail, they know Pompey will never give them the lands they've earned. Just give the word."

"Order the men to break camp and prepare to march . . . south."

Antony grinned wide. "Yes, sir. Oh, one thing. No one kills Cato except me."

The Thirteenth Legion broke camp and got into formation. The infantry was in the front, followed by the cavalry and the supply train. Caesar and Antony rode at the front. As they approached the Rubicon, Caesar halted his mount. The horse snickered as Caesar stared at the muddy stream in front of him. He stood erect in his saddle, spurred his horse, and it took a few steps into the water. Caesar turned to Antony and said, "The die has been cast."

Crossing the Rubicon made Caesar a criminal in Rome, but that didn't mean he had no friends. That night he had dinner with five well-connected Roman politicians. Not everyone was in the Cato/Pompey camp.

* * *

In Rome, Brutus was in his villa. Cato and Pompey's response to Caesar's proposal was harsh. It was as if they were goading him into invasion. A moment later, Servilia entered. "Thinking about Caesar?"

"Uh, yes Mother, I was. I fear Cato and Pompey have forced his hand. What if Caesar decides to march on Rome? Will they kill Caesar?"

"My son, Caesar is very capable. If they try to kill him, they'll find it a difficult task."

"I know you love him, Mother, and so do I. He's been a father to me. I admire him greatly, but if he marches his army to the gates of the city, I cannot abide that. I would have to side with Pompey and the Senate . . . and the law."

"I understand. You're in a difficult position. Whatever happens, remember Caesar has nothing but love and admiration for you."

As she said this, a servant entered. "Dominus, domina, I apologize for interruption. A courier has arrived with a message for dominus."

"Send him in."

A moment later a young man entered. He was out of breath. "Senator." He handed Brutus a scroll.

Breaking the seal, Brutus read the message. He stared at it for a long minute without speaking. Finally, his mother touched his shoulder. "What is it?"

"Caesar and his legions crossed the Rubicon on the tenth and took the town of Ariminum two days later."

"What does this mean?"

"We are at war."

The Senate met that afternoon to discuss the situation. Cato was his usual cantankerous self. "Well, Caesar might as well have nailed himself to the cross. He has declared war on the Republic and must be dealt with accordingly." Placing his hand on Pompey's shoulder, he said, "I move that we appoint Pompey Magnus to defend the Republic from these pirates. All in favor?" There was a roar of "ayes." No one even asked for those opposed. "What do you need from us, Pompey?"

Pompey sat stoically. "Gentlemen, we are in a precarious situation. I have legions, but they are in Spain, and it will take some weeks to bring them here. We have no confirmation as to the size of Caesar's force, but he had eight legions in Gaul. We must assume he has most of them if not all. We've just learned Caesar has taken three more towns on the Flaminian Way. Antony has taken Arretium, so they now control the Cassian Way as well. Rome is effectively cut off from the north."

Cato asked incredulously, "What are you saying?"

"Our position is untenable. We cannot defend the city. We must take what forces we can and move south. We need to stall for time until my troops arrive from Spain. Then I will meet him on the field of battle and crush him." His confidence inspired his fellow senators. No one objected to the plan.

Pompey gathered the local troops and headed south to Capua in southern Italy. The aristocratic Optimates—including Brutus, Cassius, Cato, the consuls, and their supporters—followed him. They abandoned Rome to Caesar without a fight. Little did they know Caesar only had one legion. Pompey and his senatorial forces actually numbered some ten legions. By the time Pompey ordered one of his commanders, Domitius, to stop Caesar, two more of Caesar's legions from Illyricum had arrived on scene along with over thirty-two cohorts of recruits. As each cohort numbered about 480 men, this was equivalent to about three legions. Caesar forced the senatorial army to surrender after a brief siege of Corfinium. He released their commander and the senators with him, and even gave back six million sesterces of captured money for the commander to pay his troops. In return, the three captured legions had to swear allegiance to Caesar before being sent to Sicily.

With the victory, Caesar's army continued to grow. He had three battle-hardened legions, but his volunteers had swollen to fifty-three cohorts.

* * *

Brutus and Cato called on Pompey in his command tent. He leaned over a table studying the map laid out before him. Cato said, "General, might we have a word?"

"Certainly, gentlemen. Do you speak for the Senate?"

Brutus replied, "As much as any two men could, I suppose. What is our situation? What do you propose we do now?"

"Domitius's defeat at Corfinium has put us at a disadvantage. We lost three legions. We have no choice but to move south. I've already sent for ships to meet us at Brundisium."

Brutus was surprised. "Brundisium? If we are going meet your legions in Spain, wouldn't Neapoli be the logical choice?"

"Brundisium is closer. Besides, we're not going to Spain."

Cato asked, "Then where are we going?"

"Epirus in Greece. I have allies there with money and legions. We need money as much as we need men. Those provinces are far richer than Spain."

Brutus asked, "What if Caesar follows?"

"I fully expect him to. In fact I'm counting on it. It will buy us time. He'll have to arrange transport for his legions, but before he can do that, he has to put Rome in order. All that will take time, time we'll use to raise funds and more legions. By the time he gets to Greece, his men will be exhausted, and ours will be fresh."

Brutus wasn't convinced. "I'm not so sure about this. Caesar is in a very strong position."

Pompey snorted, "Not as strong as you think. Just yesterday I received a dispatch from him. He proposed that we both sheath our swords and work together like in the old days of our triumvirate. It is the third time he has proposed such a move. He's desperate."

"Or generous."

Pompey scoffed, "Bah. Brutus, you think too highly of Caesar. I refuse to consider any such agreement. I have the Senate and the consuls.

We are the legitimate authorities of Rome. I will not let a subordinate dictate terms to me. No, we'll go to Greece, raise an army, and I'll destroy him. That is what we will do. Now, if you'll excuse me, I have an army to transport."

As they walked away, Brutus asked, "Cato, do you think his course is a sane one? I mean, what Caesar proposed was not that bad considering he has us outmanned and outmaneuvered. If we go to Brundisium and the ships do not arrive, we'll be trapped on the heel of the Italian boot. Let's not forget, Caesar has Rome and its treasury. When it comes to raising an army—and paying them—he is in a much stronger position."

Cato looked concerned but said, "I trust Pompey. He is a great general. He knows what he is doing."

"For the sake of the Republic, I hope you're right."

*   *   *

As it turns out, Cato was wrong, as was Pompey. Once Pompey and his senatorial allies boarded their ships, Caesar was in sole possession of Italy. Rather than follow them to Greece, Caesar marched west. He laid siege to the city of Massilia (the modern city of Marseille), then under control of the Optimates. Leaving one of his commanders in charge, Caesar took the rest of his army to Spain, where he defeated Pompey's legions stationed there.

Caesar returned to Rome in December of 49 BCE, where he was appointed dictator. In ancient Rome, *dictator* was an official title, a magistrate granted full authority to deal with a military emergency or some other specific duty. All the other magistrates were subordinate to him and the tribunes had very limited veto authority over him. Caesar only wanted to be dictator long enough to run for one of the two consul positions. When he won his election for consul, he promptly resigned as dictator after only eleven days.

Pompey was able to rebuild his forces and amassed a navy superior to that of Caesar. Pompey, ever cautious, was weighing his options when Caesar forced his hand by pursuing Pompey into Illyria (modern day Albania). On July 10, 48 BCE, they fought a battle at Dyrrachium. Caesar lost over a thousand of his veteran legionaries and had to retreat. Thinking it was a trap, Pompey didn't pursue him. Caesar commented, "Today the victory had been the enemy's, had there been anyone among them to gain it." Caesar was able to slip away and regroup. In Pompey's camp, the mood was mixed.

Pompey Magnus was pleased. "We really stung Caesar today. He lost hundreds of his best troops. He was lucky to escape with his skin!"

Brutus nodded. "Yes General, the gods were definitely smiling on us today. Congratulations. I have but one question. Why did you not pursue him aggressively? Why not strike the fatal blow while his troops are bloodied and in disarray?"

"Brutus, I can see why you are a senator and not a general. You'd best leave the military thinking to me."

Brutus boiled at the man's arrogance, but the situation called for diplomacy. "You'll forgive me, general. Of course, I don't mean to second-guess your decisions. Maybe you could educate me on such things."

"Certainly, my boy. You see, I know Caesar, probably better than he knows himself. He is a master of the feint. He excels in drawing his opponents into elaborate traps. He did it to the Gaul, Vercingetorix, at Alesia. I'm sure he is out there right now trying to figure out why we didn't stumble into the snare he set for us."

"But General, you said it yourself: he lost hundreds of his best troops today. Certainly you're not suggesting he sacrificed them for bait?"

"I wouldn't put it past him. He's as ruthless as he is clever."

"Whatever the reason, his forces are depleted. It seems now would be the time to force a decisive battle, before he has time to regroup or gather reinforcements. I was talking to Cato and the other senators and they agree that—"

Pompey Magnus was growing impatient with the impertinent young senator. "Posh! What does the Senate know about waging war? Let me do my job without all your second-guessing!"

Brutus shook his head and left. He'd known Caesar his entire life. Pompey was wrong. The two armies shadowed each other for the next month. Pompey was loath to engage Caesar's troops. Instead, he hoped to hem them in and starve them into submission.

After a month, Pompey became impatient and met Caesar's forces in Pharsalus. With his future sitting on a knife's edge, Julius Caesar was still concerned about his young friend and protégé, Brutus. Before the battle, he gathered his officers. "Gentlemen, I expect nothing less than a great victory today. The enemy has underestimated us at their peril. Among their group is Senator Marcus Junius Brutus. My orders to you are that he is not to be injured. If he surrenders himself, you are to take him prisoner and treat him with respect. If he fights capture, leave him alone and do not harm him."

A centurion asked, "General, are you saying that if he refuses to surrender, we are to let him go?"

"Yes. That is exactly what I am saying. Do you understand?"

The men replied in unison, "Aye, sir."

After Caesar left, one of the centurions pulled Mark Antony aside. "General Antony, may I ask a question?"

"Certainly."

Speaking in a low voice, the man asked, "What is it with Caesar and Brutus? Is there more to their . . . relationship?"

Antony smiled. "It's not like that. Caesar and Brutus's mother have been lovers for years. There was even talk the old man might actually be Brutus's father. I don't believe it, personally, but you never know. For whatever reason, Caesar thinks of Brutus as the son he never had. My suggestion to you is, if you encounter Brutus on your sector of the battlefield, make sure he lives."

Despite being outnumbered almost two-to-one, Caesar's confidence was not misplaced. His army scored a massive victory. Pompey's forces were routed, and Pompey fled the field, leaving his remaining troops to fend for themselves. Caesar's troops took Pompey's camp; the old general barely escaped with his life. Caesar's report indicated he lost only two hundred troops and thirty centurions. Pompey lost over six thousand soldiers, and most of the survivors surrendered. Pompey escaped and headed for Egypt. Brutus was captured.

Caesar was jubilant. He scored a decisive victory over his Optimates rivals. While Pompey, Cato, and others were still on the loose, they were no longer a military threat. As Caesar relaxed in his tent writing his account of the battle, a centurion entered. "General, I have word of Senator Brutus."

Caesar dropped his pen. "And?"

"He was captured, sir. He is alive and unhurt. He wrote you a letter and asked that I deliver it to you."

"Give it to me!" The man handed Caesar the parchment. Brutus surrendered himself to Caesar and accepted whatever punishment he saw fit. He also apologized for opposing Caesar, stating that his loyalties were to Rome and the Senate, not to Pompey. "Bring him here immediately!"

Brutus was shown into Caesar's tent. He was dirty and tired. His legs were muddied to the knees and his tunic smeared with blood. Caesar exclaimed, "Your tunic! Are you all right? I was told you were uninjured!"

Brutus looked down at his clothes. "Oh, that. No. It's not mine. I was trying to help a wounded centurion when I was captured. You received my letter?"

"Yes, most gracious of you. Please sit. Have some wine and something to eat. You look starved."

"Thank you, general. You're most kind."

"Bah, forget the formalities. I've been out of touch with Rome these past few months. Any word on your mother? She'll be thrilled you're unhurt."

Brutus was befuddled by his reception. "Uh, she was well, last I heard from her." A slave entered the room with a large platter of fresh fruit, cheese, and bread.

Caesar snapped his fingers. "Cipius, fetch a clean tunic for Senator Brutus. Take one from my luggage." Caesar picked up a grape and popped it in his mouth. "This is from Pompey's personal kitchen. The grapes are excellent . . . but then you must know that." He poured a cup of wine and handed it to his confused guest.

"Uh, General . . . excuse me, Caesar. I don't understand."

"Brutus, we're old friends. We shouldn't let politics get in the way of that. I was only asserting my rights as a citizen, and you've apologized for opposing me. It's all water under the bridge. We need to get back home and put all things in order. I'll need smart men like you to help me do it."

* * *

Brutus returned to Rome without penalty for having opposed Caesar. Pompey fled to Egypt expecting help from King Ptolemy XIII, the boy king of Egypt who owed a debt to Pompey for help provided to his father, Ptolemy XII. When Pompey arrived, he was murdered. Pursuing him, Caesar arrived shortly after. He was presented Pompey's head as a gift. Enraged, Caesar had those involved in Pompey's murder killed.

Cato escaped as well. Rather than flee to Egypt with Pompey, he left for Africa with former consul, senatorial general, and fellow Optimate Metellus Scipio. Scipio committed suicide after Caesar defeated him at the Battle of Thapsus in North Africa in 46 BCE. Cato wasn't at the battle, but nearby in Utica. After hearing of Caesar's victory, he disemboweled himself rather than allow Caesar to pardon him. Upon hearing the news, Caesar said, "Cato, I grudge you your death, as you would have grudged me the preservation of your life." With the leaders of the senatorial faction dead or surrendered, Caesar was firmly in charge in Rome.

* * *

By March 45 BCE, Caesar's Civil War was over. Caesar defeated the last of his enemies' armies, led by Pompey's son, Gnaeus. Brutus was back in Rome and once again a senator representing the conservative Optimates political faction. Most of the senators who opposed Caesar were back as well. The senatorial military commanders who died were killed in battle like Gnaeus Pompey, committed suicide like Cato, or, like Pompey Magnus, were murdered by people unaffiliated with Caesar. Caesar advocated reconciliation with his enemies rather than punishment. He appointed Brutus governor of Cisalpine Gaul for 47–45 BCE, one of the provinces that made Caesar among the wealthiest men in Rome. Caesar was definitely not settling old scores.

In 46 BCE Caesar was elected to one of two annual Consul of Rome positions, with the other going Marcus Aemilius Lepidus. The next year Caesar was again elected consul; this time it was *sine collega*, without a colleague. That was against Rome's constitution, but no one was in a position to argue. Caesar shared his power with no one.

Caesar had three stated goals for his stewardship of Rome. First, he wanted to restore order and end armed resistance. He did this when he defeated Pompey and his allies in the civil war. His other goals were to create a strong central government and blend all the provinces into a single, unitary nation—a Roman Empire. To do this, he needed complete control over the Roman government. He increased his authority and decreased that of other institutions, including the Senate.

Caesar threw extravagant games to celebrate his victories, but afterward got to work on reforms. He ordered a census, which saved the government money by reducing the grain dole. He declared that jurors should come only from Senate and equestrian ranks. He passed a law restricting the purchases of luxury goods. Recognizing that Italy needed to be repopulated, he subsidized families for having many children. He enacted term limits for governors and restructured debts, which eliminated about a quarter of all debt. While the Optimates boiled, the common folk were ecstatic.

His biggest reform was the calendar. Rome used a lunar-based calendar, which was not very practical, especially for farmers trying to determine when to plant their crops. When he was in Egypt, Caesar was introduced to a solar-based calendar, which he then adopted for Rome. He set the length of a year to 365.25 days, with a leap day added to February every four years, and added two months. This is the same system we use today, and it is why the month of July is named in honor of Julius Caesar.

Caesar was aligned with the Populares political faction, which supported the plebeians—the common people. To push through his agenda, he had to contend with the elitist Optimates, which included Brutus and Cassius. Since entering Rome in 49 BCE, he steadily chipped away at the authority of those who opposed him. In 48 BCE he was given permanent tribunician authority that allowed him to veto the Senate. On the rare occasion someone challenged him, they were removed from office. In 47 BCE he used his power as *censor* to appoint scores of new senators. These new senators were aligned with him and the Populares movement, which diluted influence and prestige of the aristocratic Optimates.

In 48 BCE Julius Caesar was appointed dictator for a year, ostensibly to settle the dynastic succession issues in Egypt between Caesar's lover Cleopatra and her brother, Ptolomy XIII. Two years later he was appointed dictator again, only this time for a period of ten years. His ability to act unilaterally with no check on his authority was becoming an issue for the Senate, especially the older, established Optimates faction. In late 46 BCE Cleopatra came to Rome, where she was feted and put up in Caesar's villa. By late 45 BCE Caesar was preparing for another war. This time it was against the Parthian Empire, which spanned modern-day Iraq and Iran. Since such a war would take him away from Rome for a long time, he passed a law that authorized him to appoint all magistrates, consuls, and tribunes. They would no longer be representatives of the people; they would be representatives of Julius Caesar.

* * *

Brutus's term as governor of Cisalpine Gaul ended in 45 BCE. Upon his return to Rome, Caesar nominated him for the position of *praetor urbanus*, or urban praetor, for the following year. The urban praetor presided over civil cases between citizens, defended the city if attacked, and in the absence of the consuls, was the senior magistrate in the city.

Despite the honor Caesar bestowed on him, Brutus was still torn over their relationship. Caesar had always been generous with Brutus, even after he sided with Caesar's enemies during the civil war. Maybe the rumors that Caesar was his real father were true. Maybe it was Caesar's yearslong affair with Brutus's mother, Servilia. Brutus simply could not reconcile his affection for Caesar with the man's increasingly tyrannical actions.

As Brutus sat at his desk, Servilia entered the room. "You look deep in thought, my son."

"I am. I'm in a quandary."

"Oh? About what?"

"Caesar. He has seen fit to nominate me for urban praetor. And if Caesar wills it, it will be done."

Her mood changed instantly. Though she and Caesar had been lovers for many years, they'd recently had a falling out. Upon his return to Rome, he refused to divorce his wife, Calpurnia. Then Cleopatra showed up in late 46 BCE and moved into his villa. Rumors were swirling that the son the Egyptian queen left behind in Alexandria was Caesar's. She even named him Caesarian. "That man is a disgrace. He brought that Egyptian whore to Rome and moved her into his villa. His wife is humiliated. I'm surprised Cleopatra didn't drag along that little bastard son of hers."

Brutus suppressed a smirk. This was a sore subject for his mother. "Uh, that 'whore' is the Queen of Egypt and the ruler of one of our most important client states. Chances are, the bread you ate this morning was from wheat grown along the Nile."

"Be that as it may, it is an affront to Calpurnia."

"Would this be the same Calpurnia whose husband you slept with for years and asked him to divorce so he could marry you?"

"Don't you dare disrespect me! I've known Caesar longer than her. Longer than almost anyone!"

"I'm sorry, Mother. It's just—" Brutus was relieved when a servant meekly entered the room. *Oh, thank god.* "Yes, what is it?"

"Excuse me, dominus, but your brother-in-law, Senator Cassius, is here."

Jumping up, Brutus said, "Show him in."

Servilia just shot him a dirty look. Cassius walked in and turned to make sure the servant left before he spoke. "I suppose you've heard the news?"

"Depends. What news are you referring to?"

"Caesar, of course."

"Of course. What is it now?"

"He is setting himself up to be declared king, that's what."

"Does this have to do with him not standing when he received the senatorial delegation at the Temple of Venus Genetrix?"

"They were bestowing great honors on him and he laughed in their faces! That's unconscionable! He has a total disdain for the Senate. But no."

"So, are you talking about the diadem tribunes Marullus and Flavus claim they found on Caesar's statue in the Forum? A crown on a statue does not a king make. Besides, anyone could have put that there just to smear him."

Cassius was growing frustrated. "Or he put it there to test the waters before declaring himself king. You think I'm overreacting, but the other day he was riding on the Appian Way and the crowd called him *rex.* They called him 'king!' He did nothing to correct them. He said, 'I am not rex, but Caesar.'"

"If that's not a correction . . ."

Cassius ignored Brutus's comment. "When Marullus and Flavus had the man who first shouted 'rex' arrested, Caesar accused them of stirring up trouble."

Returning to the papers on his desk, Brutus mumbled, "A fair assessment, I'd say."

"Caesar has revoked their tribuneships and their membership in the Senate! The man is out of control."

Brutus now looked Cassius in the eye. "That was an extreme response, I'll grant you. It's not right for him to simply remove senators with whom he disagrees."

"He's been doing it for years! Get your head out of the sand. You need to put aside your personal affection and recognize the man is a tyrant!"

"Cassius, you need to calm down. I do not agree with him on most things but the plebes love him. They will side with him in any conflict. So what were you referring to when you first walked in?"

"At the festival of Lupercalia, Mark Antony climbed on the Rostra and placed a diadem on Caesar's head and said, 'The people give this to you through me.' When the crowd was mostly quiet, Caesar took it off but Antony put it back."

Now interested, Brutus asked, "What happened then?"

"The crowd's response was still not positive, so Caesar took it off and set it aside. He said, 'Jupiter alone of the Romans is king.' The crowd cheered this, but I swear the man is trying that crown on for size. He wants to be king. He must be stopped."

Brutus smirked, "What do you propose? Murder him?"

"Yes."

Brutus lowered his voice. "Just speaking such things could get you crucified."

"How many indignities must Rome suffer before you'll act?"

"Apparently, at least one more." He leaned back. "I sided with Pompey and Cato against him and instead of killing me or forcing me into exile, he made me the governor of Cisalpine Gaul. He has been nothing but generous to me. I will not contemplate doing him harm."

"Well, if one more is what you require, I have it."

Brutus was confounded and more than a little scared. "What? What has he done?"

Cassius took a deep breath. "He has declared himself *dictator perpetuo*, dictator for life."

Brutus gasped. "Oh, good god. A king by any other name is still a king. You're right. We must stop him."

* * *

The plot against Caesar came together quickly. With Caesar's long-time friend Brutus as the face of conspiracy, others quickly joined, but the leaders were careful whom they selected. Since the death of Cato, Marcus Tullius Ciciero was probably the most influential senator and member of the Optimates faction. He was a prolific writer, scholar, and philosopher as well as a skilled orator. He supported Pompey in the recent civil war but was cautious. He fled the city but made a concerted effort not to alienate Caesar. After the Battle of Pharsalus, he pragmatically declined to take command of the remnants of Pompey's army and continue the war. As a result, the victorious Caesar pardoned him. While the conspirators were certain of his moral support, they felt his excess of caution could be a fatal delay in a plot that required swift action. Cicero was excluded.

One of the first men they approached was Quintus Antistius Labeo, a noted legal scholar. Brutus asked, "Labeo, is it wise for a man to put himself in danger if it means overcoming evil or foolish men?"

When Labeo responded "Yes," Brutus had him.

On March 7, 44 BCE, Labeo and Cassius then approached Decimus Junius Brutus, a distant cousin of Marcus Brutus. He was a general and politician who supported Caesar during the Gallic Wars and the war against Pompey. Caesar had appointed Decimus *praetor peregrinus,* a judge who administers justice among foreigners. Despite his closeness to Caesar (he was Caesar's second heir in his will), he too was disturbed by Caesar's efforts to consolidate all power.

Another recruit was Gaius Trebonius, one of Caesar's trusted generals and the man who secured northern Gaul while Caesar marched on Rome in 49 BCE. Caesar appointed him consul in October 45 BCE to complete the term of the previous consul who died. Trebonius called Caesar out for disrespecting the senatorial delegation at the Temple of Venus Genetrix, and Caesar was none too pleased. Cicero later wrote that Trebonius preferred the liberty of Romans over his friendship with Caesar.

Lucius Tillius Cimber was an ambitious Roman senator who joined the plot despite his recent appointment by Caesar as governor of the lucrative provinces of Bithynia and Pontus on the southern coast of the Black Sea. Another disgruntled acolyte convinced to betray Caesar was Lucius

Minucius Basilus, who served Caesar in Gaul. He was angry that, after his term as praetor, Caesar did not give him a province to govern.

The brothers Gaius and Publius Servilius Casca also sided with Brutus. Their family was loyal to Caesar, and Publius was a tribune of the Plebes. Their motives for joining the plot are not known. Pontius Aquila also served as tribune of the Plebes in 45 BCE. He and Caesar were feuding ever since Aquila refused to stand as Caesar's procession passed by during one of his triumphs. An irritated Caesar shouted, "Come then Aquila, take back the Republic from me, you tribune!" For the next several days, Caesar wouldn't make a decision without adding, "That is, if Pontius Aquila will allow me."

The conspirators considered approaching Caesar's trusted subordinate, Mark Antony. Someone suggested, "We could approach Antony. He is seen as Caesar's loyal man, but there is tension there. He owes his very existence to Caesar but he does not think so. He is a very ambitious man."

Another added, "As consul, Antony would become the most powerful man in Rome should something befall Caesar. That would certainly appeal to him." Many voices echoed this assessment.

Brutus and Cassius looked at each other. Cassius commented, "It would certainly simplify things. He could definitely keep the army in check, and no general would dare challenge him. Okay, who should do it? Who should talk to him?"

Before anyone could step forward, Trebonius spoke up. "That would not be a good idea."

Brutus asked, "Why not?"

"I approached Antony last year. There was another plot to get rid of Caesar. I will not name names, but it was being seriously considered. I asked Antony if he would consider joining the plot; he turned me down flat. That said, I assume he never told Caesar."

Cassius asked, "How can you be so sure?"

"I'm still breathing."

"Ah."

Brutus said, "Well, I'd say that precludes Antony."

Aquilla asked, "But what to do about him? He is consul and very popular with the army. If he isn't going to be part of our conspiracy, he is a potential impediment to it. You said it yourself, he would become the most powerful man in Rome, and he'll not be happy with us for killing his patron. He'll have to die too."

This issue created a rift among the men. Quintus Labeo spoke for the Optimates. "If we want to return to the days of the Republic, the days before Caesar, logic would dictate that we eliminate not just Caesar but all his men, and we rescind all his reforms."

Basilus objected. "I have no quarrel with Caesar's men. I fought with many of them. They should not be punished for his crimes. I also take issue with rolling back his reforms. They are very popular with the people, and we'll need their support." The other men who served under Caesar supported Basilus's position. He added, "I do agree, however, that Antony needs to die. He's too loyal and too powerful. If the army sides with him, and I think they will, he'll be uncontrollable."

Everyone nodded in agreement except Brutus who, in effect, saved Antony's life. "Gentlemen, we should only kill Caesar and no one else."

Cassius asked, "And why is that?"

"Killing a tyrant like Caesar is in accordance with principles of justice and the law. To kill Antony or any of his supporters would be viewed by the people as a political purge, revenge by Pompey's supporters. By preserving Caesar's popular reforms, we'll retain the support of the people and the army. To do otherwise, we risk losing the city moments after we save it."

Cassius and Labeo contemplated what he said. Labeo agreed. "Brutus is right. We need to be seen as stopping a tyrant. Even Caesar's supporters have been given pause by his recent ambitions. If we limit our action to him and him alone, they will see it as what it is—tyrannicide, not unlike what Brutus's distinguished ancestors did when they overthrew Tarquinius Superbus more than four centuries ago."

Brutus asked the group, "Then it's decided?" The others nodded in assent.

The men began seriously plotting Caesar's assassination. They knew if he found out, he would have them killed. For that reason, they limited the number of people who knew of their plan. They only met in small groups in their homes, never in the Senate or any other public building. Despite their precautions, there were rumors in Rome that a plot against the dictator was afoot. They needed to act before details got out and they were undone.

Several ideas were floated. They agreed the murder should be public to have maximum impact. Someone suggested they kill him as he walked on the Via Sacra, the most important street in the city. Another offered they might throw him from a bridge to assassins waiting in the water below. An attack at a gladiatorial game was recommended, noting armed men would not be out of place.

Finally, someone brought up an inconvenient fact. "Caesar may not have bodyguards, but he has asked his friends to protect him in public. These 'friends' usually include some capable former soldiers who are rather . . . intimidating. We're not young men, and most of us have limited combat experience. To engage these men might lead to our deaths, not Caesar's."

Tillius Cimber spoke, "The one place these 'friends' are not allowed is the Senate. Only senators are allowed in Senate chambers. Doing it there would send a message to the people that the Senate removed the tyrant."

Cassius smiled. "I like it. We have the where. Now we need the when, and it needs to be soon. Caesar is scheduled to depart Rome on March 18 for his military campaign against the Parthians."

Brutus shrugged. "The last meeting of the Senate before his departure is on March 15."

Gaius Casca said, "Then it will be the Ides of March. The day of Rome's liberation."

* * *

The Ides of March was a deadline used to settle debts, and the entire

Senate would meet. The Forum, where senators usually gathered, was being renovated, so they met at the Senate House of Pompey, a part of the Theater of Pompey completed some nine years before. The main theater was hosting gladiatorial games, and Decimus Brutus, who owned a stable of gladiators, stationed some of them in the portico. If a battle broke out, the gladiators would protect the conspirators. They could also block the entrance of the Senate House to prevent anyone coming to Caesar's aid.

They waited impatiently for Caesar to arrive, but he was late. The night before, his wife, Calpurnia, had a nightmare in which he was murdered. This came on top of a warning days earlier from a seer named Spurinna. He told Caesar to "beware the Ides of March." Calpurnia begged him not to go to the Senate and, while not superstitious, he decided to acquiesce. He sent Mark Antony to dismiss the Senate. After Brutus and the others learned of this, Decimus Brutus went to Caesar's home to change his mind. When he learned why Caesar chose not to go, Decimus teased him. "What do you say, Caesar? Will someone of your stature pay attention to a woman's dreams and the omens of foolish men?" Embarrassed, Caesar changed his mind.

As Caesar walked to the Senate with Antony, he encountered the seer and called out to him good-naturedly, "Well, the Ides of March have come!" Spurinna replied, "Aye, the Ides have come but they are not yet gone." As they walked up the steps to the Senate House, Trebonius intercepted Antony. "Excuse me, Tribune. Might I have a brief word?"

Caesar walked in alone toward his chair. As he was about to sit, Lucius Tillius Cimber presented him with a petition asking that his brother be allowed to return from exile. The other plotters gathered around to vocalize their support for the petition. Caesar had no time for such nonsense and waved Cimber away. When he did, Cimber grabbed his shoulder and pulled down his toga. Caesar was irked and snapped, "Why, this is violence!" Publius Casca pulled his dagger and stabbed at Caesar's neck but the dictator turned quickly and grabbed Casca's arm. Caesar was shocked. "Casca, you villain, what are you doing?"

Publius panicked. He yelled to Gaius, "Help, brother!"

Death of Caesar by Vincenzo Camuccini *(1804)*

Seconds later, Brutus and the rest of the conspirators descended on Caesar, stabbing him repeatedly. Caesar spun from his assailants and tried to run, but blinded by the blood in his eyes, he tripped and fell to the floor while they kept stabbing. Caesar was shocked Brutus was one of his attackers. "Et tu, Bruté?" ("You too, Brutus?") Consigned to his fate, he covered his head with his toga. He was stabbed twenty-three times, but there was only one fatal wound—a thrust to his chest that pierced his aorta. He bled to death on the floor of the Senate House.

Brutus, his dagger still in his hand, stood to address the Senate, the vast majority of which were not party to the conspiracy. He never got to speak. The unwitting senators fled the building in a panic. Brutus and the other conspirators decided to march through the city shouting, "People of Rome, we are once again free!" They were met with dead silence—not the reception they expected. Fearing they'd grossly misjudged the situation, the conspirators fled. Meanwhile, Caesar's body lay in a bloody heap on the marble floor of the Senate House. After a few hours, three slaves loaded his corpse on a litter and carried it to his house.

* * *

The reaction to Caesar's assassination was swift. The public was outraged.

A wax statue of Caesar—complete with twenty-three stab wounds—was erected in the forum. A mob started a fire that damaged the Forum and destroyed nearby buildings. Antony, detained by Trebonius, had been outside during the assassination. He immediately fled, assuming his life was in danger too. Two days later, after determining his head was not on the chopping block, Antony called a meeting of the Senate and hammered out a compromise whereby the assassins would not be punished in exchange for all of Caesar's appointments remaining valid.

Antony took full political advantage of the public outrage over Caesar's murder. He stirred up the plebes to the point that, though officially pardoned, most of the conspirators fled Rome in fear of their safety. Brutus moved to Crete and Decimus Brutus left for Cisalpine Gaul to take up his governorship. Antony directed the public animus against all the Optimates with an eye toward taking over the city for himself. As consul and Caesar's top subordinate, he was the obvious choice to rule Rome. But Caesar himself threw a monkey wrench into Antony's grand plans—from the grave.

Caesar, with no legitimate children of his own, named his great nephew, eighteen-year-old Gaius Octavius, a.k.a. Octavian, his heir. Young Octavian instantly became one of the richest citizens of the Republic. In addition, Caesar adopted the young man posthumously. With the adoption came Caesar's name and Octavian became Gaius Julius Caesar Octavianus, the son of Caesar. As Caesar's son, he also inherited the loyalty of the plebes.

Gaius Octavius, Octavian— later Caesar Augustus

The great orator, Cicero, became the de facto head of the Senate. He was not directly involved in the assassination, although he did support its objectives. In the wake of Caesar's death, Cicero and Antony were the two most important men in Rome. They were also on opposite sides of the political spectrum, and they hated each other. Antony made a number of missteps that turned

public opinion against him. When his consulship expired, he passed legislation naming him
governor of Cisalpine Gaul—a position already
occupied by Decimus Brutus, one of the assassins. He'd have to fight for his seat.

Octavian, it turned out, had considerable
political skills of his own. While Antony fought
Decimus Brutus for Cisalpine Gaul, young
Octavian consolidated and strengthened his
position in Rome. He also raised a private army,
funded with his dead father's money. Cicero

Marcus Tullius Cicero

and the other senior men of the Senate assumed the tyro would be easy
to manipulate. Cicero had him admitted to the Senate in January 43
BCE and tried to play Antony and Octavian off one another. Fighting
soon broke out between Antony and Decimus. When Antony ignored the
Senate's order to cease hostilities, Octavian and the two new consuls of
Rome took Octavian's army to fight Antony. Octavian's forces won, and
Antony fled into Transalpine Gaul, but both consuls died in the battle,
leaving Octavian in sole charge of the army and with sole credit for the
victory.

The Senate tried to give Decimus Brutus command of Octavian's
legions but Octavian wasn't having it. He sent emissaries to Rome to
demand that he and a relative be elected consuls. When the Senate refused,
he marched on Rome with eight legions. On August 19, 43 BCE, a little
more than a month shy of his twentieth birthday, Octavian was sworn in
as consul of Rome. He was the most powerful man in the empire. One
of his first moves was to rescind Antony's pardon for Caesar's killers. He
declared them murderers and enemies of the state.

Cicero thought he could handle young Octavian, but he misjudged
badly. When Antony combined forces with Marcus Aemilius Lepidus,
one of Caesar's closest allies, the Senate sent Octavian to confront them.
But instead of fighting, Octavian, Antony, and Lepidus formed a partnership—the Second Triumvirate. Its goal was the destruction of Brutus,

Cassius, and the other assassins who now called themselves the Liberators or simply the Republicans. Since fleeing Rome after the assassination, the Liberators had taken control of all the eastern provinces from Greece to Syria. The triumvirate now wanted to secure control of the entire Roman Empire and avenge Caesar's murder.

Whereas Caesar tried to reconcile with his enemies after the civil war, the Second Triumvirate wanted none of it. They opted instead for proscriptions. They went after the conspirators, their supporters, and their families. Men were killed, families exiled, and estates seized and sold to fund more legions. Upwards of three hundred senators and two thousand equestrians were proscribed.

Old political enemies were also added to the lists. Lepidus proscribed his own brother and Antony his uncle. However, Cicero sat at the top of Antony's proscription list and Octavian did nothing to spare his old ally. Forced into hiding and hunted for months, Cicero was finally captured and executed by two of Antony's soldiers. On Antony's orders, Cicero's hands were severed and his head chopped off. His hands were nailed to the doors of the Forum and his head put on display.

On January 1, 43 BCE, Julius Caesar was formally recognized by the Senate as *Divus Julius*, a divinity of the Roman state. This also made Octavian *Divi Filius*, "Son of the Divine," a convenient title for a man with political ambitions. Octavian and Antony set sail for Greece with twenty-eight legions to face the armies of Brutus and Cassius.

The two armies met in Greece and fought two battles in Macedonia at Philippi. The engagements were fought on a grand scale with each side fielding over one hundred thousand men. In the first battle on October 3, Brutus drove back Octavian's forces, while Antony got the better of Cassius. The battlefield was large and dusty, so one side could not see what was happening on the other. Cassius mistakenly believed Brutus was routed and the battle was lost. He had a servant kill him with a sword rather than be captured. Both armies reformed, but the loss of Cassius was devastating. Brutus was not as skilled a commander as his now dead brother-in-law.

The loss of Cassius also hurt morale among the Republican troops, and after three weeks of maneuvering, Brutus's army was starting to falter. Octavian and Antony's forces kept stretching the line, and Brutus's front got thinner and thinner. When his allies started deserting, he had to fight. On October 23, 42 BCE, the battle came, an extremely bloody, close-combat affair with thousands killed. The center of the Republican line failed, and Brutus was routed. He fled to the hills with only four of his seventeen legions. Defeated, he refused to be captured. He resigned himself to suicide, but not before calling down a curse on Antony, saying, "Forget not, Zeus, the author of all these crimes." He then had two of his men hold his sword while he ran onto it. His last words were, "By all means must we fly; not with our feet, however, but with our hands." When Antony's men recovered Brutus's body, he had it wrapped in Antony's most expensive purple cloak as a sign of respect. Antony did not forget that it was Brutus who had argued against his death when plotting Caesar's murder. His body was cremated and his ashes sent to his mother. Upon learning of his death, his wife committed suicide. The Republic of Rome died with Brutus just as it was born with his ancestor.

Aftermath

After the Battles of Philippi, Lepidus was marginalized, and Octavian and Antony essentially split the empire between them as their alliance grew strained over time. Antony took up with Cleopatra, and when he declared their children to be kings of Roman provinces, hostilities broke out between Antony and Octavian. After a prolonged war, Octavian was victorious when his troops defeated the combined forces of Antony and Cleopatra at Actium in 31 BCE. The following year he invaded Egypt, and with nowhere left to go, Antony and Cleopatra committed suicide in 30 BCE, leaving Octavian the sole ruler of the Roman Empire at the age of thirty-three.

For the next three years, he worked to stabilize the chaotic empire. In 27 BCE, Octavian became consul. He publicly returned power to the Senate and relinquished his control of the provinces and their armies, although no one doubted that Octavian and Octavian alone was in charge. It was the start of the *principate*, the reign of a single emperor, and it would last for 311 years. Octavian became the first emperor and changed his name to Caesar Augustus. He ruled Rome for the next forty years, and when he died he was replaced by another emperor, his adopted son Tiberius. The conspirators' actions and Caesar's assassination had been for naught.

Like the Senate, the conspirators and their supporters did not fare well in the aftermath of Caesar's assassination. Cassius and Brutus both committed suicide after being defeated in battle. But what of the others?

Quintus Antistius Labeo, the legal scholar brought in to the conspiracy early, was present at the Battle of Philippi on Brutus's side. After the defeat, he was unwilling to survive Brutus. Inside his tent, Labeo dug a hole the length of his body. He calmly settled his affairs, and sent messages to his wife and children. He took the hand of his most faithful slave and turned him round—a part of the ceremony by which a slave was freed. Labeo gave the now ex-slave his sword and presented his throat. The ex-slave killed his master and buried him in the hole he had dug.

Decimus Junius Brutus was initially made governor of Cisalpine Gaul. With Cicero's support he crossed the Alps to join Lucius Munatius Plancus in the war against Antony, but when Plancus switched sides, Decimus Brutus was forced to flee. He attempted to join his cousin, Marcus Brutus, and Cassius in Macedonia but was executed en route by a Gallic chief loyal to Mark Antony.

Gaius Trebonius was nominated by Caesar for the post of proconsul for Asia and immediately left for the province after the assassination. There, he raised money and troops for Brutus and Cassius. He was captured in Syria by Publius Cornelius Dolabella, one of Antony's allies. In January 43 BCE, Dolabella put Trebonius on trial for treason. He was found guilty, tortured, and beheaded.

After Caesar's death, Lucius Tillius Cimber left for Bithynia to raise a fleet in support Brutus and Cassius. He was last heard of shortly before the Battle of Philippi and was presumed killed during the fighting.

Lucius Minucius Basilus was killed in 43 BCE by some of his own slaves whom he had punished by mutilation. Brothers Gaius and Publius Servilius Casca committed suicide after Battle of Philippi. Pontius Aquila died in battle in 43 BCE fighting Antony at Mutina.

The Roman Senate never regained the power and influence it had during the Republic. As for Julius Caesar, his name became synonymous with *king* for centuries afterward and in many languages. The royal titles of *tsar, kaiser,* and many others are based on his name. To this day, our calendar is called the Julian Calendar, and the months of July and August were named after him and his adopted son, Augustus Caesar. He was immortalized like no man before or since. In contrast, the name Brutus, like Judas, became synonymous with villainy and treason.

Chapter 2

Cassius Chaerea, the Senate, and Caligula

—The Republic Reborn . . . or Not

It was the Ides of March in the year 37 CE. Emperor Tiberius of Rome was in his villa on the island of Capri, and he was sick. At seventy-seven years of age, he was already two years older than the previous emperor and his adoptive father, Augustus Caesar, had been when he died and left the throne to Tiberius. His attendants were scrambling. Some simply left the villa for fear of being accused of poisoning him if he died. This was not an unwarranted fear in elite Roman society where murder and intrigue were a part of everyday life. Others were more practical and sought to ingratiate themselves with his heir in hopes of securing their futures in the imperial household.

Septius asked, "Where's Caligula? Has anyone sent for him?" Septius was in charge of running the villa and had given most of his life to the job. He had held this position for Tiberius's entire twenty-two-year reign, as well as the previous ten years when Emperor Augustus owned the estate. Septius was born in Thrace and began working at the villa as a literate domestic slave. He was given his freedom by Augustus as a reward for his service, but he never considered leaving. He witnessed a lot over those years but kept his mouth shut. Knowledge was power.

Lucius replied, "I don't know. He has to be here somewhere. The emperor has forbidden him from leaving the island." The much younger Lucius was Septius's assistant and had only worked at the villa for two years.

"Of course, I know that. But it's possible he has fled or that someone . . ." He drew closer and whispered, "Killed him."

Lucius asked, "Who would do that?"

Caligula

"Anyone with an eye for the throne, you fool. The bricks of the imperial palace are mortared with the ground-up bones of relatives and rivals."

Tiberius was only the second Emperor of Rome and had assumed the throne upon the death of its first emperor, the great Augustus. Tiberius was a reluctant leader. Though he was the head of the most powerful empire in the world, Tiberius was neither happy nor pleasant. If you are going to lose 'man' you need to lose 'a' before 'happy.' Pliny the Elder, a prominent Roman of the time, called him "the gloomiest of men."

Lucius whispered, "Well, the Emperor doesn't look good. As unhappy as he is, I'd think death a welcome relief."

Septius sighed, "You don't know him like I do. Tiberius has good reason for his foul mood."

Tiberius Caesar Augustus

Lucius snorted, "Bah. He's the emperor of Rome, the most powerful man in the world. Everything he desires is at his fingertips. How many men would give everything they have to trade places with him?"

Septius said, "He did give everything he had—and for a job he never really wanted. Before he was emperor, Tiberius was a successful general and a happy man. He was married to a woman he loved deeply—Vipsania Agrippina—and they had a son, Drusus. Emperor Augustus forced him to divorce Vipsania to enter into a more politically beneficial marriage with Julia the Elder. Julia was Augustus's daughter and the widow of his favorite general and statesman, Marcus Agrippa."

Lucius was surprised. "I never heard about that."

Septius smiled. "Well, it was a long time ago. To make matters worse, Julia was Vipsania's stepmother and a cruel woman. Tiberius hated her. She was so promiscuous that her father, Augustus himself, had her exiled to save the family embarrassment. She died shortly after Augustus, and Tiberius never remarried."

Lucius quipped, "Still, he is the emperor and could have any woman he desired."

"All except the one he loved. Vipsania was ordered by Augustus to stay away since Tiberius still loved her. She later remarried and bore her new husband six sons. Even his path to the throne was marked by frustration. He was groomed to be Augustus's successor and given great power. However, it became clear to Tiberius that this was only intended to be temporary until the emperor's grandsons were old enough to rule. Over Augustus's objections, Tiberius resigned all his posts and exiled himself on Rhodes for several years. Augustus was angry with him but had to rehabilitate Tiberius after both of his grandsons died. Augustus adopted Tiberius and made him his official heir but also required Tiberius to adopt his own nephew, Germanicus Julius Caesar. The adoption made Germanicus number two in the line of succession, pushing Tiberius's own son, Drusus Julius Caesar, to third. After becoming emperor, Tiberius rectified this by having Germanicus murdered. However, his solution proved short-lived, as his own son and heir, Drusus, was poisoned by a political rival. From what I witnessed these past twenty-two years, Tiberius never actually liked being emperor."

"Is this why he abandoned Rome for Capri? I mean, he hasn't been to Rome in what—five years?"

"Six," Septius corrected. "Right after the execution of Sejanus, the corrupt praetorian prefect. Tiberius was tired and left Rome to its own devices. Fortunately, the bureaucracy Augustus gave us proved very robust. But enough history, we need to find Caligula. You search the house; I'll check the gardens."

Septius rushed down the long corridor of the expansive villa toward the gardens. A young man was sitting under a tree with his feet in the water of a fountain. Septius stopped dead in his tracks. "Caligula! Thank the gods. You must come quickly! The emperor is sick. I fear he is dying."

Caligula peered up in surprise and concern. "How bad is he? Have you summoned a surgeon?"

"He's very sick. He's in bed and having trouble breathing. And yes, we have sent for a surgeon. I don't know if he's here yet. You must go to his bedside."

Tiberius was technically Caligula's adoptive grandfather, but there was no love between them. Caligula hated the man, and only his acting ability concealed his true feelings. He'd worn that mask so long, he didn't know how to take it off. Virtually everyone hated Tiberius, yet he still feigned concern for the cruel old man. "Hand me my sandals, and we'll go."

Caligula's real name was Gaius Julius Caesar Augustus Germanicus, with the nickname Caligula given as a child. He was the youngest son of Germanicus, a successful general and Tiberius's adopted son. When he was a toddler, Caligula accompanied his father during his military campaigns

Caligae

in Germania and wore a little uniform complete with a wooden sword, leather armor, and soldier boots or *caligae*. His father's soldiers nicknamed him Caligula, which means "little boots," and the name stuck.

The two men rushed down the curtained promenade toward the main house. The Praetorian Guards posted throughout the house snapped to attention, saluted, and addressed Caligula as "Quaestor" as he rushed past. It was getting late, and the servants were lighting lamps throughout the villa. Reaching the Emperor's private chambers, he paused, took a deep breath, and pushed open the doors. On a large bed lay Tiberius, attended by two female slaves mopping his brow with a sponge and fanning him. He was pale and small. His grey hair was stuck to his scalp by sweat. His cheeks were sunken, and his body was frail and thin. Caligula barely made out the movement of his chest when he took his shallow breaths. The only noise was a slight wheezing. Caligula turned to the servants. "Where is the surgeon?"

"He should be here any minute, my lord."

Caligula turned to glance again at the stricken emperor. "I'll stay by his side until the surgeon arrives." Caligula took the Emperor's hand and cradled it with mock concern. A few minutes later, the surgeon arrived. Caligula stood and said, "I will leave you to your diagnosis. Let me know immediately what you determine."

The surgeon replied, "Yes, my lord."

Caligula and Septius left the bedchamber and retired to an anteroom. A few minutes later, Lucius joined them. He was out of breath. He had been rushing all over the huge palace searching for Caligula. "Oh, there you are, my lord. I've been looking for you."

Septius said, "I found him in the garden. I'd have told you, but I didn't know where you were. The surgeon is with the emperor." The doors to the emperor's chambers opened, and the surgeon emerged. His face was sour.

Caligula asked, "What's his situation?"

The surgeon replied, "I'm afraid it isn't good. He is consumed by vapors. For a man of his years, he is unlikely to survive. I might use leeches to remove some blood, but I'm not confident it would help. He is weak and isn't eating or drinking."

Caligula said, "He has already lived longer than Augustus Caesar, and he was an incredibly strong man. It may be best to wait for what the gods have in store for us."

The surgeon nodded. "I agree. He's sleeping now. I'll stay and check on him in a few hours. Is there some place with a couch where I can lie down?"

Lucius answered, "Of course." He snapped his fingers and a slave emerged as if from nowhere. "Show the surgeon to one of the nearest guest rooms."

Septius said, "Now we wait." Turning to Caligula he added, "My lord, there is no reason for you stay up all night. Lucius and I will attend to the emperor. We will wake you if there is any change."

Caligula smiled. "All right. Thank you."

Once Caligula left, Lucius turned to Septius and whispered, "I don't think he is as concerned as much as he lets on."

Septius smirked. "No. I don't think he is. And who could blame him?"

Lucius was taken aback. "Whatever do you mean? Tiberius adopted him and made him his heir!"

Septius led Lucius to a couch. "Sit down. If you're going to serve Caligula, you need to be familiar with his history. It's what makes him who he is."

"Well, tell me then."

Septius took a deep breath. "Caligula's father, Germanicus, was Tiberius's heir and very popular among the Roman population due to his storied military successes in Germania. Tiberius, however, viewed him as a rival. When Germanicus was serving as consul, he traveled to Syria where he got in a dispute with Piso, the Roman governor. Germanicus mysteriously fell ill, but before he died, he accused Piso of poisoning him. Piso was arrested and was put

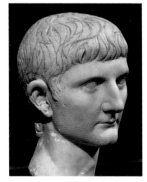

Germanicus Julius Caesar

on trial but died conveniently before it was over. Many believed that Piso killed Germanicus on orders from Tiberius and the emperor then had Piso killed before being implicated in the plot. Being suspected of the death of Germanicus undermined Tiberius's popularity among the Roman people and led to a climate of fear among the nobility. If he'd kill Germanicus, none of them were safe."

Lucius was stunned. "I wasn't aware. But then, that's the nature of Roman politics."

Septius smiled. "Caligula lost more than just his father to Tiberius's jealously and paranoia. After Germanicus's death, Tiberius refused to allow his widow, Agrippina, to remarry. She was Augustus's granddaughter, the daughter of famed general and statesman Marcus Agrippa, and very popular in her own right. As the widow of Germanicus, Tiberius feared that any man she married would become a political rival. Later, Tiberius had her and her oldest son, Nero, banished for treason. Young Caligula was sent to live with Livia, his great grandmother and Tiberius's mother. When Livia died, he was sent to live with his grandmother, Antonia Minor, the daughter of Mark Antony. About six years ago, his other brother Drusus was imprisoned for treason and murdered. His older brother Nero starved to death in prison about the same time. His mother was subjected to beatings and harsh treatment until she starved to death in prison about four years ago.

Caligula Depositing the Ashes of his Mother and Brother in the Tomb of His Ancestors by Eustache Le Sueur

Caligula certainly has reason to hate Tiberius but hides his scorn for the sake of his own life. He was forced to move here six years ago and many, myself included, expected Tiberius to kill him too, but it never happened. The emperor gave Caligula the title of quaestor and even allowed him to marry."

"I know about his wife, Junia Cladilla. She died in childbirth shortly after I arrived."

"Tiberius began pondering his own mortality because two years ago he named Caligula and his grandson, Tiberius Gemellus, coheirs—a prophetic decision, given he now appears to be on his death bed." Septius put his hand on Lucius's knee and smiled. "I am relegated to being your tutor today. Enough lessons. I'm an old man, and I need my rest. You stay with the emperor but wake me in a couple of hours."

"Yes, sir. And thank you for the lesson. It provided perspective."

The next morning, Caligula and Lucius returned to the emperor's chambers to find Septius half asleep in a chair. The surgeon was already there and looking glum. "The emperor's health has not improved. I fear the worst. You'd better make your goodbyes. Is there any other family about?"

Caligula replied, "No. Only me." He walked past the surgeon to Tiberius's bedside. The old man was even worse than the night before. His breathing was more labored. "Were it not for his chest heaving, I would think he was dead already."

The surgeon said, "It won't be long." And then, as if on cue, Tiberius gave out one hard exhale and settled still and silent into his bed. The surgeon quickly felt for a pulse and proclaimed, "The emperor is dead."

Immediately, Septius and Lucius bowed before Caligula and said, "Your imperial highness. Let us be the first to call you Augustus."

Caligula smiled slightly. "Thank you." He led the two aides out of the bedchamber and into the hallway beyond. He said to the Praetorian Guards stationed there, "The emperor is dead. Do not allow anyone to enter except us. I don't want the slaves taking morbid souvenirs." Turning to Septius and Lucius, he said, "You have been and will be trusted and loyal servants of the throne." Septius and Lucius glanced at each other and smiled. "Tell the guards and staff of the emperor's death. Then, draft a letter to the Senate advising them of Tiberius's passing and announcing my assumption of the throne. We need to make arrangements for a funeral and my return to Rome. I want to get off this damn island as soon as possible before anyone in Rome gets any ideas. And find my cousin, Tiberius Gemellus, and tell him to meet me in Rome."

Lucius answered, "Yes, my lord. It will be done." He scurried away to his office.

Caligula and Septius continued to talk in the corridor for several minutes until the surgeon came out. "Gentlemen, there is an issue."

They quickly walked back into the bedchamber and to their horror, found Tiberius sitting up in his bed. Immediately fear washed over them. Caligula had already announced that he was the new emperor. If Tiberius was still alive, what would he do in response? "Grandfather! You're alive! We feared we had lost you!" Turning to the surgeon, Caligula said, "Quick, go fetch Lucius."

"But sir," he protested, "I should really be here to treat the emperor."

Caligula replied, "I will tend to him until you return. Now go." The surgeon turned and left.

Tiberius was still weak and coughing. Caligula turned to Septius. "Maybe you should give me a few minutes alone with my grandfather." Septius didn't question him; he just turned and left.

Caligula gently pushed Tiberius back down onto the bed. "You need to rest. Don't overexert yourself. You're still very sick."

Tiberius croaked, "Planning my funeral already, were you? I'm not dead yet, you idiot."

Caligula picked up a pillow and replied, "Not yet." He pushed the pillow hard over Tiberius's face, making sure to force it onto his mouth and nose. The old man struggled but he was feeble and weak, no match for the twenty-five-year-old Caligula. "This is for my father, my mother, my brothers, and myself. Hear me when I say, old man, you are dying, and no one will shed a tear at your grave. I may even have your corpse fed to the pigs so you'll spend eternity as pig shit!" Caligula stared into the panicked eyes of Tiberius until the light faded from them. He held the pillow over his face for another minute to make sure he was really dead this time and then tossed it back onto the bed. He got up and moved toward the doors. Opening them, he walked out just as Septius, Lucius, and the surgeon were returning. "He's gone—for good this time. It appears his brief recovery was short-lived." He feigned a sniffle and a tear. "He just wanted to tell me goodbye."

* * *

Quintus Naevius Sutorius Macro was the prefect of the Praetorian Guard. Like his predecessor, Lucius Aelius Sejanus, he assumed great power in Rome while Emperor Tiberius sequestered himself in Capri. Like Sejanus before him, Macro effectively ran Rome on a day-to-day basis. Unlike Sejanus, he never provoked Tiberius enough to be executed. Macro came from more humble beginnings. Prior to becoming prefect, he served as *prefectus vigilum*, the head of Rome's fire brigade and police. Now he ran the empire.

In his will, Tiberius said both his grandson, Tiberius Gemellus, and Caligula should share power. With Macro's help, Caligula got to Rome first and quickly consolidated his position. Macro had Tiberius's will negated on the grounds of insanity, and the Senate gave Caligula the principate—the powers of the emperor. To smooth things over with Gemellus and his supporters, Caligula formally adopted Gemellus as his son and heir even though Caligula was only seven years his senior.

* * *

Cassius Chaerea was a soldier. A Roman tribune, he spent almost his entire adult life in the Legion, where he served under one of the most popular generals in all of Rome, Germanicus Julius Caesar. Germanicus had an impeccable pedigree. He was the nephew and adopted son of Emperor Tiberius. His father, Drusus, was the stepson of Emperor Augustus. His mother was the daughter of Marc Antony and Octavia, the sister of Emperor Augustus, and great niece of Julius Caesar himself. Now Germanicus's only surviving son, Caligula, was the emperor of Rome.

Cassius Chaerea was mildly famous in his own right. He was very well respected among his fellow soldiers for his bravery in battle, but his deeds off the battlefield were what earned him the attention of Rome itself. When Emperor Augustus died in 14 CE, Chaerea was stationed along the Germanic frontier. Many foreign soldiers had entered the legions for the pay and simply wanted to be on the winning side. With the great Augustus dead, many of these soldiers believed the time of Roman dominance was at an end. Some simply deserted and went home, but others recognized an opportunity. These soldiers mutinied, seized Roman lands along the frontier, and exerted power over the local populations for their own benefit. They calculated Rome would be so busy worrying about succession that it would not have the will to secure its far-flung colonies.

The mutinous soldiers miscalculated. They were thinking about Rome but not Rome's soldiers. Cassius Chaerea rallied the remaining loyal troops, organized them into a fighting force, and led them against the mutinous legions. Due to his bravery and tactics, the loyal troops prevailed, and the mutiny was put down. For his valor and dedication, Germanicus promoted him to tribune and granted him land of his own to farm and rent out. He stayed loyal to Rome and Emperor Tiberius even after his general and patron, Germanicus, was murdered and his family all but destroyed.

Chaerea was familiar with Caligula from his time serving under Germanicus. He was one of the soldiers who gave Caligula his nickname after seeing him dressed in his little soldier's uniform while visiting his father in Germania. When that little boy, Germanicus's son, became emperor in 37 CE, Chaerea volunteered his services. Based on his heroism and his history serving Caligula's father, Cassius Chaerea was commissioned as a senior tribune in the Praetorian Guard, the elite force sworn to protect the emperor. He had no idea where it would eventually lead him.

* * *

When Caligula was crowned emperor, all of Rome rejoiced. It wasn't that they loved Caligula; most knew nothing about him other than he was the son of Germanicus. They rejoiced because he wasn't the hated Tiberius. For all the animosity directed at Tiberius, he wasn't a bad ruler, and when he died, the treasury was fat. He left behind 2.7 billion sesterces, which Caligula immediately set out to spend.

Caligula started to spread around his good fortune and spent it where it would do him the most good. He paid large bonuses to the Roman military and Praetorian Guards to secure their loyalty. For the population, he put on extravagant gladiatorial games. Over 160,000 animals were sacrificed during the three months of public feasts and festivals organized to celebrate his coronation. He also forged relationships with the Roman ruling classes. He declared Tiberius's hated treason trials a thing of the past. He recalled to Rome those who had been exiled by Tiberius for real or imagined transgressions. It was into this atmosphere that Cassius Chaerea arrived in the spring of 37 CE.

"Cassius Chaerea reporting for duty, sir."

Macro put down his scroll. "So, you are the famous Cassius Chaerea who secured the German frontier against the mutinous troops when Augustus died."

Standing at attention, Chaerea replied, "I wouldn't say famous, Prefect Macro. I was only doing my duty as a loyal Roman soldier, sir."

"At ease, Cassius, we're all friends here. Don't downplay your deeds. You were clever and brave—a useful combination—for which Germanicus made you a tribune and gave you lands. That's how you get ahead in Roman society. Nothing to be ashamed of."

Chaerea relaxed a bit. "Thank you, prefect." The two men were not that different in age, but there was a significant difference in their status. Macro effectively ran the empire in the six years since the execution of Sejanus. "I'm here to serve Emperor Gaius Caesar Augustus Germanicus, just as I served his father, Germanicus Julius Caesar."

Macro smirked, "No one calls him that. He is Caligula. And how did you feel when Germanicus died? Surely you heard the rumors that he was killed on the orders of Tiberius."

"Yes, but there are always rumors about what goes on in Rome. I was on my farm in the countryside. Even if they were true, who am I to question the actions of the emperor?"

"Very good answer, Chaerea. Very . . . political. You may do well here. We in the Praetorian Guard are here to serve Emperor Caligula and to protect him. We are not privy to everything the emperor knows, so we are not in a position to question his decisions. He is descended from gods, while we are mere mortals."

Chaerea recognized false modesty. "While that may be true for most of us, others are in an entirely different position. Take yourself, for instance. It is said that you were the real power behind Rome, that you ran the empire while Tiberius stayed in Capri."

"Yes, I heard those rumors too, but they're just rumors." Macro's smile confirmed what his words denied. "I was privileged to have earned the emperor's trust, and he had me do his bidding from time to time. But now we have a new emperor, and he lives in Rome. He'll have no need for a glorified messenger such as myself. Come. Let's meet him, shall we?"

Macro led Chaerea down a long corridor to the royal chambers where the young emperor was talking to his secretaries, Septius and Lucius, whom he brought with him from Capri. His appearance was not what Chaerea expected. Germanicus was a solidly built, athletic man. In contrast, Caligula was tall and thin. He had a broad forehead and hollow eyes. His hair was brown like his father's but was already going bald on top. The lack of hair on his head was more than compensated for by that on the rest of his body. Macro approached and said, "Your highness, I would like to introduce you to one of your new praetorian tribunes. This is Cassius Chaerea."

Chaerea bowed his head and crossed his right fist across his chest. "Your highness, Cassius Chaerea at your service."

Caligula smiled. "Enough of all that. Welcome, Chaerea. I understand you volunteered for this duty. Might I ask why?"

"I served with your father on the frontier, highness. He was a great man and a great leader. I could think of no greater tribute to him than to give my service to his son."

"Well, thank you for those kind words. So you fought on the frontier? In Germania?"

"Yes, sire. You won't remember it, but we met once before, some twenty years ago. You were a boy at the time, maybe five years old. You came to visit your father in camp. He had a uniform made for you, complete with leather armor, caligae, and a wooden sword. You looked just like him. He was so proud and took you with him to inspect the troops. You even rode on my shoulders once."

Caligula smiled. "Are you the one who gave me the name Caligula when I was a child?"

"No, highness. I cannot take credit for that, but I was there when they did."

"Well, no matter. Welcome to the palace." Caligula gave a quick sideways glance to Macro and added, "It is nice to have loyal and trusted people."

"I am at your disposal, your highness."

"I want you by my side at all times. You will be my personal *tribunus militum*."

"I am honored, sire."

Turning to his secretaries, Caligula said, "Give him quarters close to the royal chambers so that I might call him when needed." Septius and Lucius bowed, and silently led Chaerea away.

* * *

The first six months of Caligula's reign were peaceful and prosperous. The young emperor was a breath of fresh air after the stodgy, old Tiberius. In addition, Caligula was actually present. Tiberius quit Rome in 26 AD for his villa in Capri and left it in the hands of Sejanus and then Macro. Now Rome had an emperor who would actually live in the city that was the seat of his empire.

Things changed in October 37 AD when Caligula fell sick. The cause was a mystery. He may have been stricken by disease, affected by epilepsy like his famous cousin Julius Caesar, or poisoned by a rival. Many inside the royal palace feared he would die. One of those most concerned was Macro. His machinations secured the principate for Caligula at the expense of Tiberius Gemellus. Now, if Caligula were to die, it was his heir and adopted son Gemellus who would inherit the crown. Given their history, this was not good news for Macro. He needed to hedge his bets.

With Caligula incapacitated, Macro was the sole power in Rome—at least temporarily. He summoned Gemellus to meet him. Gemellus was aware Caligula had fallen ill but not how serious it was.

Marco put on his best smile. "Tiberius Gemellus, I'm so glad you took the time to meet me."

"Well, one doesn't refuse an invitation from the prefect of the Praetorian Guards. What do you want?"

"It's about your father, Caligula."

"Caligula is no more my father than he is yours. He only adopted me for political advantage."

"True, but that still puts you on the throne should anything befall him."

Gemellus smirked. "What are you not telling me, Macro? Is the emperor's illness more serious than they're saying?"

Macro didn't want to tip his hand prematurely. "No. Of course not. I'm sure he'll be fine. He is young and strong—as are you, Gemellus. That said, stranger things have happened. Your own father, Drusus, died at what—thirty-seven years?"

"Thirty-six. What's your point?"

"Should something happen to Caligula, there will be others besides you who will have themselves measured for the emperor's robes. There are some who might propose Claudius. He is older and easier to manipulate. A case could be made for him based on his age and experience alone. After all, you are—"

"Too young? I am eighteen years old."

Macro smiled. "Even the great Augustus was thirty-three when he became emperor."

Gemellus smirked. "Yes, but he was only twenty when he joined Marc Antony and Marcus Lepidus to form the Second Triumvirate, and only sixteen when elected to the College of Pontiffs."

"True, but being a member of a religious body is not the same as running an empire."

"What's your point, Macro?"

"Caligula is sicker than people are being told. I am not sure he'll survive. If he doesn't, you'll need powerful friends to push your claim to the throne."

"Powerful friends like the prefect of the Pretorian Guards? Need I remind you that, were it not for you, I would already be on the throne with equal status to Caligula?"

"You don't really believe that, do you? You studied history. After Augustus defeated Marc Antony and Cleopatra at Actium, there was the question of what to do with Caesarian, Julius Caesar's child with Cleopatra. Do you recall what Arius Didymus told Augustus?"

"'Too many Caesars is not good.'"

"Exactly. You think I deposed you, but I saved you. The empire can only have one emperor. And your time may yet come. If Caligula dies, *when* Caligula dies, I will support your succession."

"In exchange for what?"

"The status quo. You become emperor of Rome, and I remain the prefect of the Praetorian Guard with all my current duties and privileges. After a suitable amount of time, say six months, you appoint me to the Senate. You're smart, Gemellus, but lack the experience and relationships. You'll need someone to help you deal with the Senate from the inside—as well as the equestrians, the military, and the plebes. Who better than the man who's been doing it for the last six years?"

Gemellus pondered Macro's offer for a long moment. It made sense. He required help to ascend the throne, and Macro required help staying in power. Macro needed Gemellus as much as Gemellus needed him. Macro was not of the senatorial or equestrian classes. He'd never sit on the throne himself. "All right. When Caligula dies, you back my claim to the throne, and you keep your current position until you join the Senate."

"Then we have a bargain." Macro extended his arm and both men gripped the other's forearm to seal the deal.

After Gemellus left, Macro summoned Cassius Chaerea to meet him. "Chaerea, Tiberius Gemellus and I have struck a bargain. When Caligula dies, I will support Gemellus's claim to the throne. In return, I will keep my position as prefect of the Praetorian Guards until such time as I am appointed to the Senate. Once I'm a senator, I will need someone to handle the day-to-day operations of the guard and the palace. I want that to be you."

Chaerea was shocked. "Macro, you talk as if Caligula is already dead. He is not."

Macro waived him off. "Bah, you've seen him. It's just a matter of time. We both know it. Do you accept my offer or not?"

"No disrespect, sir, but I cannot accept an imperial position from anyone other than the emperor. Right now the emperor is Caligula. If he should die, things will be different, but until then—"

"Ever the cautious one, eh, Cassius? This is why you will never be in charge. You must learn to take risks."

"I've always taken risks on the battlefield. Going against my emperor is not a risk, it's disloyalty . . . and suicide." Chaerea turned on his heel and left. He assumed that at the very least his military career was over—maybe even his life.

* * *

But Caligula didn't die. He recovered over the next couple of weeks, although he was a different man—not physically, but rather his personality had changed. It wasn't clear if the fever affected his brain or if the brush with mortality released the madman inside. Whatever the cause, it didn't start all at once but manifested itself in a creeping paranoia. Chaerea witnessed it firsthand. Neither the doctors nor Caligula understood the cause of his illness, but the emperor increasingly put stock in the rumors of poison. He was convinced someone was out to get him, someone close to him. He would get that someone before that person got him.

Caligula's first victim was his father-in-law, Marcus Junius Silanis. Silanis was a well-respected senator and former suffect consul of Rome. Caligula was married to his daughter, Junia Cladilla, from 33 AD until her death in childbirth in late 36 CE. Silanis still considered Caligula family and treated him like a son. Suspecting Silanis of plotting against him, Caligula had him executed in November.

His next victim was his cousin and adopted son, Tiberius Gemellus. Gemellus stood to gain the most from Caligula's death—the emperor's throne. In December he was summoned before Caligula to answer for his perceived sins.

Caligula sat on his throne peering down on the distraught Gemellus. "So, cousin, I adopt you as my son and heir, and you show me gratitude by plotting against me?"

Gemellus was flanked by two Praetorian Guards. Chaerea stood between him and Caligula in case he lunged at the emperor in desperation. "No, Caligula. I'd never plot against you. I love you as a father. Who has been spreading such lies?"

"My spies tell me when I was sick, you were at the temple praying to the gods for my demise. Is that love to you? It's treason to me."

"Who told you this? Was it Macro? He approached me to say he would support my claim to the throne over that fool, Claudius, should you die. I dismissed him immediately, of course. I didn't tell you at the time because you were still sick with fever. I was waiting until you were fully recovered so we could work together to neutralize him. He is a powerful man, after all."

Caligula sneered. "Macro told me nothing, cousin. I am glad you did, though. You confirmed my worst fears about you. Because you are my son, I will give you the option of suicide rather than have our family suffer the humiliation of your trial and execution."

"Execution? I've done nothing wrong, sire. I am a loyal servant and innocent of these heinous accusations! Besides, I am your heir!"

"The die is cast. The decision is made. My brother-in-law, Marcus Lepidus, will be my new heir. I will allow you to retire to your apartment and kill yourself with a sword like the soldier you are not. I only do this because no grandson of Augustus should die a traitor's death. You should thank me for allowing you this one last dignity. If you refuse it, you'll be publicly strangled and cast down the Gemonian Stairs like Sejanus. I won't be able to guarantee the safety of your mother or sister. When news of your treachery spreads, the plebes will demand more than just *your* blood."

Gemellus bowed his head in submission. His situation was hopeless. Macro would do nothing to save him. Tribune Cassius Chaerea and two other Praetorian Guards took Gemellus back to his quarters. They were silent as he stood quivering. Chaerea unsheathed his sword and handed it to Gemellus.

Taking the sword in his hand, Gemellus gaped at them helplessly. "I'm not familiar with the sword." He fumbled with it awkwardly while his guards stood by stoically. "How do I do this? How many men simply know how to kill themselves? How much will it hurt?"

Finally Cassius said, "Get on your knees. Put the hilt on the floor and the tip of the blade just under your bottom rib on your left side, under your heart. Then fall forward. That is the quickest way with the least pain."

Gemellus knelt on the floor and positioned the sword as Chaerea instructed. He stared up silently yet pleading with his eyes. The Praetorian Guards were emotionless. He started to lean forward but when the blade poked his soft skin, he recoiled reflexively. He started to sob as he repositioned the blade. This time when Gemellus started to lean forward, Chaerea pushed him. The blade was sharp and easily sliced through his skin and diaphragm before piercing his heart and lung. His eyes widened and rather than cry out, he emitted a soft yelp, like a puppy scolded by its mother. He fell face first onto the marble floor. Chaerea retrieved his sword and wiped it off on Gemellus's toga as a large pool of blood spread out from his lifeless corpse.

Chaerea left his men to deal with Gemellus's body and strode down the long corridor to the emperor's chamber. As he entered, Caligula commented, "Well, that was fast. Is he—"

"Yes, sire. Gemellus is dead." He placed his hand on his hilt. "With this very sword."

"Show me." Chaerea unsheathed his sword, rested it on his open hands, and bowed as he handed it to Caligula. Caligula took the sword and dabbed his finger in the fresh blood near the hilt. "Tell me, Chaerea, did he really kill himself or did you . . . *help* him?"

"He did ask for instructions, sire, but in the end, it was his hand on the sword." This was technically true but not exactly what Caligula was asking.

"I'm surprised. I assumed Gemellus would ask you to do it for him. Very well. Return his corpse to his mother."

"Yes, sire."

* * *

The next person Caligula sought to remove was none other than Quintus Naevius Sutorius Macro, the prefect of the Praetorian Guard and the man who helped him win the throne. Where Gemellus was a sheep, Macro was a lion, and his undoing would require forethought and guile. He was extremely powerful and had spies everywhere. Caligula assumed his own Imperial German Bodyguard—the *Germani Corpore Custodes*—and most of the Praetorian Guard were on Macro's payroll because they predated his coronation. There was one, however, who arrived after the young emperor—Cassius Chaerea.

Chaerea was surprised when he was summoned for a private audience with the emperor. "Chaerea, you served with my father and for that, I trust you above all others."

Chaerea bowed, "Thank you, sire. It has been my greatest honor to serve the House of Germanicus."

"You heard what my cousin said. He was approached by Macro when I was fevered, and they plotted to put him on my throne. I don't believe for a second that Gemellus refused the offer. I'm not sure that my recovery put an end to Macro's conspiracies, either. He is a very powerful man. His removal won't be easy. I don't trust your fellow Praetorians to place my interests over Macro's."

"Sire, the Praetorians are loyal to you. They'd die for you."

Caligula waived him off. "Be that as it may, I want to keep my plans from them. Do you understand?"

"Yes, sire. There are a number of new guards, men I personally brought in from your father's legions. They have no allegiance to Prefect Macro. They will support you no matter what, sire. I assure you of that."

"Very well. I'll leave that to you. Now I must find a way of disposing of Macro before he disposes of me. He would never accept exile, and he has more forces at his disposal than I do."

"Sire, if I may be so bold. Your great-grandfather Augustus was a wise ruler. He often rid himself of politically powerful but inept generals through promotion. He would make them the governor of some far-off province where they could do little harm. If they proved an able administrator, he got credit for promoting them. If they failed, he had his reason to replace them. Might you use a similar tactic with Macro?"

Caligula smiled. "You're smarter than you look, Chaerea. I thought you merely a loyal, if unimaginative, soldier but there's a brain under that helmet. I like your idea with one modification. We will use the lure of a fat governorship to get him to quit Rome. Whether he actually gets there is yet to be determined. Macro has power and power leads to wealth. It'd have to be quite the prize for him to leave Rome voluntarily."

Chaerea said, "Egypt. It is the wealthiest province outside Italy itself. He'll control the grain supply of the empire. That alone is worth millions of sesterces each year."

"Yes, you're right. King Midas himself wouldn't pass up that prize."

Cassius took his opportunity. "With Macro gone, you'll need a new prefect of the Praetorian Guard, someone you trust, someone whose fate is tied irrevocably to your reign."

Caligula smiled. "Someone like you, Chaerea?"

"Yes, sire."

"Let's see how you do with this assignment. If I'm pleased with the outcome, I'll consider you for the prefecture."

* * *

There was no action on the plot to remove Macro for the next few months. Caligula was paranoid but also clever. He couldn't simply announce that he was making Macro the new prefect of Egypt. There needed to be justification. Caligula dispatched his close friend, Herod Agrippa, the governor of Batanaea and Trachontis, to Egypt. Agrippa was to check on Aulus Avilius Flaccus, the prefect of Egypt. Caligula never trusted Flaccus, and Agrippa's report would justify his removal. The visit did not go well, and there was rioting in Alexandria. It couldn't have been better for Caligula.

The week after receiving Agrippa's report, Caligula summoned Macro to the palace. "Macro, my oldest and most trusted ally. I assume you have read Herod Agrippa's report on the situation in Egypt?"

"I have. It appears to be quite the mess down there."

"Yes, it is. We cannot have the empire's grain supply threatened by Flaccus's ineptitude. He has grown fat and lazy. What is it about Egypt that makes Romans forget they are Romans when they go there? First it was Antony and now Flaccus. We need a Roman prefect who remembers he is Roman."

"I agree. Who did you have in mind?"

"You."

Macro was stunned. "Me? I'd never even considered—"

"Macro, you can govern. You proved that when Tiberius was locked away in Capri all those years. It was you who kept the empire functioning. We need that kind of strong hand on the tiller in Egypt. I realize you're well established in Rome, so I intend to make it worth your while. How about 10 percent of all the grain revenue and 10 percent of local taxes collected?"

Macro suppressed his smile. "That's extremely generous, sire, but Egypt is a land of many troubles and bothersome people. I may need to bribe the Greek leaders and the unruly tribes to keep them in check. To simply send in the legions to destroy them is more costly than bribes and would disrupt grain shipments. Give me 15 percent of grain revenue and

20 percent of taxes, and I will guarantee peace. With peace comes prosperity. Rome will see a net increase in tax revenue and grain shipments without the cost of standing up additional legions."

Caligula smirked. "Macro, you're trying to take advantage of me. Let's say 15 percent of both and I appoint you to a seat in the Senate upon your return, agreed?"

"Agreed! When do you want me to go?"

"As soon as possible. I want you in place before the next harvest. Your wife will love it there. Ennia will be treated like Cleopatra reincarnated. I'll have a ship for you at Ostia in two weeks' time. Now go home and pack your bags."

Two weeks to the day, Macro and his wife, Ennia, arrived in Ostia with all their luggage. Macro was already counting the money he'd amass as prefect of Egypt. He had feared his dream of the Senate died with Gemellus. Now Caligula was offering redemption. With Egypt's gold for bribes and patronage, he'd be the most powerful man in the Senate—not bad for the former head of the fire brigade.

Macro's luggage filled two large ox carts. When they arrived in Ostia, he was surprised not to find his ship waiting for him.

Ennia asked, "Quintus, shouldn't there be a ship for us?"

"They may be waiting on the tide. I'm sure it will be here soon. It's a long voyage. Appreciate every moment on dry land."

They waited for an hour with no news. Finally, some soldiers approached; they were Praetorian Guards. Ennia espied them first. "Look there. Soldiers!"

Macro squinted and shaded his eyes from the sun. "They're Praetorians, my men. What are they doing here? Maybe our ship is delayed." The Praetorians were being led by Chaerea. "Cassius Chaerea, why are you here? Do you have any news about my ship?"

"The emperor asked me escort you back to the city."

"I wasn't informed of this. When did this happen?"

"Shortly after he ordered your arrest."

Macro's face went pale. "My what?"

Chaerea unrolled a scroll and read, "Quintus Naevius Cordus Sutorus Macro, by order of Emperor Caligula, I am arresting you for treason and plotting against the empire."

"What? Are you insane? I did no such thing!"

"Make your case before the tribunal, but know this: I was there when Gemellus told the emperor how you plotted to put him on the throne when the emperor was sick with fever. Only after Gemellus's confession did I understand what you were doing that day we talked. It seems *you* took a risk, but it was a bad one. Guards, place *former* Prefect Macro in custody."

Turning to Ennia, Cassius added, "Madam, the emperor told me to inform you that you have nothing to fear due to your previous service to the Crown." Chaerea didn't understand the context of the message. He was unaware that Ennia and Caligula had an affair some four years earlier.

Rather than face a trial for treason where the outcome was preordained, Macro, like Gemellus before him, chose suicide. Another of Caligula's rivals was gone.

* * *

Chaerea wasn't appointed prefect but was drawn closer into Caligula's inner circle. Caligula's madness continued unabated, and Chaerea had a ringside seat for it all. Within a year of assuming the throne, Caligula had spent almost all of the 2.7 billion sesterces Tiberius left in the treasury when he died. This led to a financial crisis in 39 AD, and Caligula needed to find new sources of income for the state and himself. He levied taxes on lawsuits, weddings, and prostitution. He auctioned the lives of gladiators. He forced Centurions who obtained property by plunder—a time-honored Roman tradition—to now turn over those spoils to the state. He also began falsely accusing wealthy Romans of crimes and levying huge fines or even killing them and seizing their estates.

While his actions angered the elites, he made a number of reforms the plebes approved of. He published a report on public funds. He presented prizes to winners of sporting events. He assisted citizens who lost property to fires and abolished some unpopular taxes. He reinstated democratic elections for local offices and appointed new members to the senatorial and equestrian classes. These acts delighted the general populace and horrified the Senate.

Caligula also exercised his ego and his lust. One of his most outlandish stunts was ordering the construction of a pontoon bridge two miles long to connect the resort of Baiae to the port of Puteoli. The late Emperor Tiberius had employed a soothsayer, Thrasyllus of Mendes, who once predicted Caligula had "no more chance of becoming emperor than riding a horse across the Bay of Baiae." With his pontoon bridge complete, Caligula rode across the bay on his favorite horse, Incitatus, while wearing Alexander the Great's breastplate just to spite Thrasyllus. The unintended consequence of this act of hubris was a brief famine. The pontoon bridge was constructed from Rome's grain barges and disrupted food deliveries to the population.

Caligula ordered the construction of two massive ships on Lake Nemi for his personal use. They were two of the largest ships in the world at that time. The smaller was a temple dedicated to the goddess Diana. The other was a floating palace 240 feet long with a beam of

Caligula's Nemi Ship

79 feet and powered by ten banks of oars. It had marble floors and was equipped with hot and cold running water. His ship was decorated with mosaics, jewels, and gilded copper roof tiles. The cost of these vessels was enormous.

Chaerea stood by as Caligula's personal war with his own family continued unabated. In 38 CE, Julia Drusilla, his favorite sister and wife of his new heir Marcus Lepidus, died of natural causes. Shortly after, his two other sisters, Livilla and Agrippina the Younger, were accused of plotting to overthrow Caligula and replace him with Lepidus, a man both women were said to be having an affair with. When Caligula discovered the plot, he had Lepidus executed and his two sisters sent away to exile.

The only close relative he had left was his uncle Claudius, Germanicus's younger brother. Claudius walked with a limp and was partially deaf. He had long been ostracized by his own family, and Caligula didn't view him as a political threat. The young emperor kept him around as a laughingstock and a target of Caligula's humiliations.

Julia Drusilla

Chaerea witnessed Caligula's cruelty extend beyond the palace. While attending the wedding of Roman Senator Gaius Piso to Livia Orestilla, the emperor became smitten with the new bride. He forced Piso to annul their marriage during the wedding celebrations, and Caligula married her instead. Orestilla remained loyal to Piso, so Caligula divorced her the next day but forbade her from returning to Piso.

Caligula next became infatuated with a woman he had never even seen. Lollia Paulina was the wife of a Roman provincial governor. Caligula was told her grandmother was a great beauty so he forced Lollia to divorce her husband and marry him. They were married for only six months when he divorced her, citing infertility. Afterward, she was not allowed to sleep with or even associate with another man.

In 40 CE, Caligula started an affair with Milonia Caesonia, a married woman with three children. When she became pregnant with Caligula's child, she left her husband and married the emperor just a month before the baby was born. Chaerea found them well suited. She was a woman who enjoyed extravagant and luxurious things and had no problem spending Caligula's money. She was also famous for her depravity and allowed herself to be paraded nude before her husband's friends. She was mother to his only natural child, Julia Drusilla, whom he named for his deceased sister.

Caligula's downfall started when he began to feud with the Senate.

He replaced the consul and even had several senators executed. Caligula reveled in publicly humiliating his rivals. He would summon senators to the palace only to make them wait for hours. Others he made run alongside his chariot as he moved about the city. For an old and powerful institution that had grown accustomed to running Rome alone while Tiberius was in Capri, this did not sit well.

In AD 40, Caligula started claiming he was a god. He ordered the heads on statues of gods throughout the city removed and replaced with his. To the outrage of the religious leaders, he appointed his horse, Incitatus, to the priesthood and announced plans to make the beast a Consul of Rome. The breaking point came when he announced he would relocate permanently to Alexandria, where he'd be worshipped as a living god in accordance with longstanding Egyptian tradition. If the Roman emperor moved to Egypt, Rome would cease to be Rome. The Senate had had enough.

* * *

Cassius Chaerea didn't escape Caligula's ire. He was never made the prefect of the Praetorian Guards, and instead, Caligula used him for sport. Chaerea was a brave soldier but cursed with a rather high, reedy voice that Caligula found effeminate. When the emperor had Chaerea kiss his ring, he often held out his hand and extended his finger like a penis, or crossed his fingers in the shape of a vagina. He also made Chaerea use degrading watchwords at the palace at night. Caligula would insist on words such as *venus,* which was slang for "male eunuch," or *priapus,* a reference to an ancient Greek fertility god and slang for "erection." Repeatedly and publicly humiliating the man who was supposed to protect him proved unwise.

* * *

Cassius Chaerea was a loyal Roman who fought for Germanicus and the empire. Now Germanicus's son was destroying that empire. The daily humiliations prodded Chaerea to overcome his reluctance and accept that Caligula had to go. Others had tried to depose Caligula and failed, but as a tribune in the Praetorian Guards, Chaerea was in a unique position. Killing Caligula was easy, but then what? He'd be cut down and Caligula replaced with some other tyrant. He needed to manage the aftermath. For that, he needed the Senate.

Without the emperor, Rome was just another city and the Senate just a gathering of wealthy old men. Before Augustus Caesar was proclaimed emperor, the Senate was Rome. They appointed the consuls and controlled the purse. The Senate raised the legions and authorized military actions. Chaerea wanted to replace Caligula's empire with a reborn Roman Republic and, in doing so, save both Rome and himself.

The rebirth of the Roman Republic had long been a dream of many a senator—albeit a secret one, to ensure against execution for treason. The man Cassius Chaerea approached was Marcus Vinicius, the consul of Rome and, as husband to the exiled Livilla, Caligula's brother-in-law. Under the Republic, a consul of Rome had real power; now it was just a ceremonial position. Chaerea approached Vinicius at his villa outside Rome. A slave showed him to the gardens to wait.

"Tribune Cassius Chaerea. To what do I owe such an honor? Did the Emperor send you to summon me?"

"No, Consul. I'm here to get your opinion on recent developments."

Vinicius was leery. More than one senator had been executed after stumbling into a trap set by Caligula to justify seizing their property. "And what recent developments might those be?"

"I'm referring to Caligula's intention to relocate the throne to Alexandria. He seems to be following in his great grandfather Marc Antony's footsteps."

"That didn't turn out so well for Antony or his Queen Cleopatra. I'm sure it will be different for Caligula. He's a capable ruler."

Vinicius was being cautious, and with good reason. Vinicius's wife, Julia Livilla, was the emperor's youngest sister and was already living in exile for plotting against him. "I must be the one to take the first step, so

I will. Caligula taking the throne to Egypt would be disastrous . . . and treasonous."

Vinicius was taken aback. "Treasonous? How can the emperor be a traitor against himself? He is Rome."

"No. The Roman people are Rome. The Senate is Rome, and Rome must be defended."

"You propose to defend the empire from its emperor?"

"I propose to defend the Republic from a madman. Imagine what evilness and debauchery he'll succumb to without the Senate or Praetorian Guard to keep him in check."

Vinicius paused. They were alone but he scrutinized the area anyway. "What you say might get us killed, dear Cassius."

"Not if we kill him first."

Vinicius liked what he was hearing but didn't trust it to be true. "You're suggesting we kill Caligula, and do what? Put another of his family on the throne in his place? That's been tried. Or don't you remember Marcus Lepidus—and my wife?"

"A republic shouldn't have a royal family. We need to get rid of the principate altogether. I would posit that not only do we kill Caligula, we put an end to his bloodline. He has no male heir. Who else is there? That old fool Claudius? Who would have him on the throne?"

"People would put a goat on the throne if it preserved their interests."

Chaerea replied coldly, "Then we kill the goat as well."

"Well, Cassius, who would be Emperor?"

"No one. We'd go back to the republic—back to the way it was before the emperors, tyrants, and madmen, back when the *consuls* were the highest authorities."

Vinicius smiled. "Because I am the current consul of Rome, not many of my colleagues would embrace me if I killed Caligula just to take over his job, if not his title."

"I'll kill Caligula. I have a group of loyal Praetorian Guards, men I hand-selected from Germanicus's legions. They are just as disgusted as I am by the shame Caligula has brought to his father's memory. What we need are senior senators to step in to fill the void. I need someone to declare the republic reborn. Given your familial ties to the Julio-Claudians, it would also appease those in that camp. Can you do that?"

"As I said before, it would be viewed as self-serving. We need someone else to be the face of the Senate, someone not connected to the throne if even by marriage. Once a republic is declared, most of the senators will fall in line to protect the sanctity and stability of the city. There's always time for political maneuvering later. We must first wrest the standard from the Julio-Claudians."

"Who might be this face of the Senate?"

"My nephew, Lucius Annius Vinicianus. He is a well-respected sena-tor with the courage to make the declaration. If he says it, the others will parrot him."

"He wouldn't have to say anything until after the emperor is dead, in case my plans are spoiled. Will he do it?"

"I'm sure. He was very upset when Caligula declared he was moving the throne."

Chaerea added, "Line up any other senators you can, but be careful. They must be loyal and, above all else, discreet. If word of this gets out—"

"I understand. I'll contact Lucius immediately."

* * *

Planning for the coup progressed quickly. Cassius convinced more of the praetorians to commit to his plan. Vinicius expanded his group of con-spirators to include a number of prominent senators and equestrians. They were prepared to act as soon as Caligula's death was announced. They planned to strike in January of 41 AD at the Palatine Games, a series of athletic games and theatrical presentations held in honor of Emperor Augustus.

It was January 24, and Cassius Chaerea had finally built up enough courage to act, but where was Caligula? Cassius had access to virtually every room in the palace, but the emperor was nowhere to be found. Panic was slowly creeping over Chaerea. Had their plot been discovered? Had Caligula been spirited away to Capri or his floating palace on Lake Nemi for safety while those loyal to him ferreted out the conspirators?

Encountering old Septius in a hallway, Cassius asked, "Septius, have you seen the emperor? I can't find him anywhere."

"Lucius said he was meeting with some actors in the cryptoporticus leading to the theater. He was singing with them or something. You know how he likes to perform."

Cassius smiled. "Yes, he does at that. Thank you."

"What do you need him for? Maybe I can help?"

"Praetorian business. Nothing for you to be worried about."

Chaerea calmly walked away but as soon has he was out of sight, he quickened his pace. He gathered his coconspirators to finalize their plans. "Marcus, you and Paulus will come with me and deal with Caligula. Julius Lupus—you, Erastus, and Casio take care of Caesonia and Claudius. There must be no ready heir to replace him. Do you understand?" The men nodded their heads. "With the gods on our side, today we end his maniacal reign and restore the Roman Republic. Now go!"

Chaerea led Marcus and Paulus down the stairs to the bowels of the palace. The cryptoporticus was a long hallway connecting the main part of the palace to the basement of the adjacent theater. A large audience gathered for the upcoming performance, and the murmur of the crowd echoed down from above. They walked quickly down the corridor, checking every room and alcove they encountered. No Caligula. Chaerea was beginning to doubt his plan. Did he act too soon? Why did he send Lupus, Erastus, and Casio to dispatch Caesonia and Claudius? What if he didn't find Caligula before his wife and uncle were killed? Panic was beginning to well up inside him. There were voices in front of him.

Moving quickly forward, they encountered Caligula chatting with a group of young actors. He was standing tall while sweeping his arms before him, reciting the lines from some play. Five young actors knelt before him, mesmerized to be audience to the emperor's performance. Caligula turned toward Chaerea as he approached, clearly irritated that he'd been interrupted. "My god, Chaerea, you've broken my concentration, you old woman." Chaerea said nothing but drew his sword. Caligula's expression changed from irritation to confusion. "What's all this? Has there been a threat against me?"

Chaerea simply replied, "Yes." He thrust his sword into his emperor's gut. Caligula let out a gasp. Marcus and Paulus joined the attack. Caligula fell to the floor. The three men set upon him, stabbing him over and over again. The young actors, now over their initial shock, got up and ran toward the theater screaming at the top of their lungs. Caligula was splayed out on the floor. He was still breathing—barely—but his wounds were mortal. His toga was stained red, and a large pool of blood formed around him. In another few seconds, he was dead.

Chaerea and his men fled back down the cryptoporticus toward the palace. In response to the screams of the actors, members of Caligula's Germani corpore custode bodyguard came running down from the theater. When they found Caligula dead on the floor, they flew into a rage and immediately set out to find and punish the conspirators.

Upstairs, Julius Lupus, Casio, and Erastus entered the royal apartment in search of Caesonia. They found her in the bath with her baby, Julia Drusilla. Julius Lupus immediately drew his sword and struck her down. He and Casio stabbed her several times to ensure she was dead. Erastus asked, "What about the baby?"

"Cassius said we are to leave no heirs alive." He grabbed the screaming baby by her feet and swung her, smashing her head against the wall. Dropping the lifeless infant on the floor, Lupus said, "We must find Claudius."

In the ensuing mayhem, Cassius Chaerea got a message to Vinicius and his Senate allies. It simply read, "Caligula is dead."

Vinicius immediately sent for his nephew, Lucius Annius Vinicianus. "The emperor is dead. It is time to announce the return of the republic."

While Vinicianus was hurrying to the Senate, Cassius left the palace to talk to the military. He didn't have the loyalty of the whole Praetorian

Guard, and the Roman army was the only institution powerful enough to stand up to them. He met with a group of generals and centurions to tell them Caligula was dead and the Senate was declaring the reformation of the republic. The reaction he received was not heartening. The military had prospered under the imperial system. They were not about to abandon it. They would wait.

In the Senate, Vinicianus solemnly announced the death of Caligula. There were shocks and gasps for appearance's sake but few mourned his passing. Vinicianus then spoke to his colleagues. "Senators of Rome, this is a truly a tragic day. But might it also be a message from the gods? Our dear Emperor Caligula has died without naming an heir. I believe it is the gods telling us that the time for hereditary leaders is over. Rome has grown to be the largest, most powerful empire the world has ever seen, larger than that of Alexander the Great, Darius of Persia, or the pharaohs of Egypt. We have achieved this through conquest, but now it must be governed by all the people of Rome, not just a few. I propose that we take this opportunity the gods have given us and reestablish the Republic of Rome."

Senator Cluvius Rufus, another member of the cabal, spoke up. "I concur with Lucius Annius Vinicianus's wise words. We would be foolish to let this opportunity—provided by the gods—go unused. I will be the first to say it. Caligula was not a kind and wise ruler like Augustus. He was not even a detached yet practical ruler like Tiberius. He was a cruel and foolish ruler. It is time we replace him with a practical and wise Senate. We are very fortunate to currently have as consul Marcus Vinicius, a calm and stable leader. Who better to lead us back to the republic?"

* * *

Back at the palace, when the Imperial German Bodyguard of the Praetorian Guard found the bodies of Caesonia and her baby, they went on a rampage. They were searching blindly for the assassins and killed several noblemen for no reason other than they *might* have been involved.

Fearing for his life, Claudius fled to his apartment to hide. The body-guards also started a frenzied looting of the palace. Their existence was tied to that of the emperor, and now he was dead. Julius Lupus, Casio, and Erastus were still trying to find Claudius. Not finding him in his apartment, they began searching the palace room by room. It wasn't long before they ran into a group of the German bodyguards. From the blood on Lupus's uniform, they determined they were the assassins and set upon them. Lupus and his men fought back but were overwhelmed. Casio and Erastus were killed but Julius Lupus was taken prisoner. One of the Germani corpore custodes tribunes, Corvis Lutori, recognized them. "These are Cassius Chaerea's men. He must be behind all this."

A few minutes later, a small group of bodyguards entered Claudius's apartment to loot it. One of the soldiers, Gratus, was shocked to discover the cowering Claudius hiding behind the curtains. Lupus and his men had simply missed him in their haste. Gratus quickly led him to Corvis Lutori. Realizing who it was, Lutori said, "Men, this is our new emperor. Hail, Emperor Claudius."

Proclaiming Claudius Emperor by Lawrence Alma-Tadema

Gratus pulled Lutori aside. "Sir, is this wise? We don't have the authority to name the new emperor."

"Gratus, think! We owe our very existence to the imperial throne. No emperor, no Germani corpore custodes. The Senate is already declaring a new Roman Republic. The army is still loyal to the imperial monarchy—for the time being—but there needs to be an emperor. Gather some men and take Claudius away."

"Take him where?"

"Take him to our camp, the Castra Praetoria. We can protect him there."

* * *

The situation was unfolding, but not exactly as planned. Cassius and his men had killed Caligula, Caesonia, and their baby, but missed Claudius. That wasn't insurmountable. Claudius was widely considered a fool. He wouldn't garner much support from the elites. While Cassius, Marcus, and Paulus escaped the palace alive, Casio and Erastus were dead and Julius Lupus captured. Well, every battle has its casualties. The Senate had moved to declare a new republic, but the army was noncommittal. Without an emperor, Cassius was convinced the army would have no choice but to fall in line with the Senate. Then he received some shocking news.

Not only was the doddering Claudius alive, the Praetorian Guard had named him emperor! This changed everything. He raced back to the Senate to find Vinicius and his nephew. "Have you heard the news? Claudius is alive and under the protection of the Praetorian Guard. They have declared him the new emperor!"

Vinicius just smiled calmly. "Yes, I know. The Praetorian Guard does not have the authority to name the emperor. Only the Senate of Rome can do that. And I assure you, we will not name that moron Emperor of Rome."

"That's all well and good, but you need to move forward on reestablishing the republic. If you do that and get the generals to concur, Claudius and the Praetorians will be moot. If not, we have a problem."

"Don't worry. We're on it. There is just some debate as to who should be the princeps."

"Princeps? What about the consuls?"

"The idea of princeps dates back to the republic—long before Augustus."

"Well, need I remind you that I have committed regicide? While you and your illustrious Senate colleagues argue over who will be the first among equals, I may be facing execution."

"You're being dramatic, Cassius. The Senate works at its own speed, but it does work. We will demand that Claudius be delivered to the Senate for approval. They will not vote to make him emperor. Once he is rejected, we will formally declare a republic."

To the shock of the Senate, Claudius refused to appear. He suspected—and justifiably so—that his life would be in danger. The stalemate dragged on, and the Senate debate over the republic and princeps devolved into petty squabbling. Eventually, the Senate caved, as they had to Julius Caesar, Mark Antony, Augustus, and Tiberius. They recognized Claudius as Emperor of Rome in exchange for a general amnesty for the more elite members of the conspiracy.

While few mourned Caligula, the brutal murders of his wife Caesonia and their infant daughter were horrifying and turned public sympathy against the conspirators. The senators successfully negotiated an amnesty from Claudius in exchange for his recognition as emperor. That amnesty did not, however, apply to Cassius Chaerea or Julius Lupus. Both men were executed to protect Claudius and act as a deterrent for anyone else contemplating such a move. Cassius Chaerea asked to be executed with his own sword, the same sword that struck down Caligula. In recognition of his prior service to the empire, his wish was granted.

Aftermath

Historians Titus Flavius Josephus, Gaius Suetonius Tranquillus, and Casius Dio suggest Cassius Chaerea and his coconspirators plotted the assassination of Emperor Caligula for a number of reasons. They sought to restore the Roman Republic and felt compelled to rid the Roman people of a maniacal and possibly insane rule. Cassius also wanted to take his personal revenge on Caligula for years of mistreatment and humiliation suffered at the hands of the emperor. While he rid Rome of Caligula and certainly avenged himself for the indignities he suffered, the overarching objective of Chaerea and his coconspirators was unmet. The new republic was stillborn, due in large part to squabbling and inaction within the Senate. Failing to act in a timely manner allowed the military to remain noncommittal and gave Claudius's supporters time to use the brutal murders of Caesonia and Julia Drusilla to stoke public outrage. Claudius ascended the throne and ruled competently for thirteen years until he was poisoned in 54 AD by his fourth wife, Agrippina the Younger—Caligula's sister. The Julio-Claudian Dynasty continued for another fourteen years until the death of Emperor Nero in 68 CE. Rome survived for another four hundred years but was never a republic again.

Chapter 3

Charlotte Corday
and Jean-Paul Marat
—The Angel of Assassination

The French Revolution of 1789 saw the people overthrow the French monarchy, which dated back to 843 and King Charles the Bald, the grandson of Charlemagne the Great. The French political system of the day, the Ancien Régime (the Old Rule), had been around since the fifteenth century and featured a hereditary monarchy and a feudal system headed by the French nobility. The revolution began in 1789, but exactly why was complicated. France had a number of problems that contributed to it. The economy was a mess. Years of profligate spending by the royal family on foreign wars and its lavish lifestyle had drained the public coffers. Multiple poor harvests led to rising prices for wheat, widespread hunger, and food profiteers who took advantage of the country's poor. Outdated infrastructure meant what food there was couldn't be efficiently moved from the countryside to the cities. Additionally, the country's population had grown from eighteen million in 1700 to over twenty-six million in 1789. Many of those people had no work. Of Paris's six hundred thousand residents, one third were unemployed.

For those who did earn money, rampant inflation meant it bought less and less. While the nobility and the church owned almost all the land, neither paid taxes. Taxes were the sole responsibility of the little people, the rural peasants, and the *sans-culottes*. The term *sans-culottes* literally means "without breeches," a reference to the fancy silk knee breeches worn by the nobility and wealthy bourgeoisie. Working-class men wore pants. Though France was a devoutly Catholic country, the church, the First Estate, was another sore point. The church collected a mandatory tithe of ten percent of each peasant's earnings, be that in coin, cattle, or crops. For that, the peasants received very little in return.

When the revolution came, few people other than the nobility were really sad to see the monarchy go. The Old Regime, the Ancien Régime, had done little to improve the life of the average Frenchman, while their kings lived ever more lavish lifestyles. King Louis XVI had more palaces than even Louis XIV, the fabled Sun King who built Versailles, the largest palace in the world. His wife, Marie Antoinette, was an Austrian princess notorious for throwing ridiculous parties paid for with the peasants' taxes.

Louis XVI, King of France and Navarre, Wearing His Grand Royal Costume in 1779 by Antoine-François Callet

To address the growing financial crisis, King Louis VXI called for a meeting of the Estates General, an assembly representing the French "estates of the realm"—the clergy (First Estate), the nobles (Second Estate), and the commoners (Third Estate). Such a meeting hadn't been called since 1614. While the clergy and the nobles initially controlled the assembly, the commoners were by far the largest group, representing 95 percent of the population. Fed up with the nobility, the commoners, along with some of the clergy, declared themselves the National Assembly. While they asked the others to join them, they would proceed with them or without them. Louis pushed back, but with massive support from Paris and other cities, the National Assembly prevailed. The king backed down, and in July 1789, a constitutional monarchy was declared.

Rumors were circulating in Paris that the king was planning to use the Swiss Guards to force closure of the National Assembly. Protesters poured into the streets, but the soldiers of the elite French Guards regiment refused to disperse them. Many of the soldiers defected and joined the protesters when on July 14 they attacked the Bastille, a fortress with arms and ammunition. Some eighty-three protesters were killed over several hours of fighting, but the governor of the Bastille eventually capitulated and was taken prisoner by the mob. He was carried to the Hotel de Ville, seat of the Parisian city government, and executed. His head was impaled on a pike and paraded around the city. Things were starting to get ugly.

* * *

Observing all this from afar was Charlotte Corday. She was born into a minor aristocratic family in Saint-Saturnin-des-Ligneries in Normandy. Her mother and older sister died when she was young, and her distraught father sent Charlotte and her younger sister to a convent, Abbaye aux Dames in Caen. While there, Charlotte had access to the convent's library and was exposed to the teachings of Plutarch, Voltaire, Rousseau, and other philosophers. Though she was not yet twenty-one years old when the French Revolution began in 1789, she was unusually learned for her time. She ardently supported the revolution

Charlotte Corday in Caen in 1793 by Tony Robert-Fleury

and the establishment of democracy to replace the French monarchy.

In 1790 religious orders were dissolved, and monasteries and convents closed. Corday moved in with her cousin, Madame Le Coustellier de Bretteville-Gouville. The two became very close, and Charlotte was named the sole heir to her cousin's estate. She became exposed to the political principles of the Club Breton and the Jacobins, loose political organizations that supported the revolution. The Jacobins were far from homogeneous and included members with a wide variety of political stripes. Two rival factions were starting to coalesce around their leaders. Jacques-Pierre Brissot, Jean Marie Roland, and François Buzot led a faction initially referred to as the Brissotins but later called the Girondins, named after Gironde, the city in Bordeaux where they were headquartered. Their sometime allies and most-time rivals were a more radical group led by Maximilien Robespierre, Georges Danton, and Jacques Hébert, with support from radical journalist Jean-Paul Marat. Over time they would come to be known as The Mountain, *La Montagne*, so named for their preference for sitting on the highest benches in the back of the National Assembly. Their members were called Montagnards.

Perusing a newspaper, Charlotte Corday asked her cousin, "Madam, have you been reading the news out of Paris?"

"I've read some of the papers, but they're usually several days old before they get to Caen. What are you referring to?"

"I don't understand why we still even

Portrait of Jean-Paul Morat by Joseph Boze

Portrait of Georges Danton

Portrait of Maximilien Robespierre

have a king. The Assembly is clearly in charge in Paris. The king is but a figurehead. He no longer has any real authority. They should just abolish the monarchy and make his evil wife return to Austria. We no longer need nobility."

Her cousin scowled at her. "The king is still the head of state. And need I remind you that *we* are nobility too?"

"I suppose we are, technically. But you and I both know our title doesn't come with any power or advantage."

"That may be, but be careful what you wish for. People may choose to take what little we have. They've seized all property from the Church. Who would have thought that possible just two years ago?"

"I've been following the political debate within the Assembly. It is fascinating to read about."

Her cousin smiled. "Do you have a favorite group? Maybe you should join one of the political clubs," adding sarcastically, "if they actually allowed women."

"Oh, I don't know. The Cercle Social supports rights for women."

"But not their membership."

"True. But at least they're republicans. They're aligned with the Society of the Friends of the Constitution."

"The Jacobin Club? The ones who use to be with Club Breton?"

Charlotte replied, "Yes, the Jacobins. One of their leaders is Jacques Pierre Brissot. Even if women can't join, at least they're allowed to attend the meetings and ask questions. It'll be interesting to see what they do as the revolution progresses. Politics are so fascinating!"

"Fascinating? That's not the word I would use."

"Did you read that the king and his family tried to flee the country? The rumor was that he was trying to meet up with General Bouillé and his loyalist troops in Montmédy. They snuck out of Paris in disguise. They almost made it, but some people in Varennes recognized him. They arrested him and sent him back to Paris."

"Charlotte, that's a lot of intrigue with little impact on us."

"But it does affect us, cousin. Brissot prepared a petition demanding the king be removed! A huge crowd gathered in the Champs de Mars prepared to sign it. General Lafayette and the National Guard were sent to disperse the people. Violence broke out, and the National Guard shot into the crowd. The paper says as many as fifty people were killed!"

"That sounds awful!"

"They're calling it the Champs de Mars Massacre. Now the authorities have closed political clubs like the Jacobins and shut down radical newspapers. People are going crazy in Paris."

"Well then, it's good we're in Caen. Now get ready for dinner."

* * *

Jean-Paul Marat was a bit of a renaissance man. He was a scientist and a doctor before deciding to dedicate his life to politics full time. He was a radical proponent of the *sans-culottes*. In September 1789 he started his own newspaper, *L'Ami du People* (The people's friend). He routinely used it to attack the powerful and influential in Paris. The next January, after slamming the French finance minister, he drew the ire of the local police and fled to England to avoid arrest. He returned in May and used his paper to criticize revolutionary leaders who were too conservative for his liking. He continued to pursue a more radical approach, and in July 1790 he wrote, "Five or six hundred heads cut off would assure your repose, freedom, and happiness."

This didn't win him many friends, especially among those whose heads he was recommending be lopped off. For the next two years he was repeatedly forced into hiding and sometimes secreted himself in the sewers of Paris. While this afforded him a certain level of security, it was not good for his health. Marat suffered from a chronic and debilitating skin disease. The condition caused him to break out in blisters filled with a watery fluid that caused extreme pain and itching. His condition was most likely aggravated by the time spent in the filthy sewers. When not running from the authorities, Marat was active in the Jacobin Club and the more radical Club de Cordeliers. One of the most influential

Jacobins was Jacques Pierre Brissot, the author of the petition that led to the Champs de Mars Massacre. Marat, along with other radicals like Maximilien Robespierre, represented the most radical faction within the club, and after the massacre, they were all forced into hiding.

Jean-Paul Marat was preparing once again to flee to the sewers of Paris. He had gathered some bread, wine, and cheese, along with a few articles of clothing, and was leaving his home in the Cordeliers section of Paris. It was the part of the city where many radicals congregated and the *gendarmerie nationale*, the National Police, would soon be combing the neighborhood for him.

"Jean-Paul, is that you?" Marat froze. It was Georges Danton, a friend and fellow radical Jacobin.

"Danton. Thank God. I thought you were the police."

"No. I just came to warn you. They've closed the Club de Cordeliers and are looking to arrest anyone connected to the incident on the Champs de Mars."

"I suppose it doesn't matter that I wasn't involved. I barely walk, due to my condition."

Danton chuckled, "Do you think that matters to Lafayette and the gendarmes?"

"No. Are you leaving too?"

"Absolutely! I don't want to see the inside of the Châtelet prison if I can avoid it. I'm leaving town. I am going to Champagne until this blows over. I have a property there. You're scurrying away again too."

"Aye. Sadly, no villa for me. I'm going back to the sewers. They're safe, and I know my way around."

Danton chuckled, "They're safe because no self-respecting policeman would step foot down there."

"Well, whatever the reason, they're safe. I appreciate your warning, but now I need to go, and so should you."

"Good luck, Marat. I'll see you when I can. Take care of yourself."

Marat gave a weak smile. "And you, as well." He strained to walk. His skin condition meant even the small bundle hanging from his shoulder caused severe pain with every step. Danton walked away as Marat shuffled off toward the Seine, where he would enter the sewers.

Having fled to the Parisian underworld for sanctuary, Marat waited for the storm of the Champs de Mars incident to blow over. When after several weeks it had not, he decamped for Britain.

* * *

The situation in France became even more confused. In August 1791, a month after the Champs de Mars Massacre, Hapsburg Holy Roman Emperor Leopold II and King Frederick William of Prussia issued the Declaration of Pillnizt in support of King Louis XVI. Leopold was becoming concerned for the safety of Marie Antoinette, his younger sister and King Louis's wife. The declaration was meant to be a "shot across the bow" for the French revolutionaries. Leopold had worded his declaration carefully. It said Austria would only go to war with France if *all* the other major European powers did as well. The British would never agree to war, so the threat was empty. The National Assembly in Paris was not so adept at interpreting such political nuance and was convinced Leopold intended to declare war. Girondin leader Jacques Pierre Brissot was eager to export their revolution to other countries in Europe. He used the declaration to increase his power inside the Assembly, and eventually as a pretext to declare war on Austria.

Dues for the Jacobin Club were more expensive than for most other political clubs, and that limited its membership to those who could afford the price of admission—professional men and wealthy bourgeoisie. Even the radical element, people like the lawyer Robespierre, were still professionals. There were other factions within the Jacobins who were far from radical and included nobility. Duc d'Orléan's son and Louis Phillippe, the future king of France, were members. It came as no surprise when the various factions started to separate.

In the fall of 1791 the Girondin faction led by Brissot dominated the Jacobin Club. They were considered radicals in that they favored the end of the monarchy but were more moderate when it came to implementation and opposed a Paris-centric view of France. They were active in the Legislative Assembly and its successor, the National Convention, and their foreign policy was aggressive. Their objective was to export revolution to other countries, and they counted famed American revolutionary Thomas Paine as one of their allies. However, they were also pragmatic and weren't opposed to using King Louis as a figurehead when it suited their needs.

A more radical faction within the Jacobin Club were the Montagnards. Their leaders were Maximilien Robespierre, Georges Danton, and Jacques Hébert. While the members were mostly middle-class and professional, they were more attuned to the demands of the urban working class, the *sans-culottes*. They focused more on the urban poor than France's rural population and believed that what was best for Paris was best for France. They also favored the end of the monarchy in any form, were opposed to the Girondin's prorevolution foreign policy, and advocated for the execution of the king.

In January 1792 Jean-Paul Marat thought it safe enough to return to Paris. He had been in London for several months and wanted to reengage in French politics. Soon after his return, the forty-nine-year-old Marat married twenty-six-year-old Simone Evrard, a woman who had lent him money and provided him with shelter when hiding from the authorities. His chronic skin condition had not improved. The disease made it extremely difficult for him to walk, and he hadn't been out in public for months. He spent a great deal of his time soaking in medicinal baths in an effort to ease the pain of his affliction. Because of this, his political activities were primarily through his newspaper, *L'Ami du People*. He placed a wide plank across the top of his bathtub, which doubled as his desk so he could continue to work while soaking in his tub.

In the spring of 1792 King Louis XVI was still officially the head of the French government. The Girondins, though not a majority in the Legislative Assembly, wielded a great deal of power. They compelled the king to name their partisans as his key ministers. Pierre Marie de Grave became the Minister of War, and Jean-Marie Roland was named Minister of Interior. Étienne Clavière was Minister of Finance, and Charles François Dumouriez was seated as the Minister Foreign Affairs. With their power consolidated, in April the Girondins forced through a declaration of war against Hapsburg Austria, citing the Pillnitz Declaration as justification.

The ambitious French war plan was to invade the Netherlands, a Hapsburg territory, at three locations simultaneously. They were routed. The first army, commanded by Théobald Dillon, simply ran away at the sight of the enemy. Dillon was wounded by one of his own soldiers before being murdered by a mob in Lille. The second army, commanded by Duc de Biron, was easily routed. These twin disasters forced the Marquis de Lafayette, the commander of the third army, to retreat. The Austrian forces in the Netherlands were too weak to invade France, so, under the terms of their recent alliance, Austria demanded Prussia help. France now found itself at war with two major powers.

At this point, Girondins and the Montagnards had similar objectives—they were both anti-monarchy, democrats and republicans, willing to push their agenda by force if necessary, and committed to the unity of France. But cracks were forming inside the Jacobin camp that were driven as much by personalities as policy. The Girondins were more willing to work within the system, while the Montagnards wanted action, often violent action.

On June 20, 1792, a mob invaded the hall of the Assembly and the Tuileries Palace, where the king and his family resided. The insurrection was put down, but it shifted public opinion in the king's favor. Over twenty thousand Parisians signed a petition supporting the king. Louis was banking that the foreign powers would put him back in power. The Girondins told Louis they'd save the monarchy—if he accepted them as his ministers. When he refused, all the Jacobins—Girondin and Montagnards included—were determined to get rid of the monarchy by force.

Giving new impetus to their efforts was the announcement of the Brunswick Manifesto. On July 25, 1792, the Duke of Brunswick, the commander of the combined Austrian and Prussian army, told the people of Paris that if King Louis and his family were harmed, French civilians would be harmed and the city would be burned to the ground. It was intended to be a warning after the actions of June 20, but it only served to further stoke the revolutionary fires. Louis had secretly received a copy of the manifesto two days before it was issued and personally approved its language. Even without this foreknowledge, many people saw the Brunswick Manifesto as proof that Louis XVI was collaborating with France's enemies.

On August 1 the Prussian forces crossed the Rhine into France. Nine days later, the Parisian National Guard and fédérés, volunteer troops from the provinces, attacked the Tuileries Palace and killed many of the Swiss Guards protecting the royal family. King Louis and his family were forced to take refuge with the National Assembly. The representatives present voted to "temporarily relieve the king." The monarchy was defunct. King Louis XVI of France was officially arrested on August 13, 1792, and imprisoned in the Temple, an ancient fortress-turned-prison. Amid all of this drama, Jean-Paul Marat appeared in public for the first time since returning to France in January.

With the monarchy gone, a new form of government had to be devised. In late August, elections were held for a new parliament, the National Convention. The split between the moderate Girondins, led by Brissot, and the radical Montagnards, led by Robespierre, Danton, and Marat, was complete. Of the 749 seats in the Convention, the Girondins held 160 and the Montagnards held 200. The Plain, a loosely organized centrist party with 389 members, was the swing vote.

The Commune, Paris's radical city government, was controlled by Marat's allies. It formed a Committee on Surveillance to secure the city from "counterrevolutionaries." The committee included Marat, Danton, and other radicals. Marat appointed himself head of the committee and used it for his own personal ends. At Marat's urging, the committee voted to round up people they felt were "suspect." More than four thousand people were arrested and sent to the prisons by the end of August. Most of those detained were just ordinary citizens who had been denounced by a neighbor or had a public disagreement with one of the radicals.

When those on the committee asked what should be done with these new political prisoners, Marat suggested they be burned alive. His proposal was rejected, but only for fear the fires would spread to houses near the prison. They settled on "butchering" instead. The committee graciously released those prisoners for whom there was reasonable doubt as to their guilt. The rest were doomed.

On August 20 Prussian forces captured the strategic French fortress city of Verdun. The road to Paris was now open. Rumors circulated that the prisoners constituted a threat to the city and would fight with the Prussians when they reached the city. Whether they honestly believed this or just found it a convenient excuse, the committee organized a group of mercenaries to carry out the slaughter. It included convicted murderers and other violent criminals released from jail specifically for this purpose. They were joined by National Guardsmen, gendarmes, and ordinary citizens. On September 2, 1792, a tribunal was set up at Prison l'Abbaye. Inmates were briefly interviewed and decreed to be "free" or "guilty." The "guilty" were led to a prison courtyard and beaten, hacked, speared, and decapitated. Some of those murdered were as young as ten years old.

On the second day of the massacres, Marat's Committee of Surveillance published a pamphlet calling on "patriots" to defend Paris against the Prussian invaders. However, it asked them to rid the city of "counterrevolutionaries" before they left home. The tract was written and signed by Marat as the head of the committee. It was then circulated in the provinces, where the murders of political opponents in Paris were suggested as a model for them as well.

Over one thousand prisoners were killed in the first twenty-four hours, and upwards of 1,450 by the time it was finished. The dead included royalists, common criminals, and "counterrevolutionary" political prisoners. The tally included 223 priests who refused to submit to the Civil Constitution of the Clergy, 81 Swiss Guards arrested at Tuileries Palace, and 40 to 80 political suspects. The mob killed thirty-three boys between the ages of twelve and fourteen. In one institution for "women, prostitutes, and the insane," thirty-five women were murdered, including twenty-three who were underage.

* * *

In Caen, Charlotte Corday was safe from the mayhem occurring in Paris, but it appalled her. Marat's pamphlet made it to Normandy, and Charlotte read it. She recognized Marat's name; he was a famous radical, after all. In her mind, the moderate Girondins were the only sign of sanity in the madness that was Paris.

"Cousin, have you read the news? There have been awful, bloody massacres in Paris. Hundreds of people have been slaughtered in the prisons. That monster Marat is responsible for it. I read a tract in his name calling on people to murder counterrevolutionaries before going to fight the Prussians."

"They were killed in the prisons? So, they were criminals then. I mean, I'm not condoning that kind of violence, but most of them were to be executed anyway, right?"

"Not necessarily. Remember when I told you about this new Committee for Surveillance in Paris? The one that arrested thousands of people for being suspected of counterrevolutionary actions? Many of those people were killed. No trials. No convictions. Just murdered."

"I am afraid that passions in Paris are out of hand."

"They murdered the queen's best friend. I don't like the queen, but being her friend should not be a death sentence."

"What was her name, Charlotte?"

Corday scanned her newspaper, "She was Princess de Lamballe."

Her cousin snatched the paper from Charlotte's hands. "That's Marie Thérèse Louise of Savoy! I knew her. She wasn't political."

"They killed her and cut off her head. They paraded it through the city on a pike. Marat and his ilk are monsters. The Girondins need to take control of this mob or the city will burn. All of France will burn."

* * *

On September 20 the French Army won a stunning victory over the Prussians and Austrians at Valmy, ending the threat to Paris. The National Convention was encouraged and two days later officially abolished the monarchy, declaring France a republic. Marat renamed his newspaper *Le Journal de la République Française* (The journal of the French Republic).

The Girondins, while anti-monarchy, never supported putting King Louis XVI on trial. They preferred to use him to their own ends. After the Battle of Valmy, the Prussians left French soil. King Louis's role as a hostage to dissuade the invasion was now moot. In November 1792 another scandal undermined the already dwindling support for the king. It was revealed there was a hidden safe in the king's bedroom in the Tuileries Palace. When Jean-Marie Roland, the Girondin minister of interior, found out, he ordered that it be opened. It contained correspondence with various ministers, financiers, and advisors and exposed a good deal of financial malfeasances. When this became public, the king's trial was inevitable.

King Louis was brought from his prison on December 11 and read his indictment. He was to be tried before the National Convention, accused of high treason and crimes against the state. Louis told his lawyers he was certain he would be convicted but was determined to act as though he could win. The convention was to vote on three questions. Was he guilty? Should there be an appeal to the people? And, if guilty, what punishment?

On January 15, 1793, the convention deputies voted. There was a mountain of evidence that Louis had colluded with the invaders, so the verdict was not a surprise. Of the 721 deputies, 693 voted guilty, 23 abstained, and no one voted to acquit. The voting on his fate took thirty-six hours. A group of 288 deputies voted against execution in favor of prison or exile. Another 72 voted for the death penalty, but with conditions and reservations. In the end, 361 of 721 delegates voted for immediate execution—a majority of one vote. His own cousin, Philippe Égalité, voted for execution, to the horror of monarchists. In a bit of irony, Égalité, the former Duke of Orléans, would lose his own head on the same scaffold before the year was out. A motion to grant the king a reprieve was raised. While 310 deputies favored mercy, 380 voted for the immediate execution of his sentence. The die was cast.

On January 21, 1793, King Louis XVI was taken to the Place de la Concord at the eastern end of the Champs-Élysées. It had been renamed Place de la Révolution in 1789 after the statue of King Louis XV, his grandfather, was torn down by a mob. A scaffolding with a guillotine was now the dominant feature of the nineteen-acre public square.

Louis was escorted by 1,200 guards and transported in a carriage versus the crude tumbrel, a two-wheeled cart in which most condemned were forced to ride. He was escorted through Paris in a slow-moving parade that took two hours to cover the three miles separating his prison from the scaffold. Thousands of Parisians lined the route to get a glimpse of the doomed monarch. Instead of jeering and howling, the crowd was eerily quiet; hardly a sound interrupted the slow methodical beat of the horses' hooves. Almost the entire army of France lined the streets—over 130,000 men. Louis got out of the carriage at the Place de la Révolution, met by a sea of faces. More than twenty thousand people filled the square to witness the execution. The king walked voluntarily and was stoic. The only change in his calm demeanor was when the executioner insisted on tying his hands. When Louis protested, the priest accompanying him said, "Sire, in this further outrage, I see only a final resemblance between your majesty and the God who will be his recompense." The king put up no further protest.

Trying to climb the steep stairs with his hands tied was difficult, and Louis struggled. Again the priest spoke, "Son of Saint Louis, ascend to heaven." Reenergized, Louis hurried up the stairs and to the platform. The commander of the Paris National Guard signaled for a drumroll, but King Louis ordered them to be quiet, and they did. He said, "Frenchmen, I die innocent. It is from the scaffold and near to appearing before God that I tell you so. I pardon my enemies. I hope that the shedding of my blood will contribute to the happiness of France and you, unfortunate people—" Before he could finish, the guard ordered a drumroll from the fifteen drummers present. Whatever else Louis said was drowned out by the noise.

There was deathly quiet as he was strapped to a board and his head lowered into the stocks. The heavy, angled blade hung above him by a taut rope. On the signal of the guard, the executioner, Charles-Henri Sanson, pulled the metal ring securing the rope. The blade

Execution of Louis XVI by Isidore Stanislas Helman

fell with a hiss, and in a brief second, Louis's head was severed from his neck and rolling in the basket below. Sanson lifted the head and showed to the crowd the king was truly dead. The crowd broke into cheers and threw their hats into the air. People lined up to dip handkerchiefs, finger, pikes, and envelopes into his blood for mementos. Revolutionary leaders declared it a great day for the French people. They spoke like it was the end of a horrible journey, but in truth, it was just the beginning.

* * *

Charlotte Corday, safely back in Caen, read of the king's conviction and execution a few days later when the news made its way north. She was against the monarchy but horrified by what she read.

"Cousin, can you believe it? They have executed the king! My God, are we no better than the British when they beheaded King Charles?"

Madame Le Coustellier de Bretteville-Gouville sat silently for a few moments before speaking. "It is a terrible day for the French people. I fear his will not be the last death. After the September Massacres, I believe the people of Paris are becoming addicted to the blood of their perceived enemies. I can't believe the Assembly voted to execute him. And his own cousin, the Duc d'Orleans, cast the deciding vote!"

"Cousin, while he did vote for execution, it was hardly him alone."

"Yes, but if he had voted for prison or exile, the king would still be alive."

"That is true."

"And what of your beloved Girondins? Why didn't they stop this? They control the ministries, or at least the important ones. What is the point of having power if you fail to exercise it for good?"

Charlotte scanned the newspaper again. "I think the radicals are in command. The Commune runs Paris, they and their National Guard. The Girondins may run the nation but are at a disadvantage in Paris."

Her cousin snorted, "Humph. Whoever controls Paris controls the nation."

* * *

The Girondins tried to reassert control. In an attempt to unite the people behind them by exporting the revolution, they declared war on Great Britain and the Dutch Republic. To man the army, they instituted the first conscription. This led to riots and open revolt in Vendee, Bordeaux, and Lyon.

In April 1793 the Committee on Public Safety was formed, and Georges Danton was put in charge. Its job was to protect the young republic against its enemies—foreign or domestic. Danton had been aligned with the Girondins but had a falling out after his fiscal mismanagement during his time as minister of justice came to light. To protect himself, he made a secret alliance with two of the Girondins' biggest detractors, Maximilien Robespierre and Jean-Paul Marat.

The Girondins, who had been considered radicals just a year before, were now the conservatives. Almost every day, Marat accused the Girondins of protecting the rich at the expense of the *sans-culottes*. The Jacobin Club was fracturing, with the Girondins increasingly on the outside. Danton and Robespierre used the club as their primary platform for attacking the Girondins. Things started getting so bad that even Danton tried to intervene to calm the rhetoric. "Citizens, now that the tyrant is dead, let us turn our energies to valiant prosecution of the war," he said. "If we must drink blood, let it be the blood of the enemies of humanity."

All the while, his erstwhile partner, Marat, stirred the pot. He continued to berate the Girondins and even suggested they should be killed. "Caesar was assassinated in the public Senate. Let us treat the traitorous representatives of the country in the same manner." The Girondins, who controlled the National Convention, had had enough. On April 14, 1793, they decreed that Marat should be tried by the Revolutionary Tribunal for promoting murder and dictatorship.

Marat was put on trial and mounted his own defense. During the trial, mobs of his supporters formed in the streets outside. They chanted, "If Marat's head must fall, our heads will fall first." The convention lost its nerve, and he was freed. Marat promptly threatened vengeance on his enemies. At the Jacobin Club, he was placed on the president's chair, and he resumed his war against the Girondins. They were already marginalized within the Jacobin Club, and now Marat demanded that they be kicked out of the National Convention altogether.

* * *

In Caen, Charlotte Corday read the newspapers in horror. "Cousin, have you read what this madman, Marat, is doing?"

Madame Le Coustellier de Bretteville-Gouville sat calmly, attending to her knitting. She was quite used to her ward's complaints. "And what would that be this time, Charlotte?"

"He has been publishing vile screeds every day accusing the Girondins in the convention of all sorts of libels."

"Such is the way of politics, my dear."

"You don't understand. Listen to this. These are his words: 'Caesar was assassinated in the public Senate. Let us treat the traitorous representatives of the country in the same manner.' He is advocating for the murder of our elected government officials! He should be in prison!"

"Well, I doubt that will happen. Not after what happened to him . . . or should I say *didn't* happen to him after the September Massacres. The man proudly claimed credit for riots that killed over a thousand people. And what happened to him? He got elected to the convention!"

Charlotte added, "Let's not forget his role in the King's execution. He bragged about that as well." Charlotte continued to read her article. "Oh, wait a minute. At the end of this article it says he's been brought up on charges of promoting murder. The indictment is nineteen pages long. It says here that even the American revolutionary Thomas Paine is in favor of his conviction."

"Nineteen pages. My, that is long."

Charlotte snorted, "Would be longer if they included the names of the people killed in September." A few days later, she learned he had been acquitted.

* * *

Back in Paris, the Girondins plotted their next move. They'd failed to silence Marat, but they had other enemies, not least of which was the Commune, the city of Paris's radical government that was the source of much of Marat, Robespierre, and Danton's power. It was a violent organization that functioned as much like a gang as a government. Girondins organized a twelve-man *commission extraordinaire* to investigate the *sans-culottes*. Since the Girondins controlled the National Convention, they dominated the commission. On May 24, the convention ordered the arrest of several Commune leaders. The Commune insisted they be released. The Girondins presiding over the convention refused and said, "If any attack is made on the persons of the representatives of the nation, then I declare to you in the name of the whole country that Paris would be destroyed; soon people would be searching along the banks of the Seine to find out whether Paris had ever existed." This only threw fuel on the fire. Marat and Robespierre came to their jailed allies' defense and rallied the citizens of Paris to revolt. A mob marched on the convention, demanding the men be freed, and they were.

The Commune declared itself in open revolt and voted to create its own army of twenty thousand men to defend the city from the convention. On June 2 a mob measuring in the tens of thousands marched on the French parliament and demanded the arrest of the Girondins' leadership. The Girondins, the men who had overthrown a thousand-year monarchy and waged war against the imperial powers of Europe, were forced to flee. The Paris National Guard detained twenty-two Girondin delegates and confined them to house arrest. Some of the deposed Girondins acquiesced, but others—like Jean Marie Roland—escaped, hoping to rally support in the provinces against the radicals in Paris. Only days before, the Girondins had been the most powerful political entity in France. Now they ceased to exist as a political force.

* * *

Reading about the arrest of the Girondins, Charlotte Corday seethed. The Girondins who escaped were trying to organize opposition to the radical Jacobins, led by the Montagnards, who were now in charge of Paris—and as such, effectively in charge of the whole country. She was still an avid supporter of the Girondins and wanted nothing more than for a fair and decent republic to take root in her country, but the Girondins had miscalculated. They needed help, and she was willing to martyr herself to provide it. The focus of her ire was the rabble-rouser, the man who stirred such hatred and venom that he inspired average citizens to commit horrific atrocities like the September Massacres, the man whom she blamed for the downfall of her beloved Girondins— Jean-Paul Marat.

She didn't tell her cousin of her plans. She wouldn't approve and would likely have her committed in order to save her. So Charlotte planned everything by herself. On July 9, 1793, the pretty twenty-four-year-old woman from Caen boarded a stagecoach for Paris and arrived after two days' travel. Corday was not an imposing person. According to her passport, she was five feet one, with auburn hair, grey eyes, a high forehead, a medium-sized mouth, and a dimpled chin on her oval face. But she was determined.

Upon her arrival in Paris, Corday bought a sharp knife with a five-inch blade. It was not a bayonet or a stiletto that an assassin might carry, but rather a simple dinner knife like one would expect to find in any kitchen. Her plan was to seek out Marat at the National Convention and kill him in his chair before God and country. The convention met at the Tuileries Palace, which she found easily enough, but Marat was not there.

Speaking to one of the delegates, Corday asked, "Excuse me sir, I was hoping to speak with Monsieur Marat, but he's not here. Do you have any idea where he might be?"

Turning to the pretty young girl, the man replied, "He isn't here today, Mademoiselle. He isn't here most days. He has a medical condition that keeps him home."

Dejected, Corday answered, "Oh, that's unfortunate. I had an urgent matter that I can only entrust to him. Do you have any notion of when he might be back at the convention?"

"I'm afraid not. However, Monsieur Marat is nothing if not a man of the people. If you need his help, he will see you. He regularly holds audience with people in his home."

Corday perked up. "That's wonderful news. Do you know where he lives?"

"Not the exact address, but he lives in the Cordeliers section."

"Cordeliers section?"

"Yes, named for the Cordeliers Convent in the sixth arrondissement. He lives on Rue de Cordeliers or near there. He, Danton, and Desmoulin all live near each other. They tend to congregate at the Café Procope on Rue de l'Ancienne Comédie. You'll find them there most nights holding court."

"Thank you, sir. You've been very helpful."

Charlotte Corday decided she'd kill Marat on July 13 and made her way to the sixth arrondissement. It was a miserably hot day, not uncommon for Paris in the summer. She purchased a local newspaper and read more disturbing news—the Montagnards in the convention were demanding execution for the Girondins arrested earlier that month. From government ministers to the guillotine in just eleven days; so much for a trial. She needed to act quickly. Donning a spectacular black hat with loud green ribbons, she walked into the Café Procope. There were only a few patrons. The raucous political discussions it was famous for were on hold until the coolness of the evening. She approached the man behind the counter and asked, "Excuse me, monsieur. I am looking for Monsieur Jean-Paul Marat. A man from the convention directed me here to find him but couldn't recall his specific address. Would you direct me to his residence?"

The man peered at her with a jaundiced eye. Marat was popular in the radical Cordeliers section of the city, and residents were protective of him. The man sized her up. She was a small, pretty woman and appeared younger than her twenty-four years. She wasn't threatening, probably just an enamored fan. "Yes, I suppose so. Out the door and turn right and then take the second left. His will be the first red door on the left side of the street."

"Thank you, monsieur. You have been very helpful."

Charlotte left and followed the barman's directions. She found the door and knocked. When it opened, there was a man standing there. "Are you Monsieur Marat?"

The man laughed, "No, mademoiselle. He lives upstairs."

"Thank you, monsieur." She started to walk past him but he stopped her.

"Mademoiselle, Monsieur Marat is not accepting visitors. He's in the bath and too sick to see anyone."

"Oh, but I'll just be a minute. I swear."

The man held firm. "No. Madame Marat said I was not to allow anyone upstairs."

"But I have important information for him!" she pleaded.

"Go away, little girl. Come back tomorrow."

It was futile, so Charlotte left. "Until tomorrow, monsieur." Drawn by the commotion, Simone, Marat's wife, stood at the top of the stairs as she left.

Corday returned to the boarding house where she rented a room. She needed to make Marat want to meet her, so she wrote him a note:

Dear Monsieur Marat.

I come here from Caen. Your love for the nation ought to make you anxious to the plots that are being laid there. I await your reply.

C. Corday

She had it delivered to Marat's house but made a mistake. She had forgotten to include her address! Even if he was so inclined, he had no way to reach her.

Recognizing her error, she returned to Marat's house that evening, and like before, she was not granted an audience. Simone recognized her and her suspicions were raised. Who was this pretty young girl so insistent on talking to her husband?

As the guard was about to kick her out, Charlotte raised her voice. "I insist on speaking to Monsieur Marat. He needs to know about the traitors in Normandy and Caen who are plotting to undermine the revolution!"

When Marat walked the streets, he did so with two pistols tucked into his belt to defend himself against political rivals out for blood. Today, however, he was upstairs soaking in his big copper bathtub. He had a painful, chronic skin disease, most likely scrofula. Scrofula was, ironically, called the "king's evil." It was a form of tuberculosis that caused glandular swelling and painful blisters. Marat's only relief was to soak for hours in a tepid bath of medicinal salts, wearing a white linen shirt with a vinegar-soaked bandana around his neck. He placed a large plank across the top of his bath, so it doubled as a desk. On it he kept paper, pen, an ink pot, and books. He thus continued to work while Simone took care of him. Hearing Charlotte's protestations from downstairs, he demanded that she be let up.

From his tub, he invited her to join him and pointed to a chair nearby. "Now child, what news do you have for me? What is going on in Caen?" Simone stayed in the doorway. She was still suspicious of this strange girl.

Taking her seat, Charlotte replied, "It's the Girondins, monsieur. There are eighteen of them who are former deputies from the convention. They rule the city in collusion with the local officials."

"Do you have the names?"

"Yes, monsieur, I do."

Excitedly, Marat laid out a fresh piece of paper and dipped his quill in the ink pot. "Tell me, tell me their names."

"Yes, monsieur. The first is . . . "

As Charlotte started to give the names, Simone was satisfied and started to leave. "I'll leave you two alone. Jean-Paul, I'm going to fetch more salts." He waved her away, not even looking up from his paper.

Charlotte scooted her chair closer to the bathtub as he scribbled away. "In a few days I will have them all guillotined." Just after he said this, Charlotte removed her knife from her corset, raised it high above her head, and plunged it into Marat's chest. The five-inch blade entered his body just under his right collarbone where it severed his brachiocephalic artery which supplied blood to his right arm, head, and neck. Blood gushed from the deep wound. Marat shouted out for Simone, "To

Death of Marat by Jacques-Louis David

me, my love, to me!" Simone rushed back into the room and grabbed her husband. Her screams attracted a nearby Army surgeon and a dentist who were rushed to his aid. But it was too late. He'd already bled to death in Simone's arms.

Charlotte made a feeble attempt to flee. A man stopped her and beat her back with a chair and then his fists. A mob quickly formed and wanted to kill her on the spot. She was rescued when the police arrested her and took her to Abbaye jail. Her only comment was, "I have done my duty, let them do theirs."

* * *

Marat was treated like a hero and a martyr of the revolution. Songs and poems compared him to Jesus Christ. His heart was removed and placed in an urn which was displayed in the Cordeliers Club like a holy relic of the church. For the next two days, thousands lined up to see it. On July 16, the day of his funeral, Marat's body was carried slowly through the streets while thousands of *sans-culottes,* many of the same people who carried out the brutal slaughter of the September Massacres, wept like little girls. Behind the body, four women carried his copper bathtub. Behind them, his blood-stained shirt was carried aloft on a pike. All the radical leaders of the Commune and the convention were there, led by Robespierre and Danton. He was buried in the garden of the Cordeliers Convent. In September 1794 the corpse of this "hero of the revolution" moved to the Pantheon, one of the most revered places in Paris. However, just four months later, his fortunes changed again. Marat was no longer considered a hero. His body was removed from the Pantheon, and his busts and sculptures destroyed.

* * *

Charlotte Corday sat in prison while her victim's body was paraded through the city. Her trial was quick. She freely admitted what she had done and showed no fear during the proceedings. She vehemently denied that anyone else had knowledge of her plans or in any way helped her. She said she was avenging the victims of the September Massacres and others whose deaths she blamed on Marat. During her trial, she said, "I have killed one man to save a hundred thousand."

Portrait of Charlotte Corday (prior to execution) by Jean-Jacques Hauer

The prosecutor asked, "Do you think you have killed all the Marats?"

She replied, "With this one dead, the others perhaps will be afraid."

She was convicted, sentenced to immediate execution, and taken to the Concierge, a Paris prison. She had but one final request. She wanted her portrait painted. It took two hours and she made suggestions to the artist on how it should appear.

Charlotte Corday (to her execution) by Arturo Michelena

That evening, she climbed willingly into the tumbrel and stood tall. The crowd that had gathered was bitter. She calmly gazed into their faces as they cursed her. As the two-wheeled cart began its journey to the scaffold, a hard rain started to fall. Maximilien Robespierre and Georges Danton watched as she approached the guillotine. Charlotte Corday was calm as the heavy blade fell and cleaved her head from her neck.

The Aftermath

Charlotte Corday's stated motives for killing Jean-Paul Marat were to avenge the deaths of the thousands of people killed in the September Massacres and afterward. In addition, she wanted to end the persecution of the Girondins, the political group she believed was France's best hope for establishing a viable republic that valued the country and its people. She read Marat's articles, tracts, and pamphlets calling on the citizenry of Paris to eliminate the "enemies" residing in its prisons, his rants against the Girondins, and public calls for their executions. In her eyes, and thousands of others', Marat was a monster who undermined almost every aspect of French civil society. She hoped killing him would return a degree of sanity to revolutionary France, and she was willing to sacrifice her own life to make it happen.

Charlotte Corday did not recognize the consequences of her actions, but others did. The reverberations of her act echoed as far as St. Petersburg, where Empress Catherine the Great discussed it in her palace. Marat the Monster had been transformed into Marat the Martyr. The *sans-culottes* and the other radicals of Commune wanted vengeance and blamed the Girondists. Rather than save the Girondins, Corday signed their death warrants. Those Girondins languishing in French prison immediately understood this. One of their leaders, Pierre Victurnien Vergniaud, commented, "She has killed us, but she has taught us how to die."

The twenty-two Girondins arrested in June were put on trial on October 24, 1793. The verdict of the Revolutionary Tribunal was never in doubt. All were convicted and sentenced to death. Seven days later, they were on the scaffold facing the guillotine. All twenty-two, including long-time leader Jacques Pierre Brissot, were beheaded in thirty-six minutes. One of the men had committed suicide the day before. Not to be cheated, the Montagnards beheaded his corpse.

Some Girondins escaped Paris for the provinces. Most were eventually captured and executed, or committed suicide. One notable Girondin was Jean Marie Roland, who had served as the minister of interior and the minister of justice and had escaped capture in June. His wife, Madam Roland, whose salon was a Girondin gathering place, stayed in Paris after her husband fled. She hoped to defend her husband but was arrested. After Marat's death, she was tried and executed eight days after Brissot and the others. Her husband was hiding in Rouen when he heard the news. On Novermber 10 he wrote a note that read, "From the moment when I learned that they had murdered my wife, I would no longer remain in a world stained with enemies." He pinned it to his chest, leaned against a tree, and stabbed himself in the heart with a sword. The Girondins were wiped out, but they would not be alone.

The death of Marat is accepted by many as the official start of the Reign of Terror. Eight days before the Girondins were put on trial, King Louis XVI's wife, Marie Antoinette, having been found guilty of numerous crimes, was guillotined. The radicals were firmly in charge of the French government and, having eliminated the Girondins, started attacking each other. Laws were passed that suspended the constitution and gave the Committee of Public Safety almost unlimited power. When the committee was reorganized in July 1793, its first leader, Georges Danton, was not included, but he still supported its centralization of power. Later that month, Robespierre was elected to the committee and became its de facto leader. Jacques Hébert criticized Robespierre and Danton for being too moderate. He was arrested and executed. In March 1794 Danton announced the end of the Terror—but a bit too soon, as it turns out. Robespierre had his old partner arrested and executed on April 5 along with several of his supporters.

Robespierre himself, drunk with power, was viewed as a threat by other members of the revolutionary government. He was arrested and executed by guillotine on July 28, 1794. His death signaled an end to the Terror. From September 1793 until July 1794, an estimated 16,600 people were tried and executed for "counterrevolutionary"

10 Morning of 10 Thermidor An II (Robespierre wounded) by Lucien-Étienne Mélingue

activities. Upwards of forty thousand additional French citizens may have been summarily executed or died in prison while waiting for their trials.

Charlotte Corday is certainly not to blame for the Reign of Terror. At worst, her murder of Jean-Paul Marat provided the impetus to execute the Girondins when they were, although they likely would have been executed eventually. Based on the subsequent actions of Danton, Hébert, Robespierre, and others, had Corday not provided an excuse to start the wholesale bloodletting, they would have certainly found another. In retrospect, there was probably nothing she could have done to save the Girondins or stop the Terror. However, the reasoning behind her assassination of Marat—stopping the mass executions and protecting the Girondins—was woefully flawed.

Chapter 4

John Wilkes Booth and Lincoln

Dear John, Don't Do Us Any Favors—the South

A handsome young man walked briskly down the street in Washington, DC. It was a cold, rainy evening, but that wasn't why his hat was pulled down over his face and his coat collar turned up. He was famous and didn't want to be recognized. He was John Wilkes Booth, the renowned stage actor and secretly a Confederate courier and spy. His pace was frenetic, and he oozed a nervous energy. As he neared 604 H Street NW, he paused to glance over his shoulder. The street was empty. He climbed the stairs, pushed open the door, and entered the parlor of Mary Surratt's boarding house. It was Friday, March 3, 1865—the night before President Abraham Lincoln's second inauguration.

Both Booth and Surratt were staunch Confederates who supported the Southern cause, believed in slavery, and abhorred the

John Wilkes Booth

Abraham Lincoln on March 6, 1865. Photo by Henry F. Warren

man who had all but destroyed their beloved South. The American Civil War was nearing an end, but a small group of conspirators refused to give up. They were hatching a plot they were sure would snatch a victory from the jaws of defeat.

"Good evening, Mrs. Surratt. Is John here?" John was her son, John Surratt Jr., and Booth's friend and coconspirator.

"Good evening, Mr. Booth. He and the others are downstairs in the kitchen. George stepped out to buy a bottle of whiskey—of course. He should be back in a few minutes."

Mary Surratt

"I wouldn't expect George back too soon. The streets are a sea of mud. Appropriate for the occasion, I'd say."

Booth walked downstairs to the kitchen, where he found the other members of his cabal— David Herold, John Surrat Jr., Lewis Powell, childhood friend Michael O'Laughlen, and old schoolmate Samuel Arnold. "Good evening, gentlemen. I'm glad you all made it. I've secured an invitation to the inauguration tomorrow through Miss Hale."

John H. Surratt Jr. in 1868. Photo by Mathew Brady

David chuckled, "If Senator Hale knew his daughter was secretly engaged to the man plotting the kidnapping of the president, he'd have a stroke!"

Booth smiled. "I suspect he would. You're all going to be in the crowd, right?"

John Jr. and Lewis nodded as David replied, "Absolutely, though I doubt our seats will be as

Lewis Payne, a.k.a. Lewis Powell. Photo by Alexander Gardner

good as yours. We'll look for his bodyguards so we can recognize them on sight."

There were footsteps on the stairs. It was George Atzerodt. "I see you started without me." He held up a bottle of whiskey. "I brought refreshments." David grabbed glasses from the shelf, and Atzerodt poured them all a drink. "Did you hear Lincoln is proposing a constitutional amendment to abolish slavery? Then what? Ex-slaves moving in next door wanting to marry our sisters and daughters? The man is a savage."

George Atzerodt. Photo by Alexander Gardner

Booth smiled. "We aren't there quite yet. We can still correct this vile wrong."

Arnold asked, "Okay, Mr. Booth, but when do we act? The situation for the South gets bleaker by the day. If we're going to turn this around, we need to act soon, or there'll be no South left to save."

Booth's expression turned serious. "I have contacts who will let us know when to strike. Things are bad, but General Lee and General Johnston are still fighting. So long as we have soldiers in the field, we have hope. That's why we must do this; we must kidnap Lincoln. Once we have Lincoln in Confederate hands, they'll have to negotiate. We'll trade him for all the Confederate prisoners being held in Union prison camps. That influx of fighting men will bolster the Confederate forces and embolden anti-war factions in the North. That will force the Union to recognize the Confederate States of America as a separate and free country."

The next day, John Wilkes Booth accompanied Lucy Hale, the daughter of New Hampshire Senator John P. Hale, to the U.S. Capitol to attend President Abraham Lincoln's inauguration. They stood in the VIP section of the gallery above the president. Booth had an excellent view. Lincoln gave an inspiring speech about reconciliation, and his closing statement was "With malice toward none with charity for all, with firmness in the right as God gives us to see the right, let us strive on to finish the work we are in to bind up the nation's wounds, to care for him who shall have borne the battle and for his widow and his orphan—to do all which may achieve and cherish a just and lasting peace among ourselves and with all nations." His words fell on deaf ears with Booth and his cabal. They were living in the past while trying to change the future.

The conspirators met again the next day. Lewis Powell said, "Old Abe gave them a good speech. All about God, slaves, and peace."

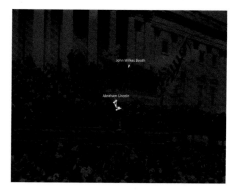

Booth at Lincoln Inauguration, 1865.
Original photo by Alexander Gardner

Booth snorted, "I wasn't listening. So much pig slop. The man is crude and boorish. His speech is indistinguishable from a cow's lowing to my ears. I must say, though, I had a great seat for the spectacle. I had an excellent chance to kill the President, if I had wished to do so."

George Atzerodt laughed and shot back, "Then why didn't ya? We'd be drinking in celebration."

Booth chuckled, "I didn't have a gun on me. Besides, not like you can swap a dead tyrant for live prisoners."

O'Laughlen added, "Fair enough. So, tell us John, what's the next step? We need to act and right soon."

"I know. Lincoln uses the Old Soldiers' Home as a country house to get away from the capital. It's three miles north of the White House in a rural area. He and his wife like to attend plays. My plan is to snatch him in transit on his way back from the theater. Most of his bodyguards and soldiers will either be at the White House or the Old Soldiers' Home. If we intercept him halfway, there will only be a couple of men at most. We can handle them, plus surprise will be on our side. I have feelers out to all my contacts in the theaters. When I find out which performance he's going to attend, we'll know when to snatch him. Once we have him, we smuggle him across the Potomac to the Confederates before anyone even figures out that he's gone."

George said, "I have acquired the necessary guns, and we'll be ready. They're stashed at Mrs. Surratt's other property, her old tavern in Surrattsville. I didn't want to keep them here at the boarding house in case the police come a-knocking. How will you get word to us?"

"I'm staying at the National Hotel at Pennsylvania and Sixth. When I learn something, I'll send a message to Surratt. We'll meet here. Be ready! I'm not sure how much warning we'll get."

The men nodded as George said, "We'll be ready."

* * *

John Wilkes Booth was funding the plot with his own money, and he had plenty. He was one of the most famous actors of his age. At twenty-six years old, he was almost a generation younger than his famous half-brother and fellow actor, Edwin Booth. Whereas Edwin was considered a patrician master thespian, John was more energetic and dashing. He was popular, handsome, and a genuine heartthrob. All this also made him wealthy. At the onset of the Civil War, John Wilkes Booth was twenty-two years old and earning approximately $20,000 a year as an actor, the equivalent of over $600,000 in 2022. As such, he self-funded his work on behalf of the Confederacy.

Booth was equally popular above and below the Mason-Dixon Line. During the war, he crossed the border between North and South regularly to pursue his trade. He acted in New Orleans and Richmond as easily as New York and Chicago. As a famous actor, his travel wasn't scrutinized by Union officials. He used this deference to smuggle the anti-malarial drug quinine into the South, where it was very difficult to obtain due to the Union blockade. He also acted as a courier and a spy reporting to Confederate intelligence officers what he learned in the North.

Booth's family was originally from Great Britain before moving to Baltimore in 1821. His parents were Shakespearean actor Junius Brutus Booth and his mistress, Mary Ann Holmes. John Wilkes Booth grew up on a farm in slaveholding Maryland. He strongly believed in slavery and wholly supported the Southern cause. He even attended the hanging of abolitionist John Brown after his raid on Harpers Ferry. In contrast, his older half-brother, Edwin, was a Unionist who resided in New York. They had many heated arguments about the war, Lincoln, and slavery until finally, in late 1864, Edwin had had enough and told John he was no longer welcome in his home.

* * *

It was almost two weeks before the plotters had their opportunity. Booth learned from his extensive contacts within the theatrical community that President Lincoln planned to attend a play, *Still Waters Run Deep*, on Friday, March 17. He wouldn't be going to a theater, however. The play was being staged at a military hospital near the Old Soldiers' Home. They'd have a limited time to act, but it would be even more unexpected.

On Friday night, Booth assembled his men. Each was armed with a revolver, and John Jr. and George had Spencer carbines. They reconnoitered the roads around the Old Soldiers' Home. They knew what roads Lincoln's carriage would have to take and selected their ambush location, a sharp turn on a country lane where the carriage would have to slow down. Their plan was simple—shoot the guards, grab Lincoln,

Dr. Samuel Mudd

and head south. Booth requisitioned food and supplies at the farm of Dr. Samuel Mudd, a Confederate sympathizer in southern Maryland. From there, they'd ride for the Potomac River, where a boat would be waiting to shuttle them across to Virginia. A string of fast horses would be waiting to speed them away to Richmond and General Robert E. Lee's Army of Northern Virginia.

The men tied up their horses in the woods near the road and took up their positions. David Herold, Samuel Arnold, and George Atzerodt were hidden on the north side of the road. Lewis Powell, Michael O'Laughlen, and John Surratt were to the south. They cut a small tree to the point where a gentle push would send it crashing across the road to stop the president's carriage. The men in the woods were to shoot any guards on horseback or on the carriage, after which Booth, ever the actor, would step out and demand the president surrender himself.

All was at the ready, and they hunkered down to wait. Booth knew the play at the hospital was to start promptly at 7:00 p.m. and last until 8:30 p.m. Assuming the president stayed to hobnob for a bit, Booth figured the president's carriage should appear sometime around nine o'clock. The night was lit by a nearly full moon. Lewis, a former sniper, had the best eyes, so he peered down the road to spot the oncoming coach.

The men sat nervously. Booth paced back and forth across the road. He wouldn't let any of the men smoke, lest the flare of a match gave away their positions. It was already after eight o'clock and the men expected Lewis to call out to them at any time. David and Michael made sure a round was chambered in their rifles and cocked the hammers in anticipation. Booth checked his watch in the pale moonlight. It was 9:00 p.m. "Any time now, boys. Look sharp." He crouched behind a thick oak tree. When the bullets started to fly, he didn't want to accidently get shot by his own men. The time crawled by. Though it was a cool night, the men were sweating. Booth checked his watch again—9:25 p.m. Lincoln was running late.

Surratt whispered, "I got 9:30 by my timepiece. When was this shindig supposed to be over?"

Booth replied softly, "At eight-thirty. Just like that lout to keep people up late with his inane gabbing. Well, we'll teach him some manners soon enough." They continued to wait. By 10:30 p.m. something was seriously wrong. "Men, I think we're screwed here. I don't believe he's coming after all."

Surratt asked, "Well, what now?"

Booth pondered this a moment. "Let's pack it in. Everyone split up;

take a different way back to town. We'll meet up tomorrow night at Surratt's boarding house and figure out what to do next."

Booth rode west before turning south and heading back into Washington. He stopped at a tavern along the way for a schooner of beer and a bite to eat. By the time he got back to the National Hotel, it was almost midnight. He wanted to determine what had gone wrong. He was assured by his contact that Lincoln would be at the hospital. Before going to his room, he approached the front desk and asked, "Any messages for me?"

Surratt's Boarding House

The night clerk responded, "Oh, hello, Mr. Booth. Let me check." After a minute he returned. "Uh, sorry, sir. No messages."

"Thank you."

The clerk added, "You should have been here. You missed all the excitement."

"Excitement?"

"Yes, sir. There was a reception here tonight. President Lincoln himself showed up! Can you believe it?"

Booth was dumbfounded. While he and his cohorts were shivering in the woods, President Lincoln was eating dinner in Booth's hotel.

* * *

John Wilkes Booth was frustrated and furious. Lincoln's last minute decision to forgo the play at the hospital cost Booth his opportunity to kidnap him. When he met with his coconspirators the next day at Mrs. Surratt's boarding house, he told them of the ironic twist of fate. The news was disheartening. It was Mary Surratt who refused to allow them to give up. "Are you men or are you children? One little setback and you're ready to pack it in? John Surratt, your father would be ashamed of you. You whine about this, but think of General Lee and his army. How good do they have it about now? No boots. No food. No blankets. You men need to buck up and soldier on."

Booth addressed his men. "Mary's right. This was just a setback. This wasn't a battle lost, it was a battle we didn't even fight. The plan was a good one. We haven't been found out. We need to just wait for the next opportunity. Everyone stay sharp, and I'll see what I can learn."

Booth continued to press his contacts for information on Lincoln, but to no avail. He learned nothing actionable of Lincoln's movements or plans. It frustrated Booth to no end that his quarry was a little over a mile from his hotel room and yet he could do nothing to stop him from destroying his beloved South.

While they waited, the South's military situation continued to deteriorate. Confederate General Robert E. Lee had been bogged down in the Siege of Petersburg south of Richmond for nine months. His army was outnumbered, outgunned, and outsupplied. Every day, Union General Ulysses S. Grant's Army of the Potomac grew stronger while Lee's Army of Northern Virginia grew weaker. With two additional Union armies soon to arrive from the Shenandoah Valley and North Carolina, Lee's position wasn't tenable, and Richmond's days were numbered. If Booth was going to affect the outcome of the war, he needed to act quickly. The conspirators met again at Mary Surratt's boarding house. Michael O'Laughlen returned to Baltimore, and after the failed kidnapping, Samuel Arnold took a clerk job near Hampton, Virginia. Their ranks were thinning.

"Gentlemen, we're in desperate times. General Lee continues to defend Richmond and Petersburg, but he cannot hold out indefinitely. We need to change the status quo. If the fates have intervened to stop us from kidnapping the scoundrel, then we shall simply kill him."

Lewis Powell asked, "And what will that accomplish? I don't mind killing him, mind you. I killed my share of Yankees when I was in the Confederate Army, and he'd just be one more. I don't see how that changes General Lee's situation, that's all."

Booth replied, "We don't just kill him, we kill Vice President Andrew

Johnson and Secretary of State William Seward too. We take out the Union leadership. We cut the head off the snake. The Union government will be thrown into disarray. That will give the Confederate government and Generals Lee and Johnston time to reorganize. The anti-war faction in the North has been held under Lincoln's boot ever since he suspended the writ of habeas corpus. With him and the others out of the way, they can rise up and assert themselves and put an end to this bloody war."

John Surratt added, "At the very least, we avenge the South. That man deserves to die for what he's done to our countrymen." The others nodded in agreement.

Booth said, "If we don't have to spirit Lincoln away to Richmond, it makes our jobs all the easier. We simply kill the sons of a bitches and melt away like a late spring snow."

George Atzerodt squirmed in his seat. "Not to throw cold water on ya, John, but that doesn't really change things much. Whether we aim to kidnap him or kill him, we still need to get next to the man."

"I know, George, I know. But killing him only requires that we get close for a few seconds."

"Yeah, but I'd prefer not to be killed in the process. They aren't going to simply bow and let us leave after we shoot the bastards."

Booth smoothed his mustache. "I understand your worry, but I've already considered that. We need a few more people to help the shooters get clear once the deed is done. I'm lining up more men."

George smiled. "I trust ya, John, but I also want to see tomorrow."

* * *

The next day was April 1, 1865, and some 150 miles to the south, the fate of the Confederacy was being determined near a rural Virginia crossroads called Five Forks. Grant's army besieging Petersburg was trying to flank Lee's army and cut the railway lines that supplied the Confederate capital of Richmond with men, food, and ammunition. The effect was to constantly force the Confederates to the extend their defenses further and further west and spread their shrinking army thinner and thinner along the line.

Union General Philip Sheridan attacked the rebel forces under the command of Confederate General George Pickett. Lee, recognizing the strategic importance of Five Forks, ordered Picket to hold it "at all hazards." Sheridan's cavalry attacked, but the Confederates initially held strong despite the fact that their two senior generals were off having lunch when the main attack began. The battle was confused on both sides, and they fought well into the night before the Confederate forces were defeated. Lee tried to reinforce his beleaguered troops, but it was too little too late. When Grant learned of the victory at Five Forks, he ordered a general attack along the front.

On April 2 the Confederate line in Petersburg was breached, and Lee had no choice but to abandon Petersburg and Richmond to the Union Army. The Confederate government loaded its archives and remaining gold onto a train, set fire to anything of value to the Union troops, and fled southwest to Danville, Virginia. Lee gathered up the remnants of his army and conducted a fighting retreat west toward Lynchburg. Union troops entered Richmond on April 3, 1865. The Confederate States of America was in its death throes.

* * *

Back in Washington, DC, John Wilkes Booth and his coconspirators were desperate. They were dismayed by the fall of Richmond and angered when Lincoln toured the fallen Confederate capital the same day it capitulated. To add insult to their injury, the city was surrendered to Union General Godfrey Weitzel, the commander of the Twenty-Fifth Corp of the United States Colored Troops. While some held delusions that the war was not yet lost, all wanted revenge on the man they blamed for the South's destruction—President Abraham Lincoln.

On April 11 Lincoln gave an impromptu speech from his window at the White House. Among those in the crowd were Booth and Lewis

Powell. This was like dangling a steak just beyond the reach of a starving dog. In his speech, Lincoln announced he favored giving former slaves the right to vote. Enraged, Booth urged Powell to shoot Lincoln on the spot. Given they were in the middle of a large crowd, Powell wisely declined. Frustrated, Booth declared this would be the last speech Lincoln ever gave.

The next day, General Robert E. Lee surrendered the Army of Northern Virginia to General Ulysses S. Grant at Appomattox Court House. Booth was at Mary Surratt's boarding house chatting with Louis Weichmann, a friend of John Surratt and a boarder in the house, when a man came in and broke the news. "Lee surrendered!"

Louis J. Weichmann, ca. 1865

Weichmann was stunned. "What? When? Where?"

"It just came in on the telegraph. Today in some place called Appomattox Court House west of Richmond. He surrendered his whole army."

Booth sat stoically. "Well, the war isn't over yet. Joe Johnston is still fighting in North Carolina. So long as there is an army in the field, there is hope."

Weichmann was incredulous. "Are you serious, John?"

"Dead serious. And I vow never to take the stage again unless it is to present *Venice Preserv'd*."

"I'm not familiar with that play, John."

"No matter." *Venice Preserv'd* was about an assassination plot.

* * *

Outwardly, Booth put on a brave face, but inside he was having doubts. Despite his efforts and extensive contacts throughout the city, all his efforts to get to Lincoln failed. He honestly believed slavery was part of God's plan, so why had God interfered with his plotting? Up to this point, the Fates had conspired against him. That was about to change.

On the morning of Friday, April 14, Booth stopped by the Surratt boarding house to chat with Mary before walking to Ford's Theater. He had performed there several times in his career, and the owner, John T. Ford, was a close personal friend who owned theaters in Baltimore and other cities. Booth preferred living in hotels and had no permanent residence, so he had all his mail forwarded to Ford's Theater, where he would retrieve it from time to time.

Booth was familiar to the staff of the theater, and no one thought anything about it when he strolled in. He walked back to the office to find Harry, John Ford's brother, sitting behind the desk. "Hello, Harry. Where's John today?"

Harry smiled broadly. "Well, if it isn't Mr. John Wilkes Booth. I haven't seen you in a month of Sundays. Where have you been?"

"Oh, here and there. Washington and Baltimore mostly. Is your no-good brother, John, around?"

"Nope. Ya missed him. He headed down to Richmond."

"Richmond? What the hell for? It's a burned-out mess."

"Yeah, I suppose it is, but that also presents an opportunity. While the warehouses and gunpowder works are gone, there are some buildings left standing downtown. John is looking at property to turn into a theater. He figures the city will come back once the war is officially over. Right now, greenbacks beat Confederate dollars all to hell. He's hunting for a bargain."

"Kind of cold blooded, ain't it? I mean the fires are still smoldering, and the Confederacy is still fighting."

"Who are you kidding, Booth? The Confederacy is finished; they just don't know it yet. What you need my brother for? Anything I can help ya with?"

"Yeah, I suppose so. I just came to pick up my mail. It's been a couple of weeks."

"Oh, of course." Harry walked across the room and opened the front of a large wooden cabinet. Inside was a grid of cubby holes above three large drawers. Reaching into the cubby hole in the upper right corner,

Harry retrieved a stack of mail. "Here ya go John." He stopped to sniff one of the envelopes. "Perfume. This one must be from one of your lady admirers."

Booth smiled. "Just one of many, Harry, one of many."

As Booth thumbed through the stack, Harry said, "We have a new play running tonight. An English farce by a fellow named Tom Taylor. It's called *Our American Cousin*. It's supposed to be a hoot."

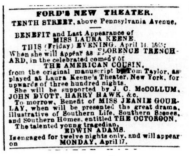

Ad for *Our American Cousin* in *Evening Star*, April 14, 1865

"Yes."

"Hell, the president himself is coming to see it tonight."

Booth stood flabbergasted. "What did you say?"

"The president. Ole Honest Abe himself. He and Mrs. Lincoln are attending tonight along with General Grant and his wife. So, you know the play?"

Booth smiled. "Yes, I am very familiar with it. Which showing is the president to attend?"

"The second. Curtain is at eight o'clock. You ought to come."

"I just may." Booth collected his mail and walked to the door. He struggled to hide his excitement and had to restrain himself from sprinting back to his hotel. After collecting a few things, he walked to Mary Surratt's boarding house. Pulling her aside, he said, "We need to gather our comrades. We finally have our opportunity to avenge the Confederacy and salvage our position."

"What are you saying?"

"Lincoln will be attending the theater tonight, where I intend to kill him. I need the others to execute the other aspects of the plan."

"You mean kill Seward and that Tennessee turncoat, Johnson?"

"Yes, ma'am. I do. I want to meet tonight no later than seven o'clock." He handed Mary a parcel he brought from his hotel. "I need this taken to your tavern. I'll retrieve it afterward. We've stashed some guns there. We'll need to retrieve them as well."

"I'll go and ask Mr. Weichmann to accompany me."

Booth had met Weichmann but didn't really know him. "Can he be trusted?"

"Yes. He and my Johnny went to seminary together. We've been friends for years."

"All right then. Are any of the other men here?"

"Just George Atzerodt. He's upstairs. Why?"

Booth took some money from his pocket and handed it to her. "Tell George to rent a room at the Kirkwood House at Twelfth and Pennsylvania. That's where Johnson is staying."

Mary replied with seriousness, "It will be done, Mr. Booth."

* * *

Booth returned to his hotel and ordered a late lunch but ate little. He was too excited. He paced around his room, checking his watch every few minutes. Finally, at about five o'clock he walked to Mary Surratt's boarding house to wait for the others. He waited impatiently for the other men to arrive. Mary had told her son, John Jr., what was going on, but the others hadn't a clue what was about to transpire. She wouldn't risk them telling someone and having their plan thwarted.

John Surratt was in the kitchen when Booth arrived. At about 6:30 p.m., Louis Weichmann and Mary returned from her tavern with the guns. Shortly after, Lewis Powell, George Atzerodt, and David Herold arrived. Lewis asked, "What's this all about, John?"

"We act tonight."

The men stood dumbfounded. George asked, "We're going after Lincoln?"

"Yes. And Johnson. And Seward. Gentlemen, this is the moment we've been waiting for. And there's a bonus."

David asked, "What's that?"

"General Grant. He's going to be with Lincoln tonight. I intend to kill them both."

John Surratt was shocked. "Grant? Really?"

Booth smiled. "The Lincolns have invited the Grants to join them tonight at Ford's Theater for a play. The curtain is in an hour. While I am at the theater, the rest of you will kill Seward and Johnson."

George Atzerodt blanched. "Are you sure? How do you know he'll be there? I mean, remember the kidnapping. He didn't show and we missed him."

"I was at Ford's Theater earlier today. Harry Ford, the owner's brother, told me himself. They are going to the second sitting of *Our American Cousin*. The curtain is at eight o'clock. I plan to shoot them both during the third act. I can get in and out of the theater without being seen. I know the place like the back of my hand."

George asked, "Both Grant and Lincoln? Do you need any help?"

"No. They will be in the president's box. I will bar the door behind me. They'll be trapped. We need to kill Johnson and Seward at the same time. George, did you get the room at the Kirkwood House?"

"I did, but I don't know why."

"Because that's where Johnson is staying. Your job is to kill him. Don't do it before nine o'clock. I don't want them to alert Lincoln or his men. He is sure to have bodyguards. I'll have to deal with them separately, but if I have the element of surprise, that shouldn't be a problem."

"How am I supposed to do that? I mean, what if Johnson has body-guards too?"

"As for 'how,' you have a pistol, but I'd use a knife if possible. Gunshots will only draw attention. I don't believe he has any bodyguards, but if he does, you'll have to deal with them. He's only been the vice president for a few weeks. Not like he's had time to make enemies."

David chuckled, "Except for us, you mean."

Booth stared intently at George. "You'll do this, right?"

George's comrades awaited his answer. "Yeah. I'll do it."

Booth turned to the others, "Okay, who wants to kill Seward?"

Lewis Powell's hand shot up. "I'll kill the son of a bitch. But I'm not that familiar with Washington. This city confuses the shit out of me."

The other men laughed. David said, "I'll go with him so he don't get lost."

John Surratt asked, "What of me and mother? What are we to do?"

"Your mother should stay here. The Union spies have been watching her, so she should make sure to be around plenty of people. If the police come to interrogate her, she'll have an alibi. She can feign cooperation and then send them off in the wrong direction. I want you to head south to the tavern. Have the guns ready. Lewis, George, and I will head there afterward to pick them up. Understand?"

John Surratt nodded. "Yes, John, I understand. After you leave, I'll head north and tell them I was nowhere around when the deed was done."

Booth added, "We'll head to the tavern to pick up the guns and then I'll go south into Maryland and then Virginia. Since I'm the most recognizable, I need to hide among friendly people. You other men need to go in different directions, but don't tell each other exactly where. That way, if one of you is arrested, he can't inform on the others under torture."

Their marching orders firmly established, the five men slipped off into the night.

* * *

Lewis Powell was the only real soldier in the group. He was from Alabama and lied about his age to join the Second Florida Infantry in 1861. He fought in several major battles before being wounded at Gettysburg. He was captured but escaped and joined Mosby's Rangers, a Confederate guerrilla force operating out of northern Virginia. He earned a reputation as a good soldier but also a violent one who always shot to kill and used the skull of a Union soldier as an ashtray.

David Herold led Powell to Secretary of State William Seward's house on Lafayette Square in Washington. They knew Seward would be home because he was convalescing from a serious carriage accident that left him bedridden with a broken jaw, a broken arm, a concussion, and other injuries. Powell was armed with a revolver and a large knife. While Herold held his horse, Powell, dressed in dark clothing, approached the house. He knocked on the door and, when the black servant answered, claimed he was a courier sent by Seward's doctor to deliver medicine. The servant was suspicious, since the doctor had left only an hour before, and ordered that Seward not be disturbed. Powell pushed his way in and up the stairs. At the top of the stairs he encountered Secretary Seward's son, Frederick. "Stop! Who are you and what are you doing here?"

"I was sent by the doctor to deliver medicine for Secretary Seward."

"What medicine? Let me see it."

Powell handed Frederick a vial, and as Frederick took it, Powell drew his pistol, put the barrel to the man's chest, and pulled the trigger. Nothing happened. The gun misfired. Powell recovered quickly and pistol-whipped Seward's son several times. Witnessing all this from the bottom of the stairs, the servant ran screaming next door to the office of General Christopher Auger. Startled by the servant's screams, David Herold panicked. He tied Powell's horse to a tree and fled.

In the house, Powell pulled out his knife and crashed through Seward's bedroom door. Seward was being tended by his daughter and a male Army nurse. Powell slashed the nurse with his knife and punched Seward's daughter in the face, knocking her to the ground. He jumped on top of Seward in his bed and starting hacking at his head and neck with the knife. Powell stabbed Seward through his cheek and opened a bloody wound on his neck but failed to kill him. Seward's canvass and metal splint for his broken jaw deflected most of the stabs. Seward's other son, Augustus, burst into the room only to be stabbed several times before he and the wounded nurse wrestled Powell to the floor. Powell was uninjured and broke free. He stabbed the nurse in the shoulder and chest and cut off a chunk of Augustus's scalp before fleeing. Running down the stairs, he collided with a State Department messenger who had just arrived and was unaware of the attack. Powell stabbed the hapless man in the back before bolting from the house and tossing his knife in the gutter. David Herold, his guide and accomplice, was gone.

"Herold, you son of a bitch." Powell swung up on his horse but, having no idea of where to go, simply rode the beast slowly away from the scene.

* * *

At the Kirkwood House, George Atzerodt sat in the hotel bar trying to screw up enough courage to go through with his part of the plot. The bartender approached and asked, "What ya drinking?"

"Whiskey." As the bartended poured the drink, George asked, "I hear the new vice president, that Johnson fella, is staying in this hotel. Is he around? Could you point him out?"

George was born in Germany, and even though he emigrated to the United States when he was only eight years old, he still spoke with a noticeable accent, which the bartender picked up on. "Uh, Mr. Johnson isn't around. Where are you from, mister?"

"Baltimore. In town on business."

The bartender was leery. "Uh, huh. That'll be two bits for the whiskey."

George put a dollar on the bar and downed his whiskey in a gulp. "Pour me another while you're here." The bartender poured another shot and walked to the other end of the bar to attend his other customers.

George stayed perched on his barstool drinking for over an hour. He checked his pocket watch. It was nine o'clock. The play was well underway. Had Booth already done the deed? No, he said he would do it during the third act. What if Booth lost his nerve? What if he was intercepted by the bodyguards before he acted? What was the point of killing Vice President Johnson if Lincoln was still alive? His second-guessing undermined what little fortitude he possessed. He ordered one last shot of whiskey, paid his tab, and left. Rather than go upstairs to Johnson's room, he exited the hotel. He had lost his nerve. Johnson would learn the next day how close he had come to death.

George was inebriated and walked the streets of Washington, DC, most of the night. He reached into his pocket; the steel of the knife was cold in his hand. Now it was a symbol of his failure and cowardice. He dropped it in the gutter. A woman walking nearby, finding it suspicious, promptly reported it to the police.

* * *

Unlike Atzerodt, Booth had not lost his nerve. He was more determined than ever. Before he had even informed his cohorts of his plan, Booth had gone to a stable near the National Hotel to rent a horse for his getaway. He had rented horses there before, and the owner, James Pumphrey, was a friend of John Surratt. Entering the stable, Booth hailed Pumphrey. "Hello, James."

"Well, hello, Mr. Booth. What can I do for you today?"

"I want to secure use of one of your animals for the evening. How about that grey gelding I rented last time? He's a fine specimen."

"I'm sorry, Mr. Booth, but someone rented him this morning. I do have a fine bay mare available. But I have to warn you, she is a mite more spirited."

"Oh, I can handle her alright. The usual rate?"

"Yes, sir."

Booth handed James the money. "I'll be back at four o'clock. I have some business to attend to at Grover's Theater, and then I want to go for quiet ride in the country."

"Well, she will do you a right service, sir."

Booth returned at four o'clock and collected his horse. James handed him the reins and warned him again, "She's a spirited animal. She'll break loose from her halter if you leave her unattended."

"Don't worry. I won't lose your horse." Booth left, but he didn't go to Grover's Theater. He returned to his hotel, where he wrote a letter to the *National Intelligencer* newspaper detailing his plan to kill Lincoln. He signed his own name to the letter and included the names of his coconspirators—Powell, Herold, and Atzerodt.

After meeting with the others at Surratt's boarding house and giving them their marching orders, Booth mounted the horse and rode to Ford's Theater. Upon arriving, Booth found Edmund Spangler, a stagehand and carpenter at the theater.

"Ed, I need you to hold my horse for a few minutes. She's a mite spirited and will break her halter if I just tie her up. I have some business inside but it shouldn't take more than a few minutes."

"Sorry, Mr. Booth, but I got work to do. I'll get Joe Burroughs to hold her for ya."

"That would be dandy, thanks." Booth flipped Spangler a quarter, tipped his hat, and entered the theater.

The Lincolns arrived late to the theater, and the play was stopped briefly while the president took his seat and the orchestra played "Hail to the Chief." Booth didn't observe the Lincolns arriving without General Grant, who declined the invitation, citing family business in New Jersey. The Grants' seats were given to Major Henry Rathbone and his fiancée, Clara Harris. Lincoln routinely was accompa-nied by bodyguards. Two men, Ward Lamon and William Crook, handled the bulk of the work. However, neither man was present on April 14. Lamon had been sent to Richmond on assignment by Lincoln, and Crook was off duty, having worked since eight o'clock that morning. Accompanying the president that eve-ning was John Frederick Parker, a Washington

President's box at Ford's Theater

Metropolitan Police officer. He was to guard the door to the president's box.

Booth drank in the theater's saloon, waiting for his chance. At inter-mission, Parker inexplicably left his post outside the president's box. He, along with Lincoln's footman and valet, went to a nearby pub for a drink, leaving the president unguarded. At 10:25 p.m. Booth made his way to the area outside the president's box. Several people recognized him, but a famous actor in a theater was not unexpected. Booth was surprised to find the door unguarded. He turned the knob and entered the president's box.

There were two doors to the box. The first opened to a small alcove. The door opened in, and Booth used a large stick to jamb it shut. Beyond the next door lay his prey. Booth was armed with a single-shot, .41-cal-iber derringer pistol and a dagger. There was a hole in the door through which Booth observed the occupants. The president was directly in front of him, but it wasn't the Grants joining Lincoln in the booth, rather some young military officer and a woman. It didn't matter. Lincoln was his real target. Booth was familiar with the play, and when an actor recited a line

Weapon used to murder Lincoln

Booth knew would draw raucous laughter, he quietly opened the door. The occupants were focused on the play. His entry was unnoticed. He placed the derringer to the back of Lincoln's head and pulled the trigger.

The bullet entered behind Lincoln's left ear and passed through his brain, lodging in the front of his skull. Lincoln immediately slumped over in his chair. The gunshot startled everyone in the box. When Rathbone turned, Booth was standing in a cloud of smoke.

Rathbone lunged at Booth, who dropped his gun, pulled out his dagger,

Booth assassinating Lincoln

and stabbed Rathbone in the arm. As Booth prepared to jump down to the stage below, Rathbone grabbed at him again. Booth's spur caught on the bunting adorning the presidential box, and he fell awkwardly to the stage below, injuring his leg. Many in the audience of 1,700 people assumed it was all part of the play. Booth regained his feet, thrust his bloody knife into the air, and shouted, "*Sic semper tyrannis!*" (Thus always to tyrants!)

The screams of Mary Lincoln and Clara Harris pierced the air. Rathbone, holding his bloodied arm, shouted down, "Stop that man!"

A military officer in the audience, Major Joseph Stewart, immediately clambered over the orchestra pit to the stage and pursued the assassin. Booth limped across the stage toward a side door, stabbing the orchestra leader when he tried to stop him. Once in the alley, he pushed past Joe Burroughs, pulled himself up on his horse, and sped away.

* * *

Pandemonium broke out inside Ford's Theater. An Army surgeon from the audience, Dr. Charles Leale, ran up to the president's box but found the door jammed until Rathbone removed the stick Booth had used to wedge the door. Lincoln slumped in his chair in the arms of his crying wife. Another doctor, Charles Taft, was lifted up from the stage to the president's box. Together, Taft and Leale began to examine Lincoln.

Since Booth had thrust a bloody knife into the air, they assumed the president was stabbed. They lowered him to the floor and opened his shirt but found no wounds. It was then that Leale discovered the bullet wound. Lincoln's breathing was labored, but when Leale removed a blood clot from the wound, it improved.

The doctors agreed it was too dangerous to take the president to the White House, so a group of soldiers carried him across the street to the home of a tailor named Peterson. Lincoln was so tall, he had to be laid diagonally across the tailor's bed. More doctors arrived, and all agreed the president's wound was mortal. Lincoln died the next morning at 7:22 a.m.

Lincoln deathbed in the Peterson House, April 15, 1865

* * *

Booth, having made his escape, headed south toward rural Maryland. To leave the city he had to cross the Anacostia River; the closest bridge was the Navy Yard Bridge, but it was closed to civilian traffic after 9:00 p.m. It was almost eleven o'clock when Booth approached the sentry guarding the bridge. The man was bored. "Halt. What's your business? This bridge is closed to civilians after nine o'clock."

Booth stopped his horse. Word of Lincoln's assassination had yet to be broadcast. "Good evening. I didn't realize the bridge was closed. That's a shame. I guess I'll have to take the long way around." Smiling at the sentry, he asked, "I don't suppose you'd just let me cross anyway? I mean, those rules are because of the war, and the war is pretty much over, ain't it?"

"Where are you headed?"

"I'm going home. I live in Charles, just across the river. I'm afraid I'm already in trouble with my wife. If I'm any later, I'll have to sleep in the woodshed."

The sentry grumbled, "Aw hell, Lee surrendered, didn't he? Go on." The sentry waved him through, and Booth tipped his hat as he rode by. Once across the river and out of sight of the sentry, Booth spurred his horse and continued on the Brandywine Pike toward Surratt's tavern some nine miles south of Washington DC.

Before reaching the tavern, a rider galloped up behind him. It was David Herold who, after abandoning Lewis Powell to his own devices, fled the city. Booth called out, "David! Is that you?"

Herold pulled his reins and his horse skidded to a stop. "Who is that?"

"It's me, John Wilkes Booth."

"Oh John. Thank God. I was afraid you were a policeman. What happened?"

Booth shifted in his saddle and grimaced as pain shot up his injured leg. "I shot the son of a bitch."

"Lincoln? You killed him?"

"I'd wager I did. I shot him in the head, but I didn't stick around to take his pulse. How about you? Where's Lewis?"

Herold shifted nervously. "I'm not sure."

"Not sure? What happened? What did he say?"

"We went to Seward's house. I was holding Lewis's horse and saw him go in. A couple of minutes later, Seward's Negro man came bolting from the house screaming bloody murder. I heard a big commotion from inside. People were starting to gather, so I left Lewis's horse for him and lit out."

"Did you hear a gunshot?"

"No. Just a lot of ruckus."

"Where's Lewis?"

"I don't know. He hadn't come out yet when I high-tailed it."

"You just left him there? He doesn't know the city at all! That's why I told you to go with him in the first place!"

The implication of cowardice was cutting and put Herold on the defensive. "I didn't know if he was alive or dead. What was I supposed to do? Wait for the police to show up? Powell is the only real soldier among us. If he survived the ordeal, he surely made his way out of the city. Hell, all he had to do was ride south and swim the river."

Herold was irritated, and Booth didn't want to alienate him. Being wounded, he needed Herold's assistance to make his escape. "Well, it doesn't matter now. What about George? How did his attack go?"

"I don't know. Wasn't like I could wait for the morning paper to come out."

Booth grimaced again. "I suppose not. I just hope he didn't lose his nerve. We were supposed to head in different directions, but I'm going to need your help. After I shot Lincoln, I jumped to the stage and landed awkwardly. I think I broke my leg."

Herold was actually pleased by this. He didn't want to go on the run alone. "I'm with ya, John. What's the plan?"

"We need to get to Surratt's tavern and pick up guns and supplies before word of the killing gets around. Then I need a doctor. We'll head to Doctor Mudd's place. That part of Maryland is friendly to our cause, and there's no telegraph service, so it'll be a while before people find out. By the time they do, we'll have slipped across the river into Virginia."

The two men continued south and reached the tavern around midnight. They retrieved weapons and supplies stashed there during the failed plot to kidnap Lincoln the month before. They pressed on to Doctor Mudd's house.

* * *

Lewis Powell was alone, desperate, and lost. He had no idea how to navigate Washington, DC. After the attack on Seward, he walked his horse north on 15th Street NW. The fact that he took a leisurely pace worked to his advantage, as no one paid attention to him. Fleeing assailants rarely just saunter away. Powell continued to move north and east through the District before stopping near Fort Bunker Hill, a temporary earthwork position constructed as part of the city's defenses. There, Powell shed his overcoat. When it was discovered, in its pockets were riding gloves, a false mustache, and a piece of paper with the name and hotel room number of a female performer at the Canterbury Music Hall. Powell ditched his horse and hid inside a local cemetery for the next three days.

* * *

After leaving the Kirkwood House, Atzerodt walked the city in a drunken stupor until about two in the morning, when he stopped at the Pennsylvania Hotel, rented a room, and went to sleep.

When news of Lincoln's assassination spread throughout the city, a worker at the Kirkwood House recalled "the suspicious man in a grey coat" (Atzerodt) who the night before had been asking about Vice President Andrew Johnson. The military police were informed, and they entered Atzerodt's room in Kirkwood House to find him gone and his bed not slept in. A search of the room turned up a loaded pistol, a bowie knife under the pillow, and John Wilkes Booth's bank book. The police now knew who they were searching for, and five days later, George Atzerodt was arrested at a cousin's house in Germantown, Maryland.

* * *

When Lincoln was shot, suspicion immediately fell upon Washington DC's Confederate sympathizers. The Surratts were high on the list. John had been fired as postmaster in Surrattsville due to his Confederate sympathies and was a known associate of Booth. Mary's tavern and boarding house were hangouts for Southern spies and adherents. The District of

Columbia police showed up at around 2:00 a.m. on April 15 searching for John Surratt and Booth. They may have been tipped off by a friend of Louis Weichmann's who worked at the War Department, but their visit turned up nothing incriminating. When asked about her son, Mary lied to the police and told them he had been in Canada for two weeks. She also omitted the fact that she had delivered a package to her tavern at Booth's request the afternoon before. While his mother dealt with the police alone, John Surratt fled to Canada.

Two days later, Surratt's neighbor contacted the police claiming to have overheard one of Mary's servants say three men had met at the boarding-house the night of the assassination and one had mentioned Booth by name. The police returned to her boarding house with orders to arrest everyone there. A search of Mary's room turned up photos of Booth and Confederate leaders, including Jefferson Davis. They also found a pistol, percussion caps, and a bullet mold. Mary was arrested for conspiracy to assassinate President Lincoln. As the police were escorting her out, a well-groomed man showed up at the door of the boarding house. It was Lewis Powell.

Powell was in disguise and using the alias Lewis Payne. Despite his polished appearance, he claimed to be a workman hired by Surratt to dig a ditch. When questioned about him, however, Surratt denied knowing him. Powell was too well dressed for a lowly workman, and his hands were manicured and uncalloused. The police searched him and found a box of pistol cartridges, a compass, a wallet with $25 (a considerable sum at the time), and a signed "Oath of Allegiance" in the name L. Paine—one of his aliases. Since none of this was consistent with his humble laborer story, the police arrested Powell as well. On April 18 Augustus Seward positively identified Powell as the man who attacked his father, Secretary of State William Seward. Powell's fate was sealed.

* * *

Booth and Herold rode deeper into southern Maryland until they came to the home of Dr. Samuel Mudd. Booth met Dr. Mudd in Bryantown,

Maryland, late 1864 while planning the escape route for his ill-fated plot to kidnap Lincoln. He claimed to be seeking investment property and ended up spending a night at Mudd's farm. They later met in Washington, DC, at Mary Surratt's boarding house, and Booth sent liquor and supplies to Mudd's farm a couple weeks before the assassination.

After stopping to rest, they reached the farm early in the morning. At Mudd's house, Booth eased himself out of the saddle and stood with his weight on his one good leg. "Go knock on the door, Dave."

Herold walked up the steps and rapped on the door. After a couple of minutes, a bearded man in his early thirties came to the door. "Uh, Dr. Mudd?"

"Yes. What can I do for you?"

"Well, I'm Dave and this is—"

Booth called out, "Hi, Sam. I'm in need of your services." Patting his horse, he added, "This infernal beast threw me last night. I think she broke my leg."

Being isolated on his farm, Mudd was unaware of the president's murder and had no reason to doubt Booth's story. "Oh my gosh! Let me help you." Turning to Herold, he said, "Help me get him inside." The two men each got under one of Booth's arms and held him as he hopped up the stairs and into the house. They sat him down on a small couch in the front room. "I'm going to cut your trousers, okay?"

"Do what ya have to, doc. I got plenty of pants."

Mudd pulled out a pocket knife, slit the cuff of Booth's left pant leg, and then ripped the cloth up to his knee. He peered at the leg, which was swollen and bruised. He gently pushed on a bulge on the side, and Booth winced. "You have a broken leg. Your fibula to be exact. It's a simple fracture, thankfully. I can splint it for you. Stay off of it for at least six weeks, and you should be right as rain."

"Thanks, doc. You have some of that whiskey I left with ya a couple weeks back?"

Mudd's wife was standing in the doorway. He turned to her and said, "Frankie, fetch me a bottle of Kentucky whiskey from that box in the pantry, if you please." She left and returned with the bottle. Booth took a long pull.

"Okay doc, do your worst."

Mudd said, "Well, I have to cut off your boot first. Your foot is too swollen." Booth nodded as he took another drink. Using his knife, Mudd carefully sliced down the side of the boot and gently eased it off his foot. "Okay, I'm ready. David, hold him under his arms." Herold did as he was instructed. "One, two, three." Mudd grabbed Booth's left heel and pulled. Booth let out a muffled scream, but the ugly bulge on his leg was now flat. "That's that. I'll splint this, and you rest."

"Uh, doc. I don't have six weeks to heal up. I have to travel. Do you have any crutches or anything?"

"No. Not here. There's a carpenter in town who I use a lot. He can throw together a pair in a jiffy. I'll also see if I can get you some laudanum for the pain. I have to run some errands anyway. You stay still until I get back."

After splinting Booth's leg, Dr. Mudd hitched up his wagon and rode to Bryantown. It was only then he learned Lincoln had been assassinated and the murderer was laying prostrate in his living room. Mudd almost panicked, but he kept his wits about him. If he turned Booth in, it would raise the question of why he went to Mudd's farm. Mudd was a Southern sympathizer. He'd been aware of Booth's plot to kidnap Lincoln and, though not directly involved, allowed Booth and his comrades to requisition liquor and supplies at his farm in anticipation of their escape. He doubted the Union authorities would make any distinction between him and Booth. He opted to say nothing and get Booth and Herold out of his house as quickly as possible.

When he returned home in the early evening, Mudd confronted Booth and Herold. "John, I heard what you did. The whole town is talking about it. I don't want to be inhospitable, but you and your man need to leave immediately. I can't risk you being caught here. I have to consider my family. You understand, right?"

Booth clapped him on the shoulder. "Oh course I do, Sam. You've done plenty for me already. We'll leave at first light. There's a man near here, Samuel Cox. Will you take us to him?"

"No, but I know a man who will."

Booth and Herold spent the night at Mudd's house and left well before sunrise. As promised, Mudd had a local man to guide them to their next destination. Booth gave Mudd twenty-five dollars for his trouble and left.

They arrived at the farm of Samuel Cox at 4:00 a.m. on April 16. Cox turned them over to Confederate sympathizer and intelligence officer Thomas Jones, who hid them in the Zekiah Swamp for the next five days until they crossed the Potomac into Virginia.

* * *

The murder of Lincoln spurred the largest manhunt in American history, overseen personally by Secretary of War Edwin Stanton. Bounties were issued for the three known conspirators still at large—$50,000 for Booth and $25,000 each for David Herold and John Surratt. Tips poured in to authorities, and thousands of soldiers and civilian police were pressed into service to search for the assassins. Federal troops concentrated their efforts on southern Maryland, a rural region with Confederate sympathies. While Booth and Herold hid, troops combed the surrounding swamps and forests.

The public reaction to Lincoln's death was a mix of grief and rage. Lincoln's funeral was public, and mourners stood seven abreast in a line over a mile long outside the White House waiting for their chance to view the slain president's body. Millions more lined railroad tracks across the country when his body was returned to Illinois for burial. The audacity of the act enraged the public, and even in the South, leaders like Generals Joe Johnston and Robert E. Lee expressed outrage and regret. Johnston called it "a disgrace to the age." While many in the South hated Lincoln and hailed Booth as a hero, others worried Lincoln's death would lead to serious retribution on the defeated South.

* * *

While Booth and Herold hid in the swamp, Thomas Jones brought them newspapers every day. Booth read about Lincoln's funeral and the outpouring of grief in both the North and the South. He also read that Seward, while badly injured, survived Powell's attack. Vice President Johnson was unscathed. Atzerodt hadn't even made an attempt. The "Tennessee Turncoat" was not only alive, he was now the president of the United States. The Southern sympathizers and anti-war faction did not rise up, but rather hunkered down even lower or changed their positions completely to avoid the wrath of Lincoln's enraged allies.

He also read that his colleagues were being arrested one by one—Mary Surratt and Lewis Powell. Even Samuel Arnold and Michael O'Laughlen were arrested, though they were not involved in the assassination plot. Things were not going as he had planned.

On April 21 it was time for Booth and Herold to move. They were now on foot. After reaching the swamp, Herold shot both of their horses, fearing they might draw attention to them. Jones provided them with a small boat and a compass to get them across the Potomac to Virginia where someone would be waiting with fresh horses. That night, they pushed the small boat out onto the water and started to row. There was only a waning crescent moon for light, and the wide, misty waters of the lower Potomac made it difficult to navigate. Pushed by the tide, Booth and Herold mistakenly headed upriver and landed, not in Virginia, but back in Maryland.

As they jumped ashore, Herold said, "John, uh, this isn't Virginia."

"What? What do you mean? Where is it?"

Herold peered into the darkness. "I know this place. I've hunted down here."

"Damn it! Are we finished?"

"No. I don't think so. The man who owns this land supports the cause. I think he'll help us." With Booth on his crutches, the two men made their way to the farmhouse. Though it was late, the old farmer greeted them warmly.

"Well, I'll be damned. David Herold, as I live and breathe. It's a mite early for duck hunting, ain't it?"

"Yes, sir. We ain't here for the ducks. We're trying to get to Virginia and got turned around on the river. Can you put us up for one night?"

The old man held up his lamp and studied Booth's face. "Mr. Booth I presume?" Booth tensed. The old man laughed, "Don't worry, I ain't going to turn you in. What would I do with $75,000 anyway? That'd buy more chewing tobacco and whiskey than I'd go through in ten lifetimes. You're welcome here."

"So you'll let us stay?"

"Yup, but in the morning, I'll give you to my son-in-law, Colonel John Hughes. He'll get ya pointed in the right direction."

Booth asked cautiously, "Can he be trusted?"

"Yes, sir. He can. He supports the cause too."

They spent the day hiding on Hughes's farm before crossing the Potomac that evening. On the morning of April 23 Booth finally landed in Virginia. He and Herold came ashore near Machodoc Creek about thirty miles east of Fredericksburg. There they were met by Thomas Harbin, another of Booth's friends privy to the kidnapping plot. He led Booth and Herold to William Bryant, a Confederate agent who gave them horses. On April 24, as Booth and Herold reached the Rappahannock River, they encountered William Jett, a former rebel soldier with the Ninth Virginia Cavalry. He led the men to the farm of Richard Garrett and left them there.

The Garrett farm was in a rural area and, with the collapse of the Confederate postal system, was cut off from most news. As such, the Garretts were unaware that Lincoln had even been assassinated. Booth was introduced to them as "James W. Boyd," a wounded Confederate soldier returning home.

Garrett Farm near Port Royal, VA

* * *

That day, in Washington, DC, a detachment of twenty-six Union soldiers from the Sixteenth New York Cavalry Regiment steamed down the Potomac River. They were commanded by Lieutenant Edward P. Doherty. With him was Lieutenant Colonel Everton Conger, an intelligence officer. They were pursuing leads that Booth was in the area. The soldiers landed that night at Belle Plain, Virginia. Conger tracked down William Jett. When interrogated, he gave up Booth and Herold. The noose around Booth's neck was tightening quickly.

The soldiers rode through the night and reached the Garrett farm before dawn. Booth and Herold were hiding in the Garretts' tobacco barn. After the troops surrounded the building, Lt. Colonel Conger came forward. "John Wilkes Booth and David Herold. You're surrounded by soldiers of the Unites States Army. Come out of the barn, and surrender yourselves."

David Herold peeked out at the soldiers. Their situation was hopeless. He whispered to Booth, "He ain't lying. There's a mess of bluecoat soldiers out there. I reckon we're at the end of our road."

"Surrender if you like, Dave. I'm not going."

"Good luck, John." He moved cautiously to the door and shouted, "Okay. I'm coming out! Don't shoot!" He opened the door a few inches and tossed his pistol out on the dirt. He walked out with his hands on his head. Two troopers quickly grabbed him, pulled his hands behind his back, and dragged him away from the barn.

Conger's men hustled the man away from the tobacco shed. It wasn't Booth. Conger had actually watched him perform on stage and would have recognized him. He called out, "Okay, Booth. Now it's your turn. Throw out your weapon, and come out with your hands high."

Booth laughed. "I prefer to come out and fight."

Conger turned to the troopers. "Secretary Stanton wants him alive. No one shoots him. Set a match to the barn. He'll come out."

One of the soldiers took a kerosene lamp from the Garretts' porch, lit it, and tossed it onto the barn. Flames slowly spread up the side of the building as the kerosene leaked out. On the other side of the barn, another trooper with a torch fired the bottom of the opposite wall. The old, dry wood caught quickly and the barn was soon engulfed. Inside, Booth choked on the thick smoke but stubbornly refused to leave. Between the rough cut boards of the barn, the soldiers saw Booth moving around inside. A couple of troopers moved closer just before a shot rang out. A Union soldier, Sergeant Boston Corbett, shot Booth in the neck. Booth collapsed and the soldiers rushed in to drag the wounded man from the burning building.

Conger was furious. "Goddamn it! Who fired that shot? I said he was to be taken alive!"

Corbett sheepishly stepped forward. "It was me, Colonel. He raised his pistol and was about to shoot."

Conger turned to Lieutenant Doherty. "Get this son of a bitch out of my sight." The soldiers dragged Booth across to the Garretts' porch. Corbett's bullet broke three of Booth's vertebrae and severed his spine. He was alive but paralyzed. Conger was afraid to move him so they left him on the porch while the medics worked on him. It was to no avail; he was dying.

Some three hours later as the end neared, he told one of his captors, "Tell my mother I died for my country." He then asked to have his hands lifted up in front of his face. Staring at them he said, "Useless, useless." He died just as dawn was breaking on April 26, 1865. A search of his body turned up a compass, a candle, his diary, and pictures of five different women. One was his fiancé, Lucy Hale, with whom he attended Lincoln's inauguration the month before. The others were actresses he knew. In his diary, he had written of killing Lincoln. "Our country owed all her troubles to him, and God simply made me the instrument of his punishment."

The same day that Booth died, in North Carolina, General Joe Johnston surrendered the last significant Confederate fighting force, the eighty-six thousand men of the Army of Tennessee, to Union General William Tecumseh Sherman. The American Civil War was over. John Wilkes Booth's last-ditch effort to save the South had failed completely.

* * *

All the conspirators, with the notable exception of John Surratt Jr., had been captured. They were tried by military tribunal and convicted. David Herold, Lewis Powell, George Atzerodt, and Mary Surratt were all hanged. Surratt had the distinction of being the first woman ever executed by the United States Federal Government. Michael O'Laughlen, Samuel Arnold, and Dr.

Execution of Lincoln Assassins, July 7, 1865 Photo by Alexander Gardner

Samuel Mudd were sentenced to life in prison. Even Edmund Spangler, the man Booth asked to hold his horse, was given a six-year prison term. Although O'Laughlen died in prison of yellow fever, the other surviving conspirators were eventually pardoned by President Andrew Johnson in 1869.

John Surratt escaped to Montreal, Canada, where a Catholic priest gave him sanctuary while his mother and friends were tried and hanged. With the help of ex-Confederate agents, Surratt assumed an alias and traveled to England before serving in the Pontifical Zouaves in the Papal States under the name John Watson. He was recognized by an old friend who alerted the U.S. minister in Rome. Surratt was arrested and imprisoned but escaped. He assumed yet another alias and booked travel to Egypt where he was arrested again by American officials who returned him to the United States to stand trial in 1867. Unlike his mother, he was tried in a civilian court. He admitted to being involved in the kidnapping plot but denied any role in the assassination. After two months, a mistrial was declared and he was released. He was the only conspirator to emerge from the ordeal essentially unscathed.

The Aftermath

The plots by Booth and his coconspirators were intended to help the South, if not win the war, at least survive it as a political entity. The kidnapping was meant to rejuvenate the Confederate military by injecting it with thousands of soldiers paroled as part of Lincoln's ransom. They also hoped the Union would be forced to recognize the Confederacy as a separate and independent nation. When the plot morphed from kidnapping to assassination, the intent was to decapitate the Union government by killing Lincoln, Johnson, and Seward, thereby giving the Confederacy desperately needed breathing room. They sought to encourage pro-Democrat and anti-war factions in the North to assert themselves politically and force a conclusion to hostilities. At the very least, they would avenge the South by killing the man most responsible for its defeat and destruction. From their perspective they did exact a modicum of revenge, but there was no benefit to the South.

Lincoln had been an advocate of a moderate approach to the reintegration of Southern states into the Union. As early as 1863, Lincoln openly stated his objectives were keeping the Union together while abolishing slavery. When a general asked Lincoln how he should deal with conquered Confederates, Lincoln replied, "Let 'em up easy." He wanted to rebuild a nation, not assign blame for its schism. For the defeated states, he wanted speedy elections under generous terms to allow them to reintegrate quickly into the Union. That same year, he issued his Amnesty Proclamation that offered pardons to anyone who was willing to sign an oath of allegiance, who had not held a Confederate civil office, and who had not mistreated Union prisoners. (Ironically, Lewis Powell had his signed oath of allegiance in his pocket when he was captured.)

Opposing Lincoln and his fellow moderates were the Radicals, led by Senator Thaddeus Stevens. They wanted to treat the Southern states as conquered provinces without rights. They favored much harsher policies, which included confiscating property of Southern land owners for redistribution to freed slaves. While Lincoln routinely bargained with the Radicals and they were technically his allies, they disagreed vehemently. Had he not been murdered, Lincoln's landslide election of 1864, the military victory over the Confederacy, and his general popularity would have given him the political capital to dictate the terms of Reconstruction.

When Lincoln was killed and Andrew Johnson became president, the battle between the moderates and the Radicals came to a head. Stevens's enmity regarding Johnson was well documented. Stevens was a hard-core abolitionist from Pennsylvania, and Johnson was a former slave owner from Tennessee. When Lincoln picked Johnson as his running mate in 1864, Stevens said, "Can't you get a candidate for Vice-President without going down into a damned rebel province for one?" This animosity culminated in the impeachment of Johnson, who survived by a single vote in the Senate.

While many of the Radicals' objectives were admirable, they brought with them harsh realities for the defeated South. Whites in the South pushed back against the harsh reforms, which led to increased violence against the freed slaves and the rise of groups like the Ku Klux Klan. The Union responded with more troops and restrictions. As a result, it was years before the Southern states were fully reintegrated. The former Confederate states would have been much better off with Lincoln than without him. By killing Lincoln, Booth caused irreparable harm to the South that lasted for years.

Chapter 5

People's Will and Tsar Alexander II
—If You Want Reform, Don't Kill the Reformer

On February 28, 1881, Ignaty Grinevitsky left his apartment at 59 Simbirskaya Street in St. Petersburg, Russia. As he left, his landlady returned home from shopping. "Hello, Mr. Elnikov. It's cold out there. Bundle up."

"I will, Mrs. Donobrev." Elnikov was his alias. As an active member of Russian revolutionary society Narodnay Volya—People's Will—he had to take precautions. The Okhrana, the Tsar's secret police, were actively trying to root out the last of the People's Will members in the city. Once on the street, Grinevitsky walked in the opposite direction of his intended destination. If an Okhrana spy was following, he didn't want to lead him to his comrades. After an hour of walking, backtracking, and jumping on and off street cars, Ignaty was convinced he wasn't being followed and proceeded to the flat where he was to meet his coconspirators to finalize their plot to assassinate Tsar Alexander II, the autocratic Romanov ruler of the Russian Empire.

He entered a nondescript apartment building on Telezhnaya Street and climbed the stairs to the fourth floor. Nearing the apartment door, he glanced down the stairs one last time before knocking lightly—*tap tap . . . tap tap tap . . . tap.* It was their signal. After a few seconds, the door cracked open. All he discerned in the darkness was an eyeball staring back at him. "Ah, Ignaty. It's you. Come in, quickly."

He slipped in the door to find most of his comrades were already there. Scanning the room, he turned to the small young woman who opened the door. "Where is your husband, Andrei Ivanovic? Is he running late?"

She wore a stern grimace on her face. "No. He was arrested two days ago."

"Arrested? What happened? And why are we still here?"

"Andrei will tell the Okhrana nothing. He was visiting Mikhail Trigoni when the police arrived. They were looking for Mikhail, but Andrei got scooped up in their net."

"Then we should act before they find out about us. I have no doubts about your husband's courage, but the Okhrana are masters of interrogation. Everyone talks eventually. Remember Goldenberg?"

She grimaced at the reference. "Well, no matter. After tomorrow, it'll be a moot point. The tsar will be dead, and the revolution will have started."

Ignaty nodded solemnly. "Yes. We will have done our duty. Is Nikolai Ivanovich ready with the bombs?"

"No, but don't worry. He's working on them as we speak. Vera Figner and I will help him assemble them this evening. They will be ready by tomorrow, as will the mine."

"If they are not ready—"

"They will be." Her confident calm reassured him. She was almost oblivious to the fact that her husband, Andrei Ivanovic Zhelyabov, was in the hands of the Tsar's dreaded secret police. He was one of the last members of the People's Will original Executive Committee to escape capture—or at least he had been until now. "The attack will be executed exactly as Andrei and I planned. We will be successful. I will consider no alternative."

"Nor I."

"If the tsar travels by Malaya Sadovaya Street, Frolenko will be in the cheese shop to set off the mine. If he travels along the canal, you and the others will use Kibalchich's bombs. Andrei's role was only a last resort. I have complete faith that you, Nikolai, Timofey, and Ivan will be successful. Now let's go over the final planning for tomorrow."

* * *

Ignaty Grinevitsky—also known by his Polish name, Ignacy Hryniewiecki—was born circa 1856 in the Minsk Governorate to a large Polish family. His father was a Catholic landowner and a member of the Polish landed gentry. Ignaty considered himself to be a Russified Pole and spoke Polish and Russian with equal fluency. After the defeat of Napoleon in 1815, Poland was partitioned, and the part abutting Russia became an autonomous

Ignaty Grinevitsky

Kingdom of Poland. It had a liberal constitution, but the Russian tsar was its king. Russia's ruling Romanov Dynasty had been in power since 1613, and its tsars ruled with an iron fist. The new kings of Poland, initially Tsar Alexander I and later Tsar Nicholas I, were not used to dealing with restrictions on their authority and generally ignored their constitutional limits. There were two failed Polish uprisings, after which the tsars cracked down, and Polish autonomy became a distant memory. This was the reality of Ignaty's world.

Ignaty graduated from gymnasium, or secondary school, in Byelostok in 1875 with high marks and enrolled at the St. Petersburg State Institute of Technology to study mechanical engineering. It was here in 1879 that he became involved with the revolutionary group the People's Will. It wasn't long before People's Will became his overarching priority, and he was kicked out of college in 1880 for not attending classes.

* * *

Tsar Alexander II—the tsar of Russia, king of Poland, and grand duke of Finland—was born in Moscow in 1818. His father, Tsar Nicholas I, was a reactionary leader. During Nicolas's reign, Russian territory increased when he conquered the Caucuses, and he oversaw impressive economic growth and the industrialization of the country. He also further centralized administrative authority and forcefully crushed any challenge to his rule. Nicholas's military and diplomatic missteps led to the disastrous Crimean War, which was still raging when Nicholas died in 1855, leaving it to his son, Alexander, to sort out.

Tsar Alexander II

No one expected much in the way of change when Tsar Alexander II assumed the throne. His father suppressed freedom of speech and any efforts at, or even discussion of, reforms. Official censorship was the rule of the day, and any criticism of the tsar or any authorities was a criminal offense. Alexander had always publicly supported his father's policies, so there was no reason to believe his son would be any different.

To the surprise of almost everyone, upon gaining the throne, Alexander began a series of radical reforms. Now that he was the tsar, Alexander was determined to do what he thought best. To accomplish his reforms, he would have to be every bit the autocratic ruler that his father was. He had to reject the establishment of any parliamentary system—at least for a while. While this was counterintuitive for a reformer, any parliament set up prior to his reforms would be dominated by the nobles, and they were not going to be happy with his directives.

Alexander had to first extricate Russia from the Crimean War. Russia was humiliated, and the prosecution of the war exposed the empire's weaknesses, including widespread bribe-taking, theft of military supplies, and general corruption. Once the war was ended, he set to work. His first major dictate was the Emancipation Reform of 1861, which abolished serfdom on private estates in the Russian Empire. Serfdom was a form of feudal slavery, but unlike slaves, serfs were not bought or sold. They were, however, sold with the land they worked. Serfs were completely reliant on and beholden to their lords. They were tied to the land and not allowed to leave of their own volition. In some cases, serfs had to have the lord's permission to marry. They were also conscripted into the military at the lord's direction. Alexander transformed the serfs into independent communal proprietors. When the law was signed in 1861, Russia's 23 million peasants became some of the last in Europe to be freed from serfdom.

After the debacle of the Crimean War, Alexander reformed the military and introduced universal conscription across all social classes. Prior to this, only the peasantry was subjected to compulsory conscription. Serfs that were drafted by their landowners served for twenty-five years. For most, this was equivalent to a death sentence. Beating, flogging, and branding of soldiers as punishment, once common, was now forbidden.

Alexander also changed the judicial system and used the French system as a model. He introduced a new penal code where criminal and civil procedures were simplified. Trials were now held in open court with a jury. Judges were appointed for life to make them less susceptible to political pressures. Justices of the Peace were introduced to handle minor offenses.

Governance itself was redesigned. Local self-governance for rural districts and large towns was introduced with elected bodies who had restricted abilities to levy and collect taxes. Rural and municipal police organizations were created under the direction of the minister of interior.

Life for the Jews of Russia had always been harsh. While they were still not allowed to own land and their travel was restricted, the special taxes levied on them were eliminated. Jews who graduated from secondary school were allowed to live outside Jewish enclaves and now eligible for jobs with the state. As a result, educated Jews moved to the major cities in large numbers.

Alexander's attention turned to foreign issues. Russia's Alaska colony had been losing money for years, and its location made it next to impossible to defend, so he sold it to the United States. As Grand Duke of Finland, in 1863 Alexander reconvened the Diet of Finland, its national assembly. He increased Finland's autonomy and let it establish its own currency. The Finnish language was elevated to a national language. Foreign investment and development increased. Finland built its first railways, which operated under Finnish control. To this day, the Finns refer to Tsar Alexander II as "the Good Tsar."

Not everyone was a fan of the new tsar, and Poland had its issues. Poles had longed for independence for years. At the very least, they wanted to return to the days before the November Uprising of 1830 when they enjoyed a liberal constitution. The failure of their uprising against Tsar Nicolas I cost them dearly. Now that Alexander was in power, they had a second chance. Russia was weakened economically, politically, and militarily by the failed Crimean War. Understanding Poland's political ambitions, shortly after coming to power Alexander issued a warning to the *szlachta*, the Polish nobility: "Gentlemen, let us have no dreams."

The Poles overestimated their support among the other great powers of Europe and rose up against the Russians in 1863. The Lithuanians joined them shortly thereafter. Not wanting to get dragged into a war with Russia, the European powers offered the Poles moral support but little else. Poland still had serfdom, and the Polish rebels tried to woo the peasantry to their side by offering them the land they worked. However, the Russians beat them to the punch. They'd already offered the peasants generous parcels of land for the asking—land that belonged to the *szlachta*. As a result, peasant support for the uprising was tepid at best.

The Russian army once again crushed the Polish rebellion. Hundreds were executed and tens of thousands of Poles were exiled to Siberia, the Urals, or other remote parts of the empire. The biggest blow to the *szlachta* was the end of serfdom in Poland. The Polish serfs were not included in the Emancipation Reform of 1861, and Tsar Alexander now corrected that in a move designed to ruin the *szlachta*. Russia confiscated 1,660 estates in Poland and 1,794 estates in Lithuania and gave the land to the serfs. Free peasants were allowed to buy land at market price. Former serfs who were granted land were allowed to sell it but only to other peasants.

Sales to *szlachta* were strictly prohibited. The Russians gave the peasants forest and pasture privileges, which further irritated the remaining land-owners. In addition, all estates had to pay a 10 percent income tax to reimburse Russia for the cost of the war. While all this was good for the serfs, it was a disaster for the *szlachta*. Tsar Alexander II had long lists of both supporters and enemies.

* * *

People's Will was a Russian socialist revolutionary political group bent on overthrowing the autocratic Russian government through assassination and revolution. It was the more violent offshoot of an earlier group, Zemlya i Volya, Land and Liberty. Ignaty Grinevitsky was drawn to the promise of action against the tsar and the Russian Empire. He was once approached by his fellow Poles, who questioned him on why he didn't get involved in Polish revolutionary groups. His response was "When you start partisan fighting, I will be with you. But for the moment, when you do nothing, I shall work for Russia's freedom."

Ignaty was clever and assumed various pseudonyms like Mikhail Ivanovich or Kotik (meaning "kitten" in Russian) to protect himself from the Department for Protecting the Public Security and Order. That name was a mouthful, so it was usually referred to as "the guard department" or "the guard"—Okhrana in Russian. Ignaty engaged in a number of anti-government activities. He started by distributing revolutionary pro-paganda to students and workers. He later established a secret printing press with which he and his colleagues published an illegal underground newspaper, *Rabochaya Gazeta*.

In 1879 a schism developed within Land and Liberty. A failed attempt by a Land and Liberty member to kill the tsar resulted in a Russian gov-ernment crackdown. Revolutionary cells in Ukraine were almost eradi-cated, and the organization was under tremendous pressure. Two factions developed—those who advocated terrorism and assassination, and those who wanted to end the use of terrorism. The anti-terrorism faction gained control of Land and Liberty's newspaper, but the terrorists gained control of its Executive Committee. Attempts to reconcile were not successful, and an amicable spit was formalized in August 1879. The terrorist wing became People's Will.

People's Will characterized terrorism as a system of mob law and self-defense. They believed assassination was merely capital punishment and self-defense against those who committed crimes against the nation. They considered killing the tsar the best way to achieve their goals. They assessed the government as weak and believed a concerted plan of assassinations and terror would cause it to fall.

People's Will was governed by an Executive Committee (EC) made up of people of various backgrounds. Andrei Zhelyabov was the son of a peasant from Odessa. His father had been a serf, and Andrei was ten when Alexander II freed his family. That fact did nothing to lessen his hatred of the tsar. His wife, Sophia Perovskaya, was another member. In sharp contrast to her husband, she was born in St. Petersburg to an aristocratic family. She was

Andrei Ivanovic Zhelyabov

descended from Empress Elizabeth and Peter the Great. Her father was the military governor of St. Petersburg, and her uncle was an advisor to the royal family. She was exposed to radical ideology in prep school and left home at the age of sixteen. Vera Figner was another member from the Russian upper class. Both of her parents were hereditary nobility, and her family owned a large estate that was worked by serfs prior to the Emancipation of 1861. She became radicalized while going to medical school in

Sophia Perovskaya

Switzerland before returning to Russia in 1875. Mikhail Frolenko was the son of an army sergeant who studied at the St. Peterburg Institute of

Technology. Aaron Zundelevich was a lower, middle-class Jew from a small town who advocated the
use of terror as a means of political struggle and
participated in a number of assassination attempts.
Lev Tikhomirov was the son of a military doctor.
Despite a conservative education, he got involved
with radical politics and was sentenced to four
years in prison for revolutionary activities. This was
the world into which Ignaty Grinevitsky plunged.

Vera Figner

* * *

Despite his reforms, animus toward Tsar Alexander
II only intensified. Political violence in Russia
increased, and there were several assassination
attempts against the tsar and other officials. Dmitry
Karakozov was a man born to minor nobility who
grew to hate his class, claiming they "suck the peasants' blood." He became a member of the revolu-

Mikhail Frolenko

tionary wing of the Ishutin Society, a group of Russian Socialist utopians
started by his cousin, Nicholai Ishutin. After being expelled from Moscow
State University, Karakozov traveled to St. Petersburg to assassinate the
tsar. He wrote a personal manifesto that he mailed to the governor of
St. Petersburg, blaming Alexander for the suffering of the poor. In his
message, he wrote, "I have decided to destroy the Tsar, and to die for my
beloved people." His note, however, never reached the governor, as it was
lost in the mail.

On April 4, 1866, Karakozov waited for the tsar outside the gates of
the Summer Garden in St. Petersburg, armed with a double-barreled pistol. As the tsar left, Karakozov stepped forward to fire his weapon. Just as
he shot, a bystander bumped his elbow and the bullet went wide. Rather
than fire his other round, Karakozov tried to run but was caught by the
guards. Throughout the ordeal, he kept one hand in his jacket pocket,

where he was holding morphine and strychnine with which to kill himself and prussic acid to disfigure his face; none of it was used. Alexander confronted his would-be assassin and asked him what he wanted. Karakozov's response was simply, "Nothing, nothing." Karakozov was sentenced to death and was hanged the following September. Ten of his accomplices were sentenced to hard labor, and twenty-five were acquitted.

The following year, there was another attempt on the tsar's life during the 1867 World's Fair in Paris. French Emperor Napoleon III, eager to showcase the city's recent renovations, invited many heads of state, including Tsar Alexander II. Anton Berezovski was the son of a Polish nobleman from the Volyn region of western Ukraine. He had taken part in the 1863 Polish uprising before emigrating to France. Berezovski believed if he killed Alexander, he'd liberate Poland. On June 6 the tsar, riding in a carriage with two of his sons and Emperor Napoleon, was coming back from a military review when Berezovski shot at him. He had a double-barreled gun, which exploded when he fired it. The bullet went astray and wounded a horse. His hand was injured in the blast, and he was immediately seized by the crowd. Berezovski claimed he only wanted to free his home country and regretted that it happened in France, a country generally supportive of the Polish cause. He was sentenced to life with hard labor in New Caledonia, a French island colony east of Australia. He was pardoned in 1906 but remained on the island until his death.

Tsar Alexander had a reprieve for several years until 1879. On April 20, he was walking toward the Square of the Guards Staff in St. Petersburg when he was confronted by Alexander Soloviev, a Russian revolutionary and member of Land and Liberty. Soloviev was armed with a revolver. Seeing the pistol, the sixty-year-old tsar fled from Soloviev, running in a zigzag pattern. His evasive maneuvers worked, and all five rounds Soloviev fired missed. Soloviev was promptly arrested. He was sentenced to death and hanged on May 28, 1879.

* * *

For the members of the newly formed People's Will, it was their turn. When still with Land and Liberty, they had conducted a successful assassination in 1878 when Sergey Stepnyak-Kravchinsky killed General Nikolai Mezentsov, the chief of Russia's Gendarme Corp and the head of the Okhrana. Stepnyak-Kravchinsky was waiting with a dagger outside Mezentsov's home when the general's carriage pulled up. As Mezentov got out, Stepnyak-Kravchinsky rushed up and plunged his knife into the general's gut and calmly twisted the blade. Stepnyak-Kravchinsky escaped in a carriage drawn by Barbarian, a beautiful black stallion used on three different occasions to help terrorists escape from prison. While the assassin escaped, Barbarian did not. He was confiscated by the police and interned in their stable. Stepnyak-Kravchinsky fled Russia and eventually settled in Britain, never to be punished for his crime. Encouraged by that success, the newly organized People's Will set their sights on the tsar. On August 26, 1879, the Executive Committee of the People's Will passed a death sentence on Tsar Alexander II.

Their first attempt came in November 1879. The tsar spent much of the fall at his vacation home in the Crimea before returning to St. Petersburg on his royal train. To get to the train, the tsar would first have to travel either by coach to Simferopol or by sea through Odessa. People's Will had a spy in Simferopol, Alexander Presnyakov, who would signal if the tsar traveled that way.

People's Will was working with a new tool—dynamite. The group acquired a supply of it in Switzerland and smuggled it into Russia. It had enough to attack the royal train when the tsar returned to St. Petersburg. Members were thorough and planned three separate attacks to cover all possible routes. They also learned the tsar and his entourage always traveled via two trains. The first carried servants and luggage and was referred to as the retinue train. The second was the imperial train and carried the tsar and his family. His personal car was the fourth car in this train.

Vera Figler was in charge of the Odessa attack. She was a beautiful woman and a member of the nobility. With Nicholai Kibalchich, the group's explosives expert, posing as her husband, she rented an apartment in a tony part of town in September 1879. She then used her charms on the governor general of Odessa to get a job as a railroad guard for her "servant," claiming his doctor prescribed outdoor work because of a lung disease. The governor general wrote a letter of recommendation, and her servant was hired as a railroad guard in Gnilyakovo, a small town outside Odessa. The guard was People's Will EC member Mikhail Frolenko. He would place a bomb on the tracks to destroy the tsar's train car.

Nicholai Kibalchich

The second attack location was near the city of Alexandrovsk. EC member Andre Zhelyabov, pretending to be a merchant, bought some land near the railroad tracks. He and his comrades then dug a tunnel under the tracks where the train traveled on a high embankment. When the train passed over their tunnel, they would explode their mine, plunging the train into the deep ravine below. They placed their explosives and waited.

The final location was near the little town of Rogozhskaya Zastava. There, Sophia Perovskaya and another People's Will member, Lev Gartman, rented a house 150 meters from the Moscow-Kursk rail line. They and other members set to tunneling from the house to the rail bed. After weeks of hard, dirty work, Perovskaya and her comrades completed their tunnel and placed their mine. Now they only had to wait for the tsar to return to St. Petersburg.

In early November the spy in Simferopol, Presnyakov, sent a coded telegram to Figner in Odessa. The tsar would not be traveling that way. In Moscow, People's Will member Grigory Goldenberg was impatient for action. Upon learning of Presnyakov's message, he traveled to Odessa to collect Figner's unused dynamite. He packed it in a large suitcase and headed back to Moscow. Though he was dressed like a wealthy man, at the train station he lugged the obviously heavy suitcase himself rather than hire a porter. This struck the porters as suspicious, and they notified the police. When approached, Goldenberg pulled a pistol and waived at anyone who approached. Police finally got the gun away from him, and the crowd attacked him. He was arrested and imprisoned at the Fortress of Peter and Paul. His interrogator was clever and played on Goldenberg's ego. He convinced Goldenberg that he might save the country if only he explained People's Will's lofty goals to the government and identified their noble members. He fell for it and wrote out 150 pages that provided names, addresses, biographies, and other information on 143 People's Will members. He warned his interrogator, "Bear in mind that if even one hair falls from the heads of my comrades, I will not forgive myself."

The interrogator replied with a laugh, "I don't know about hair . . . but I promise you that heads will fall for sure." When the naive Goldenberg realized what he had done, he hanged himself in his cell.

*   *   *

On November 18, the time finally came. The tsar's train was on its way to St. Peterburg. In Alexandrovsk, Andrei Zhelybov waited patiently as the retinue train passed his location. Less than an hour later, there was the faint sound of a second train approaching—this was the imperial train. When the tsar's train rumbled above their mine buried deep beneath the rails, Zhelybov touched the wires of the detonator, but nothing happened. He had connected the wires incorrectly. When his comrades in Moscow learned the tsar had passed through Alexandrovsk unmolested, they feared that Zhelybov had been arrested before he acted.

Later that same day, Perovskaya was waiting in Rogozhskaya Zastava when she received a coded telegram from Presnyakov. "The price of wheat is two rubles, our price is four." The tsar was coming. He was in the second train and his was the fourth car.

The royal trains were to pass through Rogozhskaya Zastava on November 19. Sophia sent all the diggers away; only she and Gartman would be there to set off the mine. She would watch for the train and signal Gartman in the house when the tsar's coach was directly above the mine. When the first train came chugging through, Perovskaya let it pass. From the message, she knew this was the retinue train. About thirty minutes later the second train followed. As the fourth car rattled by, she gave Gartman the signal. He connected the wires and a huge explosion erupted. The fourth car of the train was blasted into the air and landed upside down as the rest of the cars derailed.

Perovskaya and Gartman fled, believing they'd been successful. What they didn't know was that a mechanical problem with its locomotive caused the retinue train to be delayed. Not wanting the tsar to wait, his train went first. The train car they blew up was carrying fresh fruit from the Crimea. The tsar was unharmed.

* * *

Disappointed that their elaborate plan had failed, the members of the People's Will did not give up. In February 1880 they tried again. Stepan Khalturin, a member of the People's Will, got a job as a carpenter working at the Winter Palace, which allowed him to sleep on the palace grounds. He smuggled in small packets of dynamite every day, which he concealed in the bedding of his room. On February 17 he con-structed a bomb in the basement of the palace

Stepan Khalturin

below the dining room. Using a clockwork detonator, he set the bomb to explode when the tsar was having dinner that evening. Fortunately for Alexander, his dinner guest, the Prince of Battenberg, was late. The dinner was delayed, so the tsar and his family were not in the room when the bomb exploded. He was unharmed, although eleven Imperial Guards were killed, and forty-five other people were badly injured.

Khalturin got away and fled to Moscow before landing in Odessa. He later participated in the murder of a police general. When arrested, he and his accomplice gave fake names. They were court-martialed and hanged without Khalturin being identified as the bomber of the Winter Palace.

* * *

The multiple attempts on his life had an effect on the tsar. While he still pursued his reformist agenda, his momentum lessened, and he began to behave more like his reactionary father, Tsar Nicholas I. He started replacing liberal ministers with conservative ones. Liberal university courses were supplanted by a more traditional curriculum. Access to higher education was restricted, and after 1871 only students from *gimnaziya* (gymnasium) or prep schools were allowed to matriculate into universities. In 1879 he established governors-general with the authority to prosecute revolutionaries in military courts and exile undesirables to the far reaches of the empire.

* * *

Despite the failures, People's Will was still determined to kill him. Both previous attempts had failed, not due to poor design or execution but rather bad luck. They immediately began planning for their next attack. Tsar Alexander II was a creature of habit, and this would be his undoing. Every Sunday for many years Alexander went to the Mikhailovsky Riding Academy in the center of St. Petersburg for the military role call. He traveled with his Cossack bodyguard in an armored carriage given to him by Napoleon III and was followed by two sleighs carrying the chief of police and chief of the Imperial Guard.

In the fall of 1880 Ignaty Grinevitsky was assigned the task of monitoring the tsar's routes, which he did dutifully for a number of months. It was time to present his report. Sophia Perovskaya and her husband, Andrei Zhelybov, called a meeting to discuss how to proceed. "As you all know, Ignaty had been observing the tsar's travel patterns for some months now. Ignaty, what did you learn?"

"The tsar is a creature of habit. He travels to the riding academy every Sunday for the roll call. He most often returns via Malaya Sadovaya Street but sometimes takes Bolshaya Italyanskaya Street and then follows the Catherine Canal."

Andrei asked, "How often does he take Malay Sadovaya?"

Ignaty checked his notes. "About 75 percent of the time."

Stroking his long black beard, Andrei said, "What if we place a mine under the street like we did with the trains? Explode it under him when he passes."

Sophie turned to Nicholai Kibalchich and asked, "Do we have enough dynamite?"

"Yes, we have plenty. A carriage is much easier to blow up than a train."

Sophie mused, "But what if he changes his route? What if the mine fails to explode? What if the carriage is damaged but the tsar survives? It is said to be bomb proof. We need contingencies."

Kilbachich volunteered, "We also position men with bombs or guns to make a follow-up strike if necessary. Four men should suffice—two in front of the mine and two behind it."

Andrei said, "I'll be there as well, armed with a dagger. If all that fails to kill him, I will personally do him in with the blade. But if he takes another route altogether?"

Sophie interjected, "How long would it take the bombers to get from Malaya Sadovaya Street to the canal on foot?"

"Only a few minutes, but they would have to run to catch the carriage, and that would certainly attract the gendarmes."

Ignaty broke in, "That won't be a problem. When the tsar travels via Italyanskaya Street, it's because he is visiting his cousin, the Grand Duchess Catherine. He usually spends up to half an hour with her. That will give the bombers plenty of time to get into position near her palace."

Andrei smiled at his wife. "This could work." Turning to Kibalchich, he asked, "What sort of bombs can we arm our men with?"

"Dynamite won't work. It's too stable. I'll make up a mixture of nitroglycerine and pyroxylin. That would certainly do it."

"Pyroxylin? What's that?"

"Nitrated cellulose. Very flammable."

"What about a detonator?"

Nicholai smiled, "With nitroglycerine? Not necessary. Just throw it on the ground." His expression turned serious. "That said, if the bomber is too close, he'll blow himself up along with the tsar."

Ignaty interjected, "I'll do it. I am prepared to die. Even if I kill the tsar and survive, his Cossacks would likely cut me down. If not, then it's the executioner's rope. I'd rather die knowing I succeeded in my mission."

Sophia said, "I have no doubt about your revolutionary fervor, but we need more than one."

As soon as she said this, Nikolai Rysakov, the son of a sawmill manager, stepped forward. "I'll do it."

Nikolai Rysakov

Two other young men pushed to the front. "As will we." It was Timofey Mikhailov, a workman, and Ivan Yemelyanov, a cabinetmaker.

Sophia smiled broadly. "We have our bombers. What about the mine?"

Mikhail Frolenko raised his hand. "I'll set it off. I missed all the fun with the trains, and I need to atone."

Andrei clapped his hands together. "We have a plan. We need to find a place along Malaya Sadovaya from which to place a mine."

Timofey Mikhailov

Ignaty chimed in, "I know a place."

"Good. When we're done, you can show me. Nicholai, get started on the explosives."

Nicholai nodded slightly. "I will do so right away."

* * *

Ivan Yemelyanov

As soon as the meeting broke up, Ignaty and Andrei left for Malaya Sadovaya Street. Ignaty led him to an empty storefront. "This is the place

I was talking about. It was a restaurant. There is a shallow a root cellar for storage. It will be a perfect place to dig the tunnel. There is plenty of room to put the dirt so we wouldn't have to dispose of it."

"Good. That'll make it easier. Let's contact the landlord and arrange to rent it."

Ignaty asked, "What kind of shop will you tell him you are opening?"

Andrei mulled this for a second, then responded, "Cheese. We used to make cheese when I was a child. That also gives us a reason to close early. If it were a pub, we'd have people coming well into the evening." They rented the shop the same day and set about stocking it with various cheeses.

The People's Will plot was coming together. Kibalchich started experimenting with the mixture for his bomb. Each afternoon, a few of the men would go to the cheese shop just before closing. They were like any other customers, except they didn't leave. They proceeded to the root cellar, where they worked on the tunnel. Cheese barrels were disassembled and the staves used for cribbing to stabilize the tunnel's roof and walls.

There was, however, a bit of a problem with the bombs. Kibalchich was having difficulty finding a mixture that was volatile enough to explode when thrown but not so unstable as to blow up prematurely in the hands of the bomber. Finally he arrived at what he assessed was the proper formula, but it needed to be tested. Kibalchich told the bomb throwers to meet him on February 26 at a little-used suburban park to test smaller versions of the bombs they would use in the attack. Grinevitsky, Rysakov, and Mikhailov met him there, but Ivan Yemelyanov did not show up.

"Where is Ivan? I said I needed you all here."

Rysakov just shrugged. "I guess he couldn't get off work."

Kibalchich was uneasy. The Okhrana had been clamping down hard on revolutionaries since the assassination attempts on the tsar. He looked around nervously. "I don't feel good about this. What if he got arrested?"

Ignaty laughed, "He didn't get arrested. He just has an ass for a boss. The guy running the cabinet shop where he works thinks he is a lord and his workers are serfs. We'll test the bombs and tell him what we learn."

"Okay. Let's begin." Kibalchich reached into a cloth shopping bag and gingerly retrieved four small boxes. Each weighed a little over two pounds and was wrapped in a white cloth. "These are about half the size of what you'll use in the attack. I made these smaller for safety reasons. The more of this mixture you have, the more unstable it is. On the day of the attack, you will need to be very careful or you'll already be in hell when the tsar arrives."

Ignaty peered at the small package. "Good to know."

"Okay, all you have to do is throw the package. As soon as it hits something, the shock should make it explode. You don't have to hit stone or steel; anything should do it." He handed the first bomb to Ignaty. "Throw it in that ravine."

Ignaty took the bomb, drew a deep breath, and threw it about ten meters down the hill. When it hit the ground it exploded with loud *boom* and a large cloud of white smoke. The men were showered with sand and pebbles. There was a small crater where the bomb had landed. "Wow! That was loud. My ears are ringing! That should work."

Kibalchich handed a bomb each to Rysakov and Mikhailov. Each in turn threw his bomb while the others covered their ears. Each exploded as expected. There was one bomb left, the one for the absent Yemelyanov. "Does anyone want to throw the last one?"

Ignaty said, "Why don't you do it? It's your creation."

Kibalchich smiled. "Why not? I never get to play with my own toys." He threw the bomb and giggled with glee when it exploded. "All right, they work. But remember, the real ones will be twice as large. Make sure you throw it far from yourself to avoid the blast. We'll meet again in two days."

* * *

On February 28, 1881, Ignaty Grinevitsky was shocked when Sophia Perovskaya told him about her husband, Andrei Zhelyabov. "Arrested? What happened? Then why are we still here?"

"Ignaty, Andrei will tell the Okhrana nothing. He was visiting Mikhail Trigoni when the police arrived. They were looking for Mikhail, but Andrei got scooped up in their net."

"Then we should act before they find out about us. I have no doubts about your husband's courage, but the Okhrana are masters of interrogation. Everyone talks eventually. Remember Goldenberg?"

She grimaced at the comment. "Well, no matter. After tomorrow, it will be a moot point. The tsar will be dead, and the revolution will have started."

"Yes. We will have done our duty. Is Nikolai Ivanovich ready with the bombs?"

"No, but don't worry. He is working on them as we speak. Vera Figner and I will help him assemble them this evening. They'll be ready by tomorrow, as will the mine."

"If they are not ready—"

"They will be. The attack will be executed exactly has Andrei and I planned. We will be successful. I will consider no other alternative."

"Nor I."

"If the tsar travels by Malaya Sadovaya Street, Frolenko will be in the cheese shop to set off the mine. If he travels along the canal, you and the others will use Kibalchich's bombs. Andrei's role was only a last resort. I have complete faith that you, Nikolai, Timofey, and Ivan will be successful. Now let's go over the final planning for tomorrow."

Ignaty took a deep breath. "Okay. What do you want me to do?"

"Frolenko and I will be in the cheese shop. I want you and Rysakov at the end of the block to the south, in front of the carriage. The explosion will be large, so don't be too close. Mikhailov and Yemelyanov will be to the north end of the street, behind the entourage. When the mine goes off, make sure the tsar is dead. If he is, just walk away. If not, throw your bombs. If, for some reason, the mine does not explode, throw your bombs at the tsar's coach. It will be the first one of the three. Do you understand?"

"Yes, I understand. What if he takes the other route?"

"If the entourage continues on Italyanskaya, the gendarmes on Malaya Sadovaya will pull back. If they do, it means he is going to visit his cousin. We then move to the canal. When we are in position there, I will wave my lace handkerchief, which is your signal to proceed with the attack."

"What about the mine? What about Frolenko?"

"He can see the street through the shop window. When the tsar's carriage is over the mine, he'll detonate it. If he sees the gendarmes pull back off of Malaya Sadovaya, he'll abort."

"What about Andrei? What have you heard?"

"I don't have time to think about that. Meet me tomorrow morning at nine o'clock at the flat on Telezhnaya Street. Nicholai and I will have the bombs for you."

That night, Ignaty Grinevitsky wrote a letter. It was to no one in particular, but they would find it after the attack. He fully expected to die the next day. He wrote, "Tsar Alexander II must die. He will die and with him, we, his enemies, his executioners, shall die too. "

* * *

Sunday morning, Tsar Alexander II got up and dressed in the dark blue uniform of the Sapper Battalion, the unit that saved his father and the palace during the Decemberist Uprising of 1825. The tsar was mentally exhausted. He had been working tirelessly on his latest reforms—the first steps toward the establishment of a constitutional monarchy. The proposed reforms took the name of Count Mikhail Loris-Melikov, the minister of the interior and the project's main architect. He came to the Winter Palace that morning. A footman announced his arrival. "Your highness, Count Loris-Melikov has arrived and is waiting for you in your study."

"Thank you, Dmitry. Please tell him I'll be with him shortly."

A few minutes later, Tsar Alexander II entered his study, where his minister of the interior was waiting. The count, with his bushy mutton-chop beard, bowed. "Highness."

"Mikhail Tariolovic, no need to stand on such formality. Where do we stand on the constitutional reforms?" The reforms, though called "constitutional, " did not call for a constitution in the traditional Western sense of the word but did allow for the common people to have representation with advisory rights in the legislative organs alongside the nobility. The tsar would retain the right of legislative initiative or the right to propose a new law, but it would be an important first step, especially for such an autocratic regime.

"The document you read yesterday was approved unanimously by the consultation committee on February 16. It does not call for a formal constitution, per se."

Alexander smiled. "I am well aware of that." He laughed, adding, "If it did, I'd have to fight the nobles and the anarchists at the same time! One battle at a time, Mikhail Tariolovic." The tsar suddenly became serious again. "I have already signed the decree this very morning. I have given my approval, but I do not hide from myself the fact that it is the first step toward a constitution. The world is changing, and we must change with it or be left behind. Just like with warfare, tactics and strategies on the battlefield must change in the face of new weaponry. Crimea certainly taught us that."

"Yes, your highness."

"Make several copies of the declaration with the latest changes. I want to discuss it with the Council of Ministers in four days and then publish it. If we are going to hold this empire together, we need to defang our enemies and deprive them of the issues they use to rally opposition to us. These reforms should cool their revolutionary ardor."

"Your highness, I fear the more radical revolutionaries will never be satisfied."

"Perhaps not. But if we keep the common people on our side . . . If we just buy enough time to complete our work . . ."

"Along those lines, highness, I was informed that Andrei Zhelyabov was arrested three days ago."

"Who?"

"He is one of the leaders of the revolutionary group responsible for the bombing of the palace, and of your train before that. They call themselves The People's Will."

"Oh, yes. Of course. Good work."

"We were the beneficiaries of fortune. Our spies learned the location of another radical, a man named Mikhail Trigoni. When we raided his apartment, Zhelyabov happened to be there too."

"Two birds with one stone, eh?"

"Yes, sire."

"Well, good luck is as powerful as hard work sometimes."

* * *

While the tsar was meeting with his minister, Ignaty Grinevitsky was on his way to pick up the bomb that would kill him. He, Rysakov, Yemelyanov, and Mikhailov all arrived at the flat on Telezhnaya Street within a few moments of each other. Inside were Nicholai Kibalchich, Vera Figner, and Sophia Perovskaya. They'd been up all night preparing the bombs and looked exhausted.

Ignaty quipped, "Nicholai Ivanovich, you look like shit."

Running his hand through his dark hair, Kibalchich replied, "It was very stressful and painstaking work." He gestured to the flasks and vials scattered across the kitchen counter and table. "We first had to make the pyroxylin and then the nitroglycerine. One slip and *boom*. The ladies helped me make the chemicals, and two associates assembled the bombs." As he said this, Vera Figler walked in from the bedroom carrying a large bag. Inside were the bombs. They were made from cut-up kerosene tins and wrapped in white cloth. Each weighed at least two kilos.

Rysakov asked, "Is there anything we should know?"

"Yes, be very careful with them. They are extremely volatile. If you drop them or even bump them too hard, they will explode, and there won't be enough of you to send back to your mothers. Also, if you intend to survive the attack, throw them far. These are at least twice as powerful as the ones we threw in the park. Each of you take one. Leave one at a time. Not to sound morbid, but if one of you blows up on the street, the other three need to be far enough away to live."

Ivan Yemelyanov had brought a briefcase. He opened it, carefully put one of the bombs in it, and left. Timofey Mikhailov tucked his gently inside his coat and followed a few minutes later. Ignaty and Nicholai Rysakov had brought heavy paper bags, like workmen carried their lunches in. Each carefully placed his bomb in his bag and folded the bag shut. Sofia turned to Kibalchich. "You and Vera need to get some rest. Your work today is done. We'll take it from here." He just nodded and shuffled off into the bedroom, where he collapsed on the bed.

Rysakov asked, "Don't you need to rest too?"

"I slept some during the night. Vera insisted. My hands were starting to shake from exhaustion, and that isn't good when you're mixing volatile explosives."

"I should think not."

Sophia stood up. "Well, I'm hungry and nervous. We have some time yet. I suggest we leave and head toward the cheese shop."

"Together? But what about what Kibalchich's orders?"

She smiled nervously. "He is overly cautious. We'll be fine. After today, none of that will matter anyway." There was a sense of fatalism in her tone, as if she understood she was walking to her death. Rysakov recognized it immediately. He had the same timbre in his own voice. Ignaty's, however, was normal, almost jovial. He was totally at peace with what they were about to do.

* * *

By one o'clock, the conspirators were all in place. Two members of People's Will, posing as husband and wife, were minding the cheese shop when Mikhail Frolenko walked in with a parcel under his arm. He had volunteered to detonate the mine. Wire from the mine led back into the shop where there was a jar with a chemical solution to provide the electric charge. All he had to do was dip the wire into the solution. The mine was so large that it would likely destroy the shop and kill Frolenko in the process, but he was unconcerned. He calmly sat at a table and opened his parcel. He removed a large piece of sausage and a bottle of red wine, set them on the table, and prepared to eat.

"What is this?" the woman asked.

As he took a bite of sausage, he replied, "What? I have to be strong." The couple left and turned the shop over to Frolenko. He locked the door behind them, put a "closed" sign in the window, and returned to his meal. Thirty minutes later, gendarmes on horseback positioned themselves at either end of the street. The tsar was approaching.

Frolenko picked up his detonating wire. He peeked out the window again, expecting the royal carriage's approach—but it didn't come. Instead, the gendarmes pulled back toward Italyanskaya. The tsar was taking the other route. There would be no need for their mine today, and Frolenko would live. He poured out the solution before slipping out the back door of the shop and disappearing into the city.

On the street, the bombers and Sophia watched the gendarmes pull back. Yemelyanov and Mikhailov slowly walked west on Italyanskaya as the tsar's carriage passed them. Grinevitsky and Rysakov started to move south to Nevsky Prospect when Sophia intercepted them.

"Shall we stop at Gostiny Dvor department store? They have a wonderful sweet shop."

Rysakov stammered, "But we need to—"

She cut him off. "We have plenty of time. The tsar is visiting his cousin and spends at least half an hour with her. If he is not, he's too far ahead for us to catch up. Either way, a stop at the sweet shop won't change anything. Besides, we don't want to be loitering in the area before the tsar's arrival."

Ignaty shrugged and replied, "I'm game." The three went to the confectionery and ordered some cakes. Sophia, despite her calm outward demeanor, was too keyed up to eat. A visibly nervous Rysakov picked at his cake but ate little. Ignaty had no such qualms and downed his portion with relish. Turning to Rysakov, he asked, "Are you going to eat that?" Rysakov pushed his plate to the ravenous Pole.

After a few minutes, Sophia checked her watch. "It's time." Without another word, the three left and walked west on Nevsky Prospect toward the canal. The two men took up their positions toward the middle of the street, while Sophia walked north up the busy street from where the tsar's carriage would approach. As she did, she spotted Yemelynov and Mikahilov in the crowd. She made eye contact, and each man nodded his acknowledgment.

The men waited nervously, glanc-ing repeatedly in Sophia's direction. Her gaze was fixed eastward down Italyanskaya. At 2:15, she turned and walked back toward the quay along the canal. As she did, she waved her hand-kerchief—the attack was on. The royal carriage rounded the corner and traveled

Attack on Alexander II (first bomb)

about 150 meters along the quay when it passed the first bomber. It was Rysakov. He threw his bomb, but it detonated behind the tsar's carriage. There was a loud explosion, and a huge cloud of white smoke billowed toward the sky. Immediately, a Cossack riding behind the carriage fell to the ground, mortally wounded. A young boy delivering meat for a local butcher was cut down and seriously injured. Several other bystanders and members of the tsar's entourage were injured. Rysakov was immediately captured. Chief of Police Dvorzhitzky, who was riding in the sleigh imme-diately behind the tsar's carriage, leapt out and ran to where the bomber was being restrained. As he approached, the bomber shouted to someone in the gathering crowd. "Your turn, brother!" Dvorzhitsky instantly realized there was another assassin in the crowd, likely armed with a bomb.

For all of Rysakov's effort, the tsar was unharmed. His bulletproof carriage, a gift from French Emperor Napolean III, took the brunt of the blast. Dvorzhitsky said, "Your highness, you need to leave immediately. I fear there are more of them."

The tsar replied, "Certainly, of course." But inexplicably and despite his coachmen's pleading, the tsar got out of his carriage.

Dvorzhitsky immediately stepped in. "Your highness, you must leave. I'll have my sleigh take you back to the Winter Palace."

"Yes, that would be for the best. But first I want to have a look at this devil." The tsar walked down the sidewalk along the canal, surrounded by five of his Cossacks. When he got to where Rysakov was being held, he gave the young man just a cursory glance. Upon learning he was not a noble, he snorted, "A fine one." He shook his finger at Rysakov and turned to leave.

Dvorzhitsky again pleaded with the tsar, "Your highness, you must leave! It is not safe!"

"All right, but first show me the site of the explosion." A platoon from the Eighth Naval Equipage arrived on the scene, and along with the Cossacks, surrounded the tsar as he walked to inspect the scene of the explosion where the dead Cossack and wounded boy lay on the street. Less than two meters away, Grinevitsky was leaning against the canal fence, carrying his bomb wrapped in a handkerchief. When someone asked the tsar if he was injured, Alexander replied, "Thank God, I'm untouched."

Ignaty shouted, "It is too soon to thank God yet!" He turned toward the Tsar, raised the bomb over his head with both arms, and slammed it at his feet. The bomb exploded with a roar. Grinevitsky and the tsar both were blown to the ground. At least twenty people nearby were wounded, including Police Chief Dvorzhitsky, and one was killed.

Assassination of Alexander II (second bomb)

Tsar Alexander lay on the ground, leaning on his right arm. Both of his legs were shredded below the knee. His abdomen was torn open, and his face mutilated. Next to him lay Grinevitsky, also badly wounded, and the mortally wounded butcher's boy, now the victim of a second bomb.

The Tsar was bleeding profusely from his legs. Ivan Yemelyanov, clutching his briefcase, was nearby and ready to throw his bomb if the first two failed. He joined the bystanders who rushed to the tsar. Alexander was mortally wounded. Ivan's bomb would not be necessary.

The snowy street was covered with blood and debris. There were sabers, epaulets, and chunks of flesh strewn about. Grinevitsky lay in a pool of blood, alive but dying. The tsar was conscious but fading fast. In a weak voice he said, "I'm cold." The tsar's brother, Grand Duke Mikhail Nicholayevich, came racing up in a carriage. Drawn by the first explosion, he headed straight for the scene from the Mikhailovsky Palace. He arrived in time to hear his brother say, "Take me home quickly." Alexander lost consciousness immediately after.

In the confusion, the tsar wasn't taken to the nearby military hospital but straight to the palace. Neither were his wounds bound to stop the bleeding. Aided by members of the crowd, the shattered tsar was lifted into Dvorzhitsky's sleigh. One of those helping was Ivan Yemelyanov. In a further bit of irony, the horse pulling the sleigh was none other than Barbarian, the People's Will steed who had been captured and pressed into service for the police after the assassination of Mezentsov some two years earlier.

The sleigh rushed the tsar back to the palace, but the door was too narrow to carry him through, so the soldiers broke it down. They carried the dying man up the marble staircase to his study. This was the same room where he had signed the emancipation manifesto freeing the serfs twenty years earlier and where, just that morning, he had laid the groundwork for a new constitution. The tsar's family rushed to the scene. He was given holy communion and last rites before drawing his last breath around 3:30. Tsar Alexander II, emperor of Russia, king of Poland, grand duke of Finland, the emancipator of twenty-three million serfs, "The Good Tsar," was dead.

* * *

Ignaty Grinevitsky lay unconscious in the street as the tsar was hustled away. Ivan Yemelyanov came near in the hope he might spirit his comrade away in the confusion but immediately recognized that was not an option. Ignaty was taken to an infirmary attached to the Winter Palace. He woke up at 9 p.m. Police immediately started to interrogate him, but Ignaty didn't even give up his name. He was not given any painkillers for his injuries, and lingered in agony until his death at 10:30. He was arguably the first suicide bomber in history.

In police custody, Nikolai Rysakov cooperated with investigators in an attempt to save his own life. He gave up reams of information on his accomplices, which enabled the police to raid the People's Will flat on Telezhnaya Street. At the time of the raid, two other People's Will members, Hesya Helfman and Nikolai Sablin, were there. Helfman was arrested, and Sablin committed suicide after wounding three police in a shootout. Rysakov confirmed the identities of the other conspirators one by one as they were arrested. Despite his cooperation, he was put on trial with his comrades, convicted, and sentenced to hang. He was hanged last and had to watch all his fellow conspirators meet their fate before a crowd of one hundred thousand on the Smenovsky Regiment parade grounds before meeting his own.

Hesya Helfman

Nikolai Sablin

Ivan Yemelyanov was captured in April 1881, tried, and sentenced to death. His sentence was commuted to a life of hard labor, and he was exiled to Siberia. His sentence was commuted again to twenty years, and he was pardoned in 1895. He died in 1915.

The fourth bomber, Timofey Mikhailov, was arrested two days after the assassination at the Telezhnaya Street flat. He was armed with a revolver and wounded three police officers before being subdued. He pled not guilty to participating in the assassination, but Rysakov identified him in court. He was convicted and sentenced to hang with his comrades.

Sophia Perovskaya, the daughter of the military governor of St. Petersburg, was arrested on March 22. In a letter to her mother she wrote, "I have lived as my convictions dictated, and it would have been impossible for me to have acted otherwise." She was convicted and sentenced to hang with the others. She was the first woman in Russia to be executed for terrorism.

Nikolai Kibalchich, the group's explosives expert, was arrested about two weeks after the assassination and charged in the conspiracy. Instead of worrying about his defense, Kibalchich spent his time in prison working on the design of a missile. He had come up with a concept for a powder rocket engine with the ability to control the direction of flight by changing the engine angle. He wrote up his findings and asked that it be given to scientists for examination. His paper was simply placed in an envelope and filed in the police archives. Kibalchich was hanged with his friends. Some thirty-six years later, a Russian engineer rediscovered the manuscript in the archives and published it. Ten years after Kibalchich's death, similar ideas were independently developed by a German aerospace pioneer.

Andrei Zhelybov did not actually take part in the assassination, since he had been arrested a few days before. However, he demanded to be tried along with his comrades. He was convicted and sentenced to be hanged alongside Perovskaya, Kibalchich, Mikhailov, Rysakov, and Helfman, the woman arrested in the apartment. They were called the Pervomarovtsi—"those of March 1." They were hanged together, except for Helfman, who was pregnant. Her execution was scheduled for forty

Hanging of the Assassins of Alexander II

days after the birth of her child. Her sentence was later commuted to life in a penal colony, but she died of complications from childbirth before serving her sentence.

Vera Figler escaped St. Petersburg after the assassination. After the Okhrana cracked down on the People's Will, she became the only free member of the original Executive Committee. She became the de facto leader of the organization, but her luck ran out in February 1883. She was captured, tried, and sentenced to death. The sentence was commuted to perpetual penal servitude in Siberia, and later twenty years in the fortress at Schlüsselburg. After completing her sentence, she was sent into internal exile to Arkhangelsk, then Kazan, and finally Nizhny Novgorod. After the Russian Revolution, she published her memoir and several biographies before dying in 1942 at the age of eighty-nine.

Mikhail Frolenko, the man willing to die while detonating the mine but saved by the change in route, was arrested in March 1881. He was tried and convicted. He was originally sentenced to death, but his sentence was later changed to eternal hard labor, which he served from 1882 in the Schlüsselburg fortress where Figner was imprisoned. He was released in 1905, later joining the Communist Party, and died in 1938 at age eighty-nine.

The Aftermath

The members of The People's Will thought the death of Tsar Alexander II would result in a revolution that would overthrow the monarchy and end the empire. It did not and brought repression instead.

The Tsar Alexander II's son and heir, Alexander Alexandrovich, came to power upon his father's death. He was a completely different man with very different ideas about how to run the country. Any hope for a constitution died with his father. Just before his death, Alexander II signed a decree setting up "consultive commissions" to advise the tsar. Alexander III canceled the policy before it was published. He would not allow his autocracy to be curtailed by anyone.

He then set about reversing his father's liberal initiatives. He returned to Tsar Nicholas I's policy of Orthodoxy, Autocracy, and Nationality. He weakened the authority of the local elected bodies his father had created. Peasant communes were placed under the supervision of landowners selected by the government. He forced the teaching of the Russian language in German, Polish, and Finnish schools and pressured people of other faiths to accept Eastern Orthodoxy. The new tsar was hostile to the country's

Jews, and the anti-Semitic May Laws were passed, which restricted where Jews were allowed to live. They forbid the issuing of mortgages or deeds to Jews and forbid registering them as lessees of real property or giving them power of attorney to manage or dispose of property. The laws also forbid Jews from transacting business on Sunday or Christian holy days.

The situation for People's Will was not much better. Armed with information, first from Grigory Goldenberg and later Nikolai Rysakov, the Okhrana went after the organization with a vengeance. By the end of the year, all but one member of its original Executive Committee were either in prison or dead. Having killed the father, surviving members of the People's Will set their sights on the son, but they no longer had the organization or manpower to make it happen. Tsar Alexander III died at age forty-nine, but of completely natural causes. The horror of Alexander II's death and their general reliance on violence and terror turned public opinion against them. They were hard-pressed to mount any effective action against the government and only managed to assassinate one more government official in the next year. The Okhrana infiltrated the organization at multiple levels, which led directly to the arrest of Vera Figler, the last original Executive Committee member. Attempts to revive the group ultimately failed, and it slid into obscurity without ever achieving its primary goal.

Years later, other revolutionary groups did overthrow the Romanov Dynasty and Alexander III's son, Tsar Nicholas II, and his family paid the ultimate price; this came more than thirty years after the People's Will ceased to exist. History can only speculate what would have happened in Russia if Alexander II's reforms had been allowed to continue. They might have developed into a constitutional monarchy like Great Britain. Other countries under Russia's sphere of influence might have enjoyed more freedom and autonomy, like Finland and Bulgaria. They might even have avoided the disaster of World War I. What is not open to speculation is that Russia after the death of Tsar Alexander II was much less free than before.

Chapter 6

The Black Hand, Gavrilo Princip, and Archduke Franz Ferdinand

—17.5 Million Dead People Later ...

I f you were to pick someone out of a crowd to be the one to change the world, Gavrilo Princip would not be that person. He was not rich or powerful. He was not a military man, an inventor, an adventurer, a philosopher, a great thinker, or a leader. He was a small, thin young man from poor parents living a harsh existence. Gavrilo was born in 1894 in the

Gavrilo Princip

small village of Obljaj in Bosnia and Herzegovina. His Serbian family were Eastern Orthodox Christians living in a land officially owned by the Muslim Ottoman Empire but occupied since 1878 by the Catholic Austro-Hungarian Empire. By the measure of anyone's socioeconomic totem pole, the Princips were at the bottom.

Gavrilo's father, Petar, worked a four-acre farm to support his family, with a third of his meager income given to his Muslim landlord. Petar was a devout man who never cursed or drank. His piety only earned him the ridicule of his neighbors. He was a Serb nationalist who had fought

in the Herzegovina Uprising against the
Ottoman Empire in the mid 1870s. His
wife, Marija, had given him nine children,
with only three surviving infancy. A sickly
infant, Gavrilo was the second of their surviving offspring. He was to be named after
his late uncle Spiro, but to inspire a bit of
divine intervention, their Eastern Orthodox

Marija and Petar Princip (1927)

priest suggested Gavrilo. The priest claimed that naming the weak child
after Archangel Gabriel, Gavrilo in Serbian, would increase his chances
of survival.

And survive he did. Against his father's wishes, Gavrilo started school
at the age of nine and, after a slow start, became a very good student.
He still helped his father on the farm, but he had higher aspirations. Just
after Gavrilo's thirteenth birthday, his older brother Jovan came home for
a visit. He lived in Sarajevo, the capital of Bosnia and Herzegovina. As a
modern city, Sarajevo was two hundred miles and five hundred years away
from Obljaj.

Jovan pulled his little brother aside and said, "Gavrilo, you should
come live with me. There is more for you in Sarajevo. You can further
your education there."

"I'd like that very much. The school here is okay, and I really like the
headmaster, but there's a limit to what I can learn. What kinds of schools
do they have in Sarajevo?"

Jovan replied, "All kinds, I suppose."

"But they cost money, and I have none."

"Most do, that is true. But not all."

"What school doesn't cost money?"

"I did my research. There is a military school that, if they accept you,
they pay all costs."

Gavrilo was surprised. "Military school? You mean an Austro-
Hungarian Imperial military school, do you not?"

Jovan laughed, "Well, I don't mean an Ottoman one. The Austrians are in charge, and they don't intend to give us back to the Turks anytime soon."

"No, I suppose not. Do you think father will approve?"

As he said this, Petar Princip walked in from outside. "Approve of what?"

Jovan replied, "I think it would be good if Gavrilo came with me to Sarajevo to further his education. He has learned all he can at the local school."

"Bah. Education is a waste of time. I'll teach him what he needs to be a farmer."

Gavrilo interjected, "But what if I don't want to be a farmer?"

"Why wouldn't you? I am a farmer, just like my father and his father before him. What else would you do?" Motioning to Jovan, he added, "Besides, I already lost one son to the city. I can't afford another."

"You always say I'm too small to be of much help anyway. Maybe I'll find something else to do, something that doesn't require much physical strength."

"Like what? A shopkeeper? They still have to lift boxes, barrels, and the like."

"I was thinking more like the law or something where I use my brain more than my back."

By this time Marija had entered the room. She knew her husband and what he was likely to say. "Now Papa, let the boy have his dreams. You always complain he does not work anyway, so let him not work in Sarajevo. He'll be Jovan's problem, not yours."

"Well that is the first sense I've heard anyone speak all morning. If you go, how would you pay for school? How would you support yourself?"

Gavrilo started to respond, but Jovan cut him off with a knowing look and answered first. "I've already looked into it. There are some schools with patrons, so the costs are low. I've been working a lot and saved some money. I have friends who will give him work when he isn't in school. It'll cost you and mama nothing."

Petar just snorted. He glanced at his wife. Her eyes told him he was clearly outnumbered. "Well, one less mouth to feed." He turned and walked outside. That was the closest to a "yes" they were going to get.

Marija said to Jovan, "I am trusting you to take care of your little brother and keep him out of trouble, do you understand?"

"Yes, mama."

"And both of you need to come visit. I know it is far, but I need to see my boys."

She returned to the kitchen, leaving the boys alone. Gavrilo asked in a whisper, "Why didn't you tell father about the military school?"

"I didn't want to start a fight. He hates the Austrians almost as much as the Turks. I have to leave tomorrow to go back to work. The school term starts next month. I will arrange everything." He shoved a few bills into Gavrilo's hand. "For the train."

* * *

When Gavrilo traveled to Sarajevo the next month, he was shocked to learn that Jovan had changed his mind. A confused Gavrilo asked, "What do you mean I'm not going to the military school? It was your idea in the first place!"

"I know, I know. I thought it'd be good for you, I really did. But I started asking some of my friends about it, and what I heard disturbed me."

"What did they say?"

"My friend, Danelo, told me graduates from the military school are commissioned into the Austro-Hungarian Army, the emperor's army. If the Bosnian people . . . rather, *when* the people rise up and fight for their freedom and independence, it'll be the army the emperor will dispatch to put them down. My friend told me it was not right for me to make you an executioner of your own people."

Gavrilo pondered this. "I can't argue with that, but what am I to do instead? I don't want to go back to Oblja—not now, not after seeing a real city."

Jovan smiled. "I won't make you do that. I understand how you feel. Father would shackle you to him and the farm. Why do you think I left? I've arranged for you to attend a merchant school. I've saved enough money to pay for your tuition."

"How?"

"I've been working in the forests, hauling logs to the lumber mills in the city. It's hard work, but the pay is pretty good. Of the two of us, you're the smarter. When you become a successful businessman, just give me a job," he chuckled, "but I demand top pay."

"You'll have it!"

Gavrilo loved living in Sarajevo. The city was vibrant and bustling. It was a crossroads between the old world of the Ottoman Turks and the modern world of Europe. Oddly, Princip didn't really belong in either. The next year, the Austro-Hungarian Empire officially annexed Bosnia and Herzegovina. To most Bosnian Serbs this was no momentous event. They were merely trading Ottoman overlords for Austrian ones. There was an active Slavic separatist movement in Sarajevo that included mostly Serbs but also Croats, Bosniaks, and even some Muslims. All resented the Austrians and supported the establishment of a South Slavic state. Two Croatian bishops coined the term to describe this as-yet-unestablished state—Yugoslavia.

During a visit to his parents' home, Gavrilo broached the topic with his father. Petar was sitting in his chair by the fire smoking his pipe. "Papa, did you hear? We've been annexed into the Austro-Hungarian Empire. We're no longer part of the Ottoman Empire."

Petar snorted, "Makes no difference. The Turks haven't ruled this land in over twenty-five years anyway. Believe me when I tell you, boy, the Austrians are no better. The only reason they annexed us was to keep us divided."

"What do you mean?"

"There's talk that the Young Turks are revolting in Istanbul. They're trying to force the Sultan to reinstate the constitution. They also talk about giving Bosnia and Herzegovina autonomy within the Ottoman

Empire. Were that to happen, we'd be but a step away from our rightful place as part of the Greater Serbian Empire. Emperor Franz Joseph is afraid of a united and powerful Serbia, so he annexed our country to keep us divided. We have only traded the Sultan for the Emperor. We're no better off."

"But father, aren't the Austrians better than the Ottomans? At least they're Christian."

"Bah. In name only. They betrayed us before and will do it again."

"Betrayed us? How?"

"Twenty years before you were born, we rose up against the Turks."

Gavrilo nodded. "I know. The Herzegovina Uprising. We learned about it in school."

He grumbled, "School. What a waste of time. I should never have let you go to Sarajevo. You should've worked in the fields with me and learned how to farm, not waste time with silly books."

"But I like school, and I'm good at it. Besides, how else would I learn about history? Certainly not from you."

Petar looked up at his son. "History? You want to know about history, eh? Did you know I fought under Colonel Despotović when he cleared south Bosnia of all the Muslims? Our success inspired the Serbians and Montenegrins. The Russians and the British intervened on their behalf and, as a result, both countries became fully independent. We, however, were betrayed. Rather than winning our freedom, we were given to the Austrians like a prized cow. We were still technically part of the Ottoman Empire but occupied by new Austrian masters. Now, the Young Turks rebel in Istanbul. Bulgaria declares itself independent. And us? Instead of freedom, the Austrians annex us into their empire. Remember, my boy, no one will willingly give you your freedom. If you want it, you must be prepared to fight for it."

Gavrilo declared proudly, "As you fought the Turks, then I will fight too—for Yugoslavia!"

Petar scoffed, "You? Fight? Look at yourself. You're just a boy, and a scrawny one at that. You aren't big enough to even carry a rifle, let alone fire one. Leave the fighting to soldiers. Maybe you should just stay in school." Dejected, Gavrilo slinked away. He respected his father, and his rebuke was cutting.

Gavrilo returned to Sarajevo determined to work hard in school and prove himself worthy of his father's respect. After three years at the merchant school, he earned a position at a local gymnasium (preparatory school). Here, he was steeped in Bosnian Serb separatist ideology, specifically Yugoslavism, which advocated the union of all South Slavic territories. He also became an adherent of Bogdan Žerajić.

Eight years older than Princip, Žerajić was a law student at the University of Zagreb in Croatia, also part of the empire. As a Bosnian Serb revolutionary and one of the leaders of the Serbian secret society Freedom, he was angered by the empire's annexation of Bosnia and Herzegovina and considered the new Austro-Hungarian parliament in Sarajevo to be illegitimate. In an independent act of rebellion, on June 15, 1910, Žerajić attempted to assassinate the Austro-Hungarian governor of Bosnia and Herzegovina, Marijan Varešanin, on the opening day of parliament. Armed with a pistol, Žerajić fired at Varešanin. While ardent, he was no marksman and missed with every one of the five rounds he fired. With his last bullet, he killed himself. To most people he was a lunatic, but to Gavrilo Princip, Bogdan Žerajić was a hero and role model.

* * *

Archduke Franz Ferdinand Carl Ludwig Joseph Maria of the ancient House of Habsburg was the heir to the throne of the Austro-Hungarian Empire, albeit a reluctant one. He was the nephew of the emperor, Franz Joseph I of Austria. He became heir, not because he was the emperor's favorite or the most capable but because everyone else kept dying. The emperor's only son, Crown Prince Rudolf, died in 1889 in a scandalous manner. Though married to the daughter of King Leopold II of Belgium, the thirty-year-old Prince Rudolf began a torrid affair with the seventeen-year-old daughter of an Austrian baron. Their affair lasted only three months and ended when their bodies were found at Rudolf's hunting lodge, victims of an apparent murder-suicide. He was shot through the heart and from behind, she through the temple.

With the death of Prince Rudolf, the next in line was Archduke Karl Ludwig, Emperor Franz Joseph's younger brother and Franz Ferdinand's father. But Karl died in 1896 after returning from a trip to Palestine and Egypt. While in Palestine, he drank from the holy waters of the River Jordan, contracted typhoid, and died shortly after returning to Vienna. That put Franz Ferdinand next in line, and the House of Habsburg began grooming him for the throne. Unfortunately, Archduke Franz Ferdinand fell in love with the wrong woman.

Archduke Franz Ferdinand

Franz Ferdinand met Countess Sophie Chotek at a ball in Prague in 1894 while he was stationed at the city's military garrison. Sophie was a very

Emperor Franz Joseph I of Austria

pretty girl of twenty-six, and he fell for her immediately. She was a lady-in-waiting for Archduchess Isabella, the wife of Archduke Freidrich, a senior military officer and wealthy member of House of Hapsburg-Lorraine. Franz Ferdinand regularly visited Freidrich's Halbturn Castle to visit Sophie. When he contracted tuberculosis, she wrote him regularly while he convalesced on an island in the Adriatic Sea. They successfully kept their relationship a secret for some time. They were so successful that people assumed he had fallen in love with Freidrich's oldest daughter, Archduchess Maria Christine. One day, Archduchess Isabella found Franz Ferdinand's watch on the tennis court. Expecting to find her daughter's photo inside, she was shocked find a photo of Sophie instead. That's when the trouble started.

Sophie, although a countess, was not of sufficiently high birth. To marry a member of the Imperial House of Habsburg-Lorraine, one had to be descended from one of the reigning or formerly reigning dynasties of Europe. Sophie did not meet the criteria. Emperor Franz Joseph pressured Franz Ferdinand to cast Sophie aside in favor of a more suitable wife.

"Franz Ferdinand, nephew, you must renounce this Chotek woman and find a more suitable wife, one eligible to be empress consort and bear you an heir."

"Uncle, these traditions are archaic. I should be free to marry whomever I wish. Besides, Sophie may not be dynastic, but she is still royal. She is a countess, and her family has been royal since the fourteenth century! Surely that is long enough."

"It is not! We must ensure the strength of our bloodline. We cannot allow it to become diluted with that of lesser nobles. For this reason, you must select a more suitable consort."

"I am sorry, uncle, but I will not. I love her."

The emperor scoffed. "Nonsense. Love has nothing to do with it. It is about ruling an empire and producing heirs. If you really feel that strongly about her, keep her as a mistress. I don't normally approve of such things—I find them tawdry—but I will not object if you choose to do so."

Franz Ferdinand turned red with anger. "I will not treat the woman I love like some whore, and I will not allow you to talk of her like that! Besides, that strategy didn't end so well for Rudolf."

Now it was the Emperor's turn to erupt. "How dare you tarnish the memory of my son! You should treat your betters with more respect!"

Franz Ferdinand had overplayed his hand. "Your highness, I meant no disrespect of my cousin. I was just pointing out that a man who marries for love has no need of a mistress. I have always looked to you and Empress Elizabeth, may God rest her soul, as examples of what marriage should be, since my own mother died so young. Will you fault me for that?"

The emperor was not buying the argument. "Nonsense. It is just as easy to fall in love with a woman of dynastic birth as any other. I will not allow you to marry this woman. The House of Habsburg-Lorraine is more important than any woman, or man for that matter. The matter is settled. I will not discuss it further."

Franz Ferdinand stormed off. He was not willing to accept his uncle's edict no matter who he was.

Franz Ferdinand continued to court Sophie and flatly refused to consider marriage to any dynastic noble in Europe. It was a constant point of irritation between him and his uncle, but both men were very stubborn and refused to yield. Finally, a third party had to step in to break the deadlock.

Archduchess Maria Theresa was a formidable person. She was Franz Ferdinand's stepmother and the widow of Archduke Karl, making her the emperor's sister-in-law. He was ten when his father married her. She was only eighteen. When Franz Joseph's wife, Empress Elizabeth, withdrew from public life after the death of her son Rudolf, Maria Theresa assumed her public role. She was a strong woman with a lot of influence.

Entering the emperor's offices, Maria Theresa said, "Your highness, we need to talk."

"About what?"

"Your presumptive heir and Sophie."

The emperor turned away and pretended to read some papers on his desk. "The matter is settled. As I understand it, the young lady in question has voluntarily entered a convent."

"Yes, I know. I fetched her back myself. She is here in Vienna."

Franz Joseph flashed red. "On whose authority!"

"My own! You said she entered the convent voluntarily. She left it voluntarily too." Maria Theresa understood too well that Sophie had left Vienna due to pressure by the emperor, but she had not been ordered—at least not officially.

The emperor could not correct her without admitting he had been meddling in the first place. "She should go back to her own people. She should not be here."

"She is here because this is where the man she loves is living. You need to give up this silly notion that she is unworthy of Franz Ferdinand. He is determined to marry her or no one at all. Either way, he will produce no heir that fits your standard."

"He will . . . in time."

"My dear brother-in-law, we are not young anymore. As evidenced by the demise of my own husband, death comes without warning. Do you really want to leave the fate of the House of Habsburg-Lorraine to vagaries of your own health, or do you want to have some influence on the problem?"

"Why should I let him marry that woman? Love? Nonsense. This is not about love; it's about duty."

Maria Theresa smiled. She had her opening. "Oh really? Did you marry Empress Elizabeth out of a sense of duty? I seem to recall you were madly in love with her. You made no effort to remarry a dynastic noble after her death. Admit it, dear brother-in-law, you married for love. What would you have said if the court tried to forbid you from marrying her? It wouldn't have been a pretty scene. What a beauty she was. Do you remember what she looked like at your wedding? She was what? Sixteen years old?"

Franz Joseph smiled to himself. "She was the most beautiful woman in all of Europe. No, the world. She didn't really like me much, not at first. But I was persistent."

"Would you have accepted it if they had told you that you couldn't marry her?" He said nothing. "Of course not. So how do you expect your nephew to?"

Emperor Franz Joseph took a deep breath. "All right. I will accede to his request to marry this woman—with conditions."

Maria Theresa bowed slightly, acknowledging his concession. "What are they?"

"Theirs will have to be a morganatic marriage. She will be given a suitable title, but she will never be empress. Her position in court will be limited to that dictated by her family's rank. Finally, their children will not be dynasts and will not be eligible to inherit the throne. If my nephew agrees to these conditions, I will not stand in his way."

Maria Theresa bowed. "Your highness, I am sure my stepson will find your conditions acceptable."

Archduke Franz Ferdinand married Countess Sophie Chotek on July 1, 1900. Per the emperor's wishes, their marriage was morganatic, a marriage between people of unequal social rank. Their descendants had no right of succession to the throne, and Sophie would not share Franz Ferdinand's rank, title, or privileges. She was not allowed to appear in public beside him, ride in the royal carriage, or even sit in the royal theater box. Neither Emperor Franz Joseph I nor any of Franz Ferdinand's brothers attended. From Franz

Archduke and family

Ferdinand's side of the family, only Archduchess Maria Theresa and her two daughters, his stepsisters, attended the wedding. Their marriage was a happy one and in the ensuing years, Sophie bore him three children—Sophie, Maximilian, and Ernst.

* * *

Archduke Franz Ferdinand was thirty-two when his father's death changed his future. Wild swings in fortune were not uncommon for him. When he was seven, his mother died tragically of tuberculosis at the age of twenty-eight. Four years later, a distant royal cousin, Duke Francis V of Modena, died and named Franz Ferdinand his heir, making him one of the richest "men" in the empire at the tender age of eleven. He found love at the age of thirty, but it caused a rift in his family. The death of his father made him next in line to become emperor, but his beloved wife would not share in his glory.

Franz Ferdinand was an avid hunter and amateur adventurer, which his wealth allowed him to indulge. He circumnavigated the world when he was in his late twenties. He hunted big game in Europe, Africa, Asia, Australia, and North America. His diaries logged over 250,000 kills, and he displayed nearly one hundred thousand trophies in his Bohemian castle. This was not to say his life was limited to leisure. In accordance with family tradition, he enlisted in the Austro-Hungarian Army at a young age and was commissioned as a lieutenant at the age of fourteen. His promotions came quickly, and by age thirty-one was a major general. His influence exceeded his rank, and by the early 1900s he was hand-picking the chief of the General Staff. He reached his peak of military power in 1913 when he was appointed inspector general of all the armed forces of the Austro-Hungarian Empire, a position that would give him command of the military in wartime.

Politically, Franz Ferdinand was somewhat liberal, at least for the time. He butted heads repeatedly with his reactionary uncle and other old-line leaders. The Austro-Hungarian Empire was a massive multiethnic and multicultural behemoth with three official languages and at least thirteen others commonly spoken by its citizens. It spanned from Russia in the east to Italy in the west, and from Germany in the north to Serbia and Montenegro in the south.

Franz Ferdinand was a reformer and pushed for more federalism within the empire. Specifically, Franz Ferdinand was a proponent of *trialism* a political movement whose goal was to move the empire from bipartite to tripartite. It proposed uniting the Slavic regions into a separate state—the Kingdom of Croatia—with status equal to that of Austria and Hungary. By adding a third Slavic crown to those of Austria and Hungary, he hoped to quell the Slavic unrest that threatened to tear the empire apart. Unfortunately for Franz Ferdinand, this also gave the Serbian separatists even more motivation to be rid of him, as his plan undermined their dream of a new state of Yugoslavia.

Another problem for him was the Kingdom of Serbia, which had come into existence less than a hundred years earlier and only achieved full independence in 1878. As a Slavic nation, it was naturally aligned with Russia. To the old guard in Vienna, the upstart and expansionist Kingdom of Serbia was an impediment to their stability, as it continually stirred up trouble among the Empire's Slavic minorities. Franz Ferdinand had no love for Serbia but warned the more hard-line members of the Austro-Hungarian General Staff that any attempt to bully or attack Serbia risked war with Russia and disaster for all involved.

* * *

The failed assassination of Marijan Varešanin and death of Bogdan Žerajić in 1910 only further radicalized Gavrilo Princip. Princip so idealized Žerajić, he made regular pilgrimages to his grave, often spending the entire night sleeping on the cold ground. The following year, he joined Young Bosnia, a Serbian society that advocated for Bosnia leaving the Austro-Hungarian Empire and uniting with the Kingdom of Serbia. Political tensions continued to rise in Sarajevo, and students were barred from forming any nationalist organizations or clubs. Young Bosnia ignored the edicts and instead moved underground. Away from the prying eyes of the local government, they discussed a wide range of topics, including literature and politics, but revolution was never far from the front.

In 1912 Gavrilo helped organize a public demonstration against the empire. "Colleagues, we need to stand up for our rights and our freedom. Join me tomorrow for a protest in the city square."

A student named Andrej asked, "What exactly are we protesting?"

"We are protesting the empire trampling on us and enslaving us. We are all free Slavs and are entitled to determine our own destinies."

"No one has trampled or enslaved me. I have no intention of standing around shouting about the empire with the likes of you. Besides, I think it's going to rain tomorrow."

Gavrilo was smaller than Andrej but there was a red-hot rage behind his sunken, dark eyes. "We all need to show up. If we are there, they have to notice. They have to listen to us. You will be there!"

Andrej was a little intimidated at first but pushed back. "Get out of my face, you runt. Who are you to order me around? You are just a peasant from the sticks. You're nobody."

Gavrilo grimaced at Andrej while he reached into his pocket. He slipped a pair of brass knuckles on his right hand, made a fist, and brought it to Andrej's nose. "Either you stand with us for Yugoslavia, or I will put you down like the dog you are!"

Andrej stepped back. "Okay, okay. I'll be there."

Addressing the other boys in the room, Princip said, "I expect to see all of you there." He slammed his armed fist into the open palm of his left hand. "Anyone who doesn't show up will have to deal with me afterward."

Gavrilo was a short, skinny youth, but he looked and sounded crazy. No one else challenged him. He went to the next classroom and repeated his threat. By that afternoon, word had reached the school authorities, and he was summoned to the administrator's office.

Mr. Jonovich was the stern headmaster in charge of Gavrilo's gymnasium. "Mr. Princip, please have a seat."

"Yes, sir. Why am I here?"

Jonovich sat behind his desk and peered at Gavrilo, who was almost swallowed by his large leather chair. "Serious allegations have been made against you which, quite honestly, I find hard to believe. One of your fellow students claims that you were trying to encourage other students to leave school tomorrow to attend a protest. That is bad enough, but he also alleges that you threatened those who declined. Is this true?"

Gavrilo sat up in his chair. "Who said this?"

"That's not important. What is important is the truth. Did you do this?"

Gavrilo shrugged. "I admit trying to encourage my fellow Slavic students to attend a political rally. But as to threatening them? How? I am probably the smallest boy in my class. Who would be afraid of me?"

"They said you had a weapon. A knuckle duster, I believe. Is that true?"

"A knuckle duster? I'm not even sure what that is."

Mr. Jonovich opened the center drawer of his desk, removed the brass knuckles, and dropped them loudly on his desk. "Does this look familiar?"

"No. Should it?"

"Mr. Vuković found it in the cloakroom—in your coat pocket."

Gavrilo started to panic. "Someone planted it there! Someone is try-ing to set me up!"

"Mr. Princip, we have multiple witnesses, we have your own admis-sion about the protest, and we have an illegal weapon in your position. You're a young man, and I admire your passion. I'm not to report you to the police, but we cannot allow you to continue with this institution. You are expelled—effective immediately. Gather your belongings and leave. I am sorry it has come to this, but we will not tolerate such anti-social and anti-imperial behavior in this school."

After his expulsion, Princip left Sarajevo and headed for Belgrade, the capital of the Kingdom of Serbia. He had little money and walked the entire 170 miles. Once he crossed the Serbian frontier, he fell to his knees and kissed the earth. Eager to prove himself, upon arrival in Belgrade, Gavrilo sought out active nationalist groups to join. Princip learned about a Serbian guerrilla group that was fighting the Ottoman Turks. The group was commanded by Major Vojislav Tankosić, a member of the Black Hand.

Vojislav Tankosić

The Black Hand was the more common name for Unification or Death, a secret society formed in 1901 by Serbian mil-itary officers. Their aim was to unify all the southern Slavic peoples of Balkans into a single country ruled by Serbia. The unification of Italy under Giuseppe Garibaldi and the creation of the German state by Otto von Bismarck were their blueprints for the formation of a Greater Serbia. Doing this would entail fighting against the Ottoman Turks, the Austro-Hungarians, and any Slav who lacked their patriotic fortitude. In 1903 the King of Serbia himself fell into the latter category. Angered over King Alexander's cozy relationship with—and the kingdom's growing reliance on—Austria-Hungary, the Black Hand and a group of army officers bru-tally murdered King Alexander and his wife. King Alexander was replaced by the more compliant King Peter.

When Princip volunteered his services, it didn't go as he expected. He asked around and was directed to a nondescript room above a shop in downtown Belgrade. The door was ajar when he walked up the stairs and he cautiously knocked. A voice replied, "Enter." Gavrilo opened the door and walked in. There was a man sitting behind a simple wooden desk. He was in civilian clothes but had a distinctly military air about him. "What do you want?"

Gavrilo stood erect to make himself as tall as possible. "My name is Gavrilo Princip. I am here to volunteer for your military force and fight against the Turks."

The man behind the desk flashed a brief smile, like someone privy to an inside joke. "You want to fight the Turks? Really? Have you any military experience?"

"No sir. But I am a quick study."

The man began to size him up. "How old are you? Thirteen? Fourteen? You're no more than a boy."

"I am sixteen, sir."

"You don't look it."

"Well I am, sir. I was recently expelled from my gymnasium for organizing protests against the Austrians."

"Well, you're too scrawny for us. We need men, not boys."

Gavrilo grew agitated. "But I can fight! I wasn't completely honest before. I wasn't expelled for motivating my fellow students to attend the protest. I was kicked out of school for threatening with brass knuckles the cowards who refused to go."

The man chuckled. "Well, good for you, but it doesn't alter the facts. You are too small."

"No, I'm not. I'll prove it to you!"

The man was beginning to get irritated. "Listen, boy. A Mauser Model 1871 rifle weighs ten pounds. Your pack and bed roll weighs up to fifty pounds. Add to that a bayonet, cleaning kit, shovel, rain gear, ammunition, knife, and all the other kits you'd have to carry, and your gear would weigh more than you! Now run along. Go bother someone else."

Gavrilo stood as tall as his slender frame would make him. "Who is your superior officer? I wish to speak to him directly."

The man laughed. "That would be Major Vojislav Tankosić. He will be here tomorrow, but he'll tell you the same thing. He makes the rules, not me."

"Very well! I'll be back."

The next day, Princip returned as promised. When he arrived at the room, there were three men inside: the man from the day before, a solidly built man in his early twenties in a simple soldier's uniform, and a striking man in his midthirties wearing the tunic of a Serbian Army major. He cut a dashing figure with a strong straight nose above a long mustache with ends that curled up. He had a high forehead, thick jet-black hair, and a strong jaw. He looked like a soldier. This was Major Tankosić.

"I'm looking for Major Tankosić. I assume that is you?"

"I am he. What can I do for you, boy?"

"I came here yesterday to volunteer, and your man here rejected my offer. I ask you to reconsider."

Tankosić smiled. "Yes, David told me about you. I admire your grit, but as he told you, you're simply too small for our unit."

"I can fight, and I will carry whatever physical load is required to help establish a free Yugoslavia. I can—"

Tankosić cut him off with the wave of his hand. "No one is questioning your bravery or patriotism, but we have physical standards that must be met by all volunteers. We accept less than one in five volunteers. Many of those we reject have prior military experience and, I dare say, all are more . . . physically suited than you. There is no appeal of my decision. I suggest you try to find some other way to further our cause."

Princip recognized that to argue was futile. Just like his father, the guerrillas thought he was too small to fight. Dejected and embarrassed, Gavrilo Princip left Belgrade and returned to Sarajevo, where he moved back in with Jovan. He did not give up, however, and spent the next several months shuttling back and forth between Sarajevo and Belgrade searching for a group that would take him.

Finally, on one of his trips to Belgrade, Gavrilo Princip met a man willing to give him a chance. "Hello. I was told I'd find Mr. Živojin Rafajlović here."

"I'm Rafajlović. What do you want?"

"My name is Gavrilo Princip. I am a Bosnian Serb from Sarajevo. I want to volunteer for service."

Rafajlović studied the skinny teenager before him but, unlike the others, he wanted to hear the boy out. "What kind of service?"

"Fighting for a Greater Serbia. I'm small, but I have heart. My father fought the Turks during the Herzegovina Uprising. I am a member of Young Bosnia and was expelled from my gymnasium in Sarajevo for organizing protests against the Austro-Hungarian Empire and threatening students who lacked sufficient . . . patriotism. Now I am here in Belgrade to volunteer my service for whatever action Greater Serbia requires."

He sized up Princip and asked, "Exactly how did you threaten these students? No offense, but I wouldn't find you very intimidating."

"With this." Gavrilo reached into his pocket and pulled out a pair of brass knuckles. "I needed an equalizer, if you will."

Rafajlović laughed. "Well, heart means more than size. A small man who will pull a trigger is worth more than a big man who won't. How old are you? Princip, was it?"

"Yes, sir. I am seventeen, sir."

There was something in the young man Rafajlović liked. "Have you any military training? Can you shoot a gun or use explosives?"

Anticipating another rejection, Princip replied sheepishly, "No sir, I don't."

Rafajlović smiled. "Well, that can be remedied. We can train you to shoot, but bravery is something you cannot teach. We're looking for Bosnian Serbs to send back to fight the Austrians. Are you interested?"

"Yes, sir! Absolutely!"

"Okay. Come back tomorrow at noon. And pack your bag."

Živojin Rafajlović was one of the founders of the Serbian Revolutionary Organization or Serbian Chetnik Organization. The Chetniks had been organized in 1902 with the goal of liberating historically Serbian lands from the Ottoman Empire. They operated both political and paramilitary groups and actively engaged in fighting against those perceived to be enemies of a Greater Serbia.

The next day, Princip returned and, along with fifteen other Young Bosnia members, was sent to a paramilitary training camp near Vranje in southern Serbia. The camp was operated by Mihajlo Stevanović-Cupara. During his stay, Princip lived in Cupara's house while he was being taught how to shoot, use bombs, and fight with a knife. Upon completion of his training, he returned to Belgrade before being sent on to Sarajevo.

In 1913 the Austro-Hungarian Empire declared a state of emergency in Sarajevo and implemented martial law throughout the city. Tensions ran high, and the empire assumed control of all schools and banned all Serbian clubs and cultural organizations. Sarajevo was already a powder keg, and the empire was trying its best to light the fuse.

* * *

In Vienna, Emperor Franz Joseph ordered Archduke Franz Ferdinand, in his role as inspector general of the armed forces, to attend military maneuvers to be held in Bosnia the following summer. In conjunction with his military purpose, he would also visit Sarajevo for the opening of the new state museum. Since he would be traveling in his military vice, his wife, Duchess Sophie, could accompany him. The visit to Sarajevo was scheduled for June 1914 and announced to the public.

* * *

Danilo Ilić had been a bank teller and school teacher but by 1913 was back to living with his mother in her small boarding house. He was also the leader of the Black Hand cell in Sarajevo. Near the end of 1913 he traveled to Belgrade to meet with Colonel Dragutin Dimitrijević, more commonly known by his code name Apis. Apis was the chief of

Serbian military intelligence and a leader of
the Black Hand. Ilić suggested it was time
to take action against Austria-Hungary, and
Apis agreed. Shortly after, Major Tankosić,
Apis's adjutant and the man who had dismissed Princip the year before, called for a
Black Hand planning meeting in France in
January 1914. One of those in attendance
was Muhamed Mehmedbašić, a carpenter
from Herzegovina whose father was a poor
Muslim noble. Mehmedbašić was a Black
Hand member who was eager to "revive the
revolutionary spirit of Bosnia." During the
meeting, multiple assassination targets were
discussed, including Franz Ferdinand. At the
end of the meeting, however, it was agreed
they would target Bosnian Governor Oskar
Potiorek, and Mehmedbašić would be sent to
kill him.

Danilo Ilić

While traveling from France to Bosnia-
Herzegovina, Mehmedbašić was spooked by
a police inspection of the train he was riding and threw his weapons out the window.

*Colonel Dragutin
Dimitrijević, a.k.a. Apis*

Upon arrival in Sarajevo, he had to locate suitable replacements, which
delayed his assassination attempt. Before he acted, he was informed by Ilić
that the attempt against Potiorek had been called off. Mehmedbašić's new
target was Franz Ferdinand. The Black Hand tasked Ilić to recruit people
to help with the effort. One of those was Gavrilo Princip.

At the time, Princip was living in Belgrade. He was recruited
along with two other Bosnian Serbs—Trifko Grabež and Nedeljko
Čabrinović. Unbeknown to the three, Ilić also recruited two Serbian
youths in Sarajevo—Vaso Čubrilović and Cvjetko Popović. Along with

Mehmedbašić, these seven men would be the assassination team targeting the archduke.

In Belgrade, Major Tankosić provided the assassins a pistol with which to practice—a FN Model 1910 .380 APC. The ammunition for the weapon was rare and expensive, so they only had a few rounds to practice with in a park near the city. They later received four more Model 1910 pistols, six hand grenades, money,

Trifko Grabež, Nedeljko Čabrinović and Gavrilo Princip

suicide pills, and map of Sarajevo marked with the locations of the local gendarmes.

Princip, Grabež, and Čubrilović were smuggled into Bosnia-Herzegovina by agents of the Black Hand and Narodna Obrana, another Serbian nationalist organization with tentacles that extended deep into the Serbian government. As the men were moved from safe house to safe house, reports on their progress were briefed to Serbian Prime Minister Nikola Pašić. In Tuzla, one of the assassins, Nedeljko Čabrinović, ran into a friend of his father. His father was a Sarajevo police officer, and the friend was Sarajevo Police Detective Ivan Vila. Čabrinović casually asked about the date of the archduke's planned visit to Sarajevo, and Vila told him. The following day, Čabrinović told his comrades the date of assassination would be June 28.

The three assassins arrived in Sarajevo on June 4 and immediately split up. Princip visited his family briefly before returning to Sarajevo on June 6 and moving in with Ilić. Grabež stayed with his family in Pale, while Čabrinović moved to his father's house. Midmonth, Ilić fetched their weapons from an agent in Tuzla and hid them under the sofa in his mother's boarding house. All they had to do now was wait.

* * *

Over the weekend of June 12–14, Archduke Franz Ferdinand was at his favorite home—his hunting lodge at Konopischt. Joining him there was Kaiser Wilhelm II, the ruler of Germany. Franz Ferdinand wanted to talk to the kaiser about Serbia, a thorn in the side of the Austro-Hungarian Empire. Serbia fought two Balkan wars in 1912 and 1913, which doubled its size and increased its population by 50 percent, to 4.4 million people. Austria-Hungary had not gotten involved in the wars, and as such, its interests were not considered during the settlements of those conflicts. Its victories and favorable peace terms only emboldened Serbia. The Ottoman Turks were in retreat and to Serbia, it was only fair that the Slavs—not Austria-Hungary—take over the vacated lands in the Balkans. Franz Ferdinand needed an ally in the region and wanted the kaiser's advice on whether to approach Romania or Bulgaria.

Following his uncle's orders, on June 23 Franz Ferdinand left Vienna for Bosnia to observe military maneuvers. The Fifteenth and Sixteenth Corps of the Austro-Hungarian Army were on maneuvers for both training and politics. It was a show of force intended primarily for the Serbians to reaffirm the empire's resolve to defend its southern territories. On June 26 Franz Ferdinand and Sophie went shopping in Sarajevo. The couple were surrounded by a dense throng of well-wishers and had been treated warmly. No one had reason to suspect any problems. The next day they took the train to Ilidža Spa a few miles west of the city before returning to Sarajevo the morning of June 28 to celebrate their fourteenth anniversary.

* * *

While Franz Ferdinand and Sophie visited the spa, the assassins met to finalize their plot. Danilo Ilić had kept the three from Belgrade, Pincip, Grabež, and Čabrinovic, isolated from the local recruits, Čubrilović and Popović. They met each other for the first time on June 27 along with Mehmedbasić. After introductions, Ilić produced a hand-drawn map. "Gather around. I want to show you where you'll be. The Archduke's people were kind enough to tell us the route in advance." Turning to

Mehmedbasić, he said, "Muhamed, you're the most experienced, so you will take the first position." Pointing to the map he said, "This is the Mostar Café. It's on the north side of the street. I want you to be in front of it, near the garden. You will have a grenade. When the archduke approaches, throw your grenade into his car."

"How will I know which is his?"

"He is here in a military capacity, not a royal one. That is why his wife is accompanying him. He will be in his military uniform, and his hat has a very large plume. His security detail should be in the first car, maybe two. He will probably be in the third or fourth vehicle." Mehmedbasić nodded.

"Čubrilović, I want you positioned down the street but close to him in case his grenade doesn't explode or he misses. You'll have a grenade and one of the pistols. If the archduke's car is disabled, finish him off with the pistol."

Čubrilović replied, "You can count on me."

Ilić continued, "Any number of things can go wrong, so the rest of you will be positioned further along the route. Čabrinović, there is an electrical box on the opposite side of the street along the river. That's where I want you. If the first two fail and alert the guards, they will most likely be drawn to the north side, so you will have time to act. You'll have a grenade."

Čabrinović nodded. "It will be done."

Ilić continued, "Popović, you and I will be here on Ćumurija Street directly across from the bridge. You will have a grenade, and I will have a pistol. Grabež, you and Princip are the last. I want you next to the Latin Bridge. You will both have a pistol and a grenade. If they get past us, it's up to you to stop them. Do you understand?"

Princip replied, "They won't get past us."

Ilić smiled. "Okay. After I pass out the weapons, I want everyone to go home and get a good night's sleep. We all need to be sharp tomorrow when we make history."

The archduke's schedule and route had been made public in advance. He and Sophie were met at the train station by General Oskar Potiorek, the governor of Bosnia and Herzegovina, with six cars. The first car carried local police and the head of the archduke's security detail. The second car carried the mayor and chief of police of Sarajevo. The third car was a Gräf & Stift 28/32 PS convertible sports car, which carried the archduke, Sophie, Governor Potiorek and Lt. Colonel Count Franz von Harrach. Their first stop was a military barracks, where the archduke made a quick inspection before continuing on to city hall via the Appel Quay along the Miljacka River.

A little after ten o'clock, the motorcade turned east onto the Appel Quay. The first assassin the motorcade approached was Mehmedbašić. As instructed, he was standing in front of the Mostar Café. His hand cradled the grenade in his pants pocket. The murmur of the crowd to his right signaled the motorcade's approach. He briefly stepped into the street for a better view. The archduke's large plumed hat was clearly visible in the third car. As the cars approached, Mehmedbašić gripped the grenade tightly. The first car rolled past, but instead of pulling out his grenade, he did nothing. He froze. He lost his nerve. Čubrilović was just to his left, waiting for Mehmedbašic to act. His hands were in his jacket

Archduke and Sophie just before assassination

pockets, the pistol in his right, the grenade in his left. When Muhamed stepped back, turned, and walked away, Čubrilović was confused. He too lost his nerve. The motorcade passed unmolested. The next man in line was Nedeljko Čabrinović on the opposite side of the street near the river. He was armed with a grenade. He did not lose his nerve.

At 10:10 a.m., the Gräf & Stift approached. The car's convertible top was down, and Franz Ferdinand was clearly visible. Čabrinović threw his grenade, but instead of exploding in the car, it bounced off the folded convertible top onto the street behind it. The delay fuse caused it to explode under the next car. The trailing car was disabled, and the explosion left a crater in the street a foot across and over six inches deep. While more than a dozen people were wounded, the archduke and his party were unscathed. The driver reacted immediately. He stomped on the accelerator and sped away. The other conspirators gaped helplessly as the car raced past them at high speed.

Čabrinović was trapped between the motorcade and the river. Policemen piled out of the last two cars and ran toward him. "Shit!" He swallowed a cyanide pill Major Tankosić had given him and jumped into the river, but his suicide plan, like his assassination attempt, was flawed. First, the cyanide didn't kill him. It apparently was so old it only made him vomit. And as for drowning himself in the river, it had been a hot, dry summer, and the Miljacka River was less than six inches deep. He was plucked from the river by the police and badly beaten by a mob before being arrested.

The archduke continued to the city hall to give his speech. He was not in a good mood and interrupted Mayor Fehim Curčić's welcome by saying, "Mr. Mayor. I came here on a visit and I am greeted with a bomb. This is outrageous!" The text of Archduke's speech had been in the damaged car. When it finally arrived, it was wet with the blood of one of the victims. After his speech, there was some question as to what to do next. The archduke's chamberlain, Baron Rumerskirch, spoke first. "Your highness, I recommend you and the Duchess stay here in city hall until troops are summoned to secure the streets."

Governor Potiorek chimed in, "Nonsense. The troops are on maneuvers and are in battle uniforms. They will not have their dress uniforms, as a royal guard is required to wear."

Rumerskirch protested, "This is no time for protocol! An attempt has been made on the archduke's life!"

Potiorek silenced him with a wave of his hand. "Do you think that Sarajevo is full of assassins?" Actually, it was.

While the men continued to argue, Franz Ferdinand was conferring with his wife. "Gentlemen, all this is academic. The Duchess and I will visit those wounded in the bombing at the local hospital."

"But your highness, it is too dangerous!"

"I think the danger has passed. We are off our schedule, so if there are more assassins out there, they won't know where we are going or when. I'll wager any others fled as soon as they saw their cowardly attempt failed."

Potiorek was in no position to argue. "Of course, your highness. But may I make one suggestion? Let's avoid the crowds of the city center and drive along the Appel Quay. That route will be unimpeded."

Count Harrach stepped up. "I will stand on the left-side running board to protect the Archduke from any attack from the south side of the street. That is the side the cowards attacked from before."

Potiorek said, "Then it's settled. I will ride with the royal family for added security, but I'm sure the route along the quay will be much more secure." The problem was, no one told the drivers about the change to the route.

As the motorcade drove along the river, rather than stay on the quay as Potiorek wanted, the first two cars turned right at the Latin Bridge onto Franz Joseph Street. The archduke's driver dutifully followed. Potiorek immediately yelled at the driver to stop and go back. The driver stopped the car, but when he started to back up, the motor stalled.

After the failed attack, Gavrilo Princip moved in front of Schiller's delicatessen near the Latin Bridge and waited. He reasoned that if they returned along the same route, he might still have a chance to assassinate the archduke. He was standing there when the first two cars in the motorcade rumbled past.

Murder weapon

When the third car, carrying the royal couple and governor, screeched to a halt right in front of him, he couldn't believe his luck. When the motor stalled, Princip drew his FN Model 1910 .380 ACP, stepped on the running board, and shot Archduke Franz Ferdinand and his wife, Sophie, Duchess of Hohenberg, at point blank range.

Princip's first round struck Franz Ferdinand in the neck, severing his jugular vein. His second hit Sophie in the abdomen. Princip tried to shoot himself but was immediately set upon by bystanders who wrestled him to the ground. The other members of the entourage initially believed the royal couple was unhurt. Then a spurt of blood shot from the Archduke Franz Ferdinand's neck and splashed onto Count Harrach's cheek. Harrach attempted to stop the bleeding with his handkerchief. Turning to her husband, Sophie said, "For Heaven's sake! What happened to you?" Then she collapsed onto her husband's lap. Franz Ferdinand was now bleeding profusely. Potiorek took charge. "Driver! Proceed immediately to my residence with the utmost haste! The archduke has been injured!"

The Archduke seemed oblivious to his own injuries. As the car sped away, he pleaded, "Sophie, Sophie! Don't die! Live for our children!" Her unconscious body lay splayed out across his knees.

Count Harrach was still standing on the running board with the bloody handkerchief pressed to the Archduke's neck as blood poured over his uniform. "Your highness, how bad is your injury?"

Franz Ferdinand replied, "It is nothing. It is nothing." These would be his last words. He choked violently on the blood and passed out. When they arrived at Potiorek's residence, Countess Sophie was already dead. Archduke Franz Ferdinand, heir to the Habsburg throne, died ten minutes later. The fuse of the Balkan powder keg was well lit.

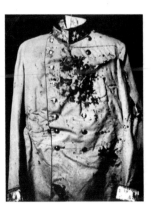

Franz Ferdinand's blood stained uniform

* * *

News of the assassination spread quickly, and violent anti-Serb riots swept through Sarajevo and other cities in Bosnia and Herzegovina. Similar acts of violence broke out in Croatia and Slovenia. Over five thousand prominent Serbs were arrested, and hundreds died in prison. Another 460 Serbs were sentenced to death. A Bosniak special militia called the Schutzkorps was organized to persecute the Serbs.

The assassination led to what was called the July Crisis, a month of furious diplomatic efforts involving Austria-Hungary, Russia, Germany, France, and Great Britain. Austria-Hungary rightly believed Serbia was behind the plot but had no proof. With Franz Ferdinand dead, the hawks in Vienna were firmly in charge. They issued an ultimatum to Serbia with ten demands they knew would not be accepted. They weren't supposed to be; they were supposed to provoke a war. And they did.

Serbia actually agreed to most of the demands, but not before mobilizing its military forces. Austria-Hungary broke off diplomatic relations with Serbia and ordered a mobilization of its own. On July 28, 1914, a month to the day after the assassination, Austria-Hungary declared war on Serbia. World War I had begun.

In Sarajevo, the conspirators were quickly rounded up and put on trial. Gavrilo Princip said he was sorry he had killed Sophie; he had meant to kill Potiorek. That said, he was still proud of his actions. "I am a Yugoslav nationalist, aiming for the unification of Yugoslavs, and I do not care what form of state, but

Trial of the conspirators (1914)

it must be free of Austria." Under Habsburg Law, no person under the age of twenty could be sentenced to death. Gavrilo was twenty-seven days shy of that mark. Too young to receive the death penalty, he was sentenced to twenty years in prison at the Small Fortress in Terezín.

Like Princip, Nedjelko Čabrinović and Trifko Grabež were both under twenty years old and were sentenced to twenty years in prison. Both men died in prison of tuberculosis within two years of their sentencing. Vaso Čubrilović and Cvjetko Popović, also minors, were sentenced to sixteen and thirteen years, respectively. Both men survived the war and lived well into old age. Danilo Ilić, Veljko Čubrilović, and other coconspirators were hanged. Muhamed Mehmedbašić escaped but was later arrested and court-marshalled in Serbia, along with Colonel Dragutin Dimitrijević, a.k.a. Apis, for plotting against Serbian regent Alexander. Mehmedbašić was sentenced to fifteen years in prison; Apis was executed by firing squad. Vojislav Tankosić was never tried in connection to the assassination but was killed in battle by Austro-Hungarian forces in 1915.

For Princip, prison conditions were extremely harsh. Gavrilo was chained to a wall in solitary confinement. He contracted tuberculosis, which attacked his bones, and his right arm had to be amputated. In 1916, he tried to hang himself but failed. He finally died in prison of tuberculosis on April 28, 1918. At the time of his death, he weighed only eighty-eight pounds.

The Aftermath

The goal of Gavrilo Princip, his coconspirators, and their Black Hand masters was the creation of a Slavic nation (Yugoslavia) by cleaving off the southern reaches of the Austro-Hungarian Empire and annexing them into the Kingdom of Serbia. In August 1914 Austria-Hungary invaded Serbia and was repulsed with heavy losses. The Serbian plan appeared to be working. However, in 1915, a second invasion was launched with Austro-Hungarian, German, and Bulgarian troops under German command. The Serbians were crushed, and their country divided between the Austro-Hungarian Empire and Bulgaria. Eventually Austria-Hungary, Germany, and their allies lost the war. A new Kingdom of Yugoslavia was declared, with Serbia and Montenegro assuming the dominant positions. In the long term, the conspirators were successful, but at great cost.

The conflict between Serbia and Austria-Hungary quickly expanded. The Russian Empire sided with Serbia, as did Britain, France, Belgium, Japan, and Montenegro. Eventually Italy, the United States, Romania, and many other countries joined the Allies. Austria-Hungary was joined by Germany, Bulgaria, the Ottoman Empire, and a number of smaller nations to make up what would be called the Central Powers. The war lasted over four years and resulted in over thirty million military casualties, of which almost ten million were killed. In addition, there were an estimated 7.7 million civilians killed. Serbia suffered the highest casualty rate in the war. Of the Serbian army, 58 percent were killed—some 243,600 men. Total casualties were estimated to be in excess of one million—25 percent of Serbia's prewar population and 57 percent of its overall male population. Of all the combatant countries, Serbia suffered the highest casualty rate in World War I.

The Kingdom of Yugoslavia was created from the ashes, but it did not last. The monarchy ended when Nazi Germany invaded the country in 1941. After World War II, the Socialist Federal Republic of Yugoslavia was declared, and it survived within the Soviet orbit until the early 1990s, when the country broke up after the fall of the Iron Curtain. Ten years of fighting followed. In the end, Yugoslavia was no more. Its component states—Serbia and Montenegro, Macedonia, Bosnia and Herzegovina, Croatia, and Slovenia—had all become independent nations. With the independence of Kosovo, Serbia was even smaller than before.

Chapter 7

Mercader, Stalin, and Leon Trotsky
—How Far Away Is Far Enough?

It was September 21, 1935, and Jaime Ramón Mercader del Río was in Madrid. Spain was two months into its civil war, which started when a group of senior military officers led by General Francisco Franco staged a coup to overthrow the leftist government of President Manuel Anzaña. Mercader was on the side of Anzaña's Second Spanish Republic, whose coalition government was led by the left-leaning Popular Front and included anarchists, communists, socialists, and anarcho-syndicalists, as well a mix of separatist groups. Mercader was not a member of the Popular Front, nor was he an anarchist or a separatist. He was a communist.

Being a communist in 1936 didn't mean one was all alone on the left. There were several competing factions. The oldest leftist party was the Spanish Socialist Worker's Party, Partido Socialista Obrero Español (PSOE). A division within PSOE in 1921 spawned the formation of the Spanish Communist Party, Partido Communista de Español (PCE), a Stalinist party and part of the Soviet controlled Communist International. In 1935, the Worker's Party of Marxist Unification, Partido Obrero de Unificación Marxista (POUM), was formed as an anti-Stalinist communist party aligned with the "permanent revolution" philosophy of exiled Bolshevik leader Leon Trotsky. Just as Stalin and Trotsky vied for power in the Soviet Union after Lenin died, the Stalinist PCE and Trotskyist POUM were vying for power inside the Spanish Republican government.

Ramón Mercader was an unlikely communist. He was born into a family of wealth and privilege. His father, Pablo Mercader Marina, was from Badalona in Catalonia, where his family owned a successful textiles company. His mother was born Eustacia María Caridad del Río Hernández in Santiago de Cuba. Caridad was the daughter of an affluent merchant from Cantabria. Caridad Mercader became an ardent communist after she divorced her husband. She took her children and decamped for Paris, where Ramón followed in his mother's political footsteps. She was a member of the Unified Socialist Party of Catalonia, Partido Socialista Unificat de Catalunya (PSUC), a regional communist party aligned with the PCE.

Before the Spanish Civil War even started, Caridad and Ramón returned to Spain to fight for leftist causes. When the shooting started, they joined the Republican Army. Caridad fought alongside male soldiers in the field and suffered severe injuries during an aerial attack near Aragon. After leaving the hospital, she was sent to Madrid to recuperate and visit her son.

There was a knock at her door. She opened it to find her son dressed in his uniform. "Ramón, you're so grown up!"

He hugged her. "I am, mama. I am twenty-three now. I'm in charge of my own squad of soldiers."

"How have you been? Not doing anything too crazy, I hope?"

"No. We've been in a few skirmishes, but nothing serious. How are you? How goes your recovery?"

She smiled. "Oh, I'm fine. Back to my normal self. Ready to go back to work. In fact, that's what I wanted to talk to you about."

Ramón paused. Work for his mother didn't mean cooking meals or wrapping bandages; it meant fighting. "Are you fit enough for . . . work?"

Caridad laughed, "I'm not going back to the front, if that's what you mean. I have other work. I'm being sent to Mexico on behalf of the party."

He was relieved she wasn't going back into the line but also suspicious. "The party? Why would the PSUC send you to Mexico?"

"No, not the PSUC or even the PCE. *The* party. The Soviets. They've asked me to go to Mexico on a propaganda mission, and I accepted."

"The Soviets! Wow. You're moving up in the world."

"Ramón, I've been in contact with the Soviets since Paris. I just couldn't tell you."

Ramón shrugged. "I understand. The work of the party requires discretion."

"Indeed, it does. I don't know how long I'll be gone, so there's someone I want you to meet. If you need to contact me, he'll get a message to me and from me to you."

"Okay, who is this Mexican postman?"

A voice from behind him said, "Not Mexican, Russian." Ramón spun around to find a stocky man with black hair and a small black mustache. "Hello, my name is Lev Leonidovich Nikolaev, but call me Lev. I'm with the Soviet Embassy. I've only just arrived in Spain. I was sent to establish patriotic guerrilla groups to fight behind enemy lines. It was my idea to use your mother for the propaganda mission. I met her in Paris, and she's very capable. She's also very stubborn and would return to the front before she fully recovers if given the chance. This solves both our problems."

Ramón bowed slightly. "Thank you, sir. I appreciate you tending to my mother. Left to her own devices, she'd be driving a tank tomorrow."

Lev laughed, "Yes, you're probably right. Don't worry, this mission will be nothing like that. She should be back within a few months. In the meantime, if there's anything you need, please don't hesitate to contact me. Consider me a friend."

Taking Lev's calling card, Ramón put it in his pocket. "And me as well."

"I understand you were in jail recently."

"Yes, I was arrested for my 'anti-reactionary activities'—something

I'm quite proud of. I was released when the Popular Front came to power and joined the army when the war started."

"I admire your revolutionary zeal. There are a lot of groups within the Republican coalition. Not all are created equal."

Ramón glanced at his mother, who just nodded. "I think I understand what you're saying. The anarchists, separatists, and even the Popular Front cannot be trusted to guide Spain into the future; only the communists can."

"And not even all of those. There are some who call themselves communists who don't have the best interests of the people or the party in their hearts."

"I assume you're referring to the Trotskyists. Well, I assure you, I am not one of them."

Lev smirked, "How do you know I'm not a Trotskyist?"

"Because my mother hasn't killed you."

Lev roared with laughter. "That's a very good point." With his jacket on his arm, he walked toward the door. "Well, I'll let you say goodbye to your mother. I'm sure we'll see each other around."

Ramón didn't know it, but "Lev" was not his real name. It was one of the many aliases used by Colonel Alexander Mikhailovich Orlov from Naródnyy Komissariát Vnútrennikh Del, the People's Commissariat for Internal Affairs, the Soviet secret police known simply by its initials— NKVD. Orlov, code name SCHWED, was the NKVD rezident in Madrid and the NKVD liaison to the Spanish Ministry of Interior. He was telling the truth about the guerrilla operations, but he had another, more important mission.

Joseph Stalin, NKVD chief Nicholai Yezhov, and Yezhov's deputy Lavrentiy Beria, didn't trust the Soviets already in Spain. They suspected that Vladimir Antonov-Ovseyenko, the consul general in Barcelona, and Mikhail Koltsov, an NKVD officer undercover as a journalist, harbored hidden Trotskyist sympathies. Antonov-Ovseyenko had been expelled from the Communist Party for being a Trotsky supporter but later reinstated. Needless to say, Stalin didn't trust him. In actuality, the NKVD was more interested in rooting out and murdering Stalin's enemies than defeating Franco's Nationalists. Orlov's primary objective was to eliminate anti-Stalinists among International Brigade commanders, the Republican government, and the Soviets working in Spain. Of those in the Republican government, the Trotskyist POUM officials were at the top of his list.

* * *

By 1936 Leon Trotsky was in Norway—his fourth exile location. Trotsky was one of the original Bolsheviks and Vladimir Lenin's right-hand man. He negotiated Russia's exit from World War I, turned the volunteer Red Army into a first-class fighting force, and defeated the last vestiges of the White Army to win the Russian Civil War. That earned him Lenin's admiration but others' jealousy—particularly Joseph Stalin. Trotsky may have been a better organizer and general, but Stalin was the better politician.

Leon Trotsky (early 1920s)

After Lenin died in January 1924, Trotsky was repeatedly outmaneuvered by Stalin until he was completely marginalized. In October 1927 he was expelled from the Central Committee and a month later from the Communist Party itself. He was too high profile and too popular to simply kill, so in January 1928 Trotsky was sentenced to internal exile in Alma Ata, Kazakhstan. A year later, he was expelled from the Soviet Union altogether.

Joseph Stalin (1937)

In 1929 Leon Trotsky, his wife Natalia Sedova, and their son Lev Sedov were sent into exile in Turkey, while their other son Sergei decided to stay in Russia. While in Turkey, they were joined by his daughter Zinaida and her son, Seva. After Turkey, it was France. Then Norway. Along the way, Lev went to Germany for university and Zinaida committed suicide, leaving Leon and Natalia to raise Seva. By the summer of 1936 Leon and Natalia were living in the house of Konrad Gustav Knudsen, a Norwegian painter and parliamentarian.

Leon sat outside the Knudsen home in Norderhov, gazing out over the rolling pastures and fields, when his wife approached. "What are you thinking about, Leon?"

"I was admiring the countryside. It reminds me of Ukraine when I was a boy."

Natalia chuckled. "Except there are no mountains in Ukraine."

"This is true. I was just thinking about our lives, how we got here. Do you ever regret it?"

"No. I mean, it's been hard, certainly, but I don't regret standing up for what we believe."

Trotsky sighed. "I regret how it has been for the boys. Lev is safe in Paris, but I worry about Sergei."

Natalia tried to assure him. "Sergei is using my family name, not yours."

"Scant protection. The boy is apolitical, but that won't matter to Stalin."

"Like you said, he's apolitical. Hurting him serves no purpose." Peering out over the countryside, she added, "I like Norway more than France. It's more like home."

A few moments later, Konrad Knudsen exited the house. "Ah, there you are. I have news."

Trotsky peered up at him and replied, "Judging from your face, I'd gather it isn't good."

"It's the French."

"The French? What do they want? Do I owe them rent? They already expelled me after signing that ridiculous Franco-Soviet Treaty of Mutual Assistance. If they think that's worth anything, they're fools. Stalin's only interest is Stalin."

"They're complaining through the press that your newspaper articles encouraged the recent French labor strikes."

Trotsky scoffed, "Bah, nonsense. The French workers were plenty frustrated before I wrote a word."

Knudsen replied, "Be that as it may, Prime Minister Nygaardsvold is not as predisposed to your presence here as Justice Minister Lie was. He isn't happy with what he sees as your meddling in the affairs of a country to which you hold no allegiance."

"My allegiance is to the workers, not the government."

"Well, you need to tone it down, for your own sake. Vidkun Quisling, the head of the fascist Nasjonal Samling Party, is grumbling. He and your old Soviet comrades are putting pressure on Nygaardsvold to do something about you. The prime minister is getting pressure from both sides."

Trotsky stubbornly stood his ground. "I refuse to temper my political views or my comments in deference to fascists and tyrants."

"Leon, old friend, I'm not your enemy. I'm just trying to warn you."

On August 5, 1936, Leon and Natalia joined the Knudsens for a trip to the seashore. While they were gone, a group of fascists from Nasjonal Samling broke into the Knudsen home. They were searching for Trotsky's current writings as well as his extensive personal archive. The thieves were interrupted by the Knudsens' daughter and only managed to escape with a few papers they scooped from a table on their way out. The burglars were caught, and the materials they took were used as evidence against them. Given the politics involved, the recovered materials were also used as evidence against Trotsky.

Nine days after the burglary, TASS, the Soviet news agency, announced that a "Trotskyist-Zinovievist" plot had been uncovered. Trotsky was put on trial in absentia along with sixteen of his old comrades, including original Bolshevik revolutionaries Grigory Zinoviev and Lev Kamenev. All were convicted and sentenced to death, including Trotsky in absentia. The sixteen were executed on August 25, 1936. The next day, policemen arrived at the Knudsen home demanding that Trotsky sign a document detailing new conditions for his exile in Norway—no writing, no interviews, and no correspondence without police inspection. When Trotsky refused, he was told they'd be moving to another house.

On September 2, Norwegian Minister of Justice Trygve Lie, the man who first granted Trotsky asylum, ordered Leon, Natalia, and Seva be moved to a farm in rural Hurum where they'd be under house arrest. In December 1936, the Trotskys were officially deported from Norway. They were placed aboard the *Ruth*, a Norwegian oil tanker bound for Mexico, with a Norwegian police officer in tow to make sure they reached their destination.

They arrived in Tampico, Mexico on January 9, 1937, twenty-one days after leaving Norway. Their reception was markedly different. They were met at the dock by famous Mexican artist Frida Kahlo. The president of Mexico, Lázaro Cárdenas, welcomed the Trotskys to the country and ferried them to Mexico City aboard his presidential train, *The Hidalgo*. For the Trotskys, 1937 was already a huge improvement over 1936.

* * *

In early 1937 Ramón Mercader met a Soviet journalist, Mikhail Koltsov, in Madrid. Koltsov was a short, stocky man with a rather large head and expressive face. He enjoyed danger, which was evident in both his work as a war correspondent and his notoriously indiscreet love affairs. While the encounter appeared random to Mercader, it was not. Koltsov was also an NKVD agent.

"So tell me, Ramón, why did you come back to Spain?"

"To fight the fascists, of course. To save the country. To ensure the establishment of communism for the people of Spain."

"Well, certainly. But you were living in Paris not too long ago. Imagine what your life would be like if you'd just stayed? Sipping coffee every morning along the Seine. Drinking wine with a pretty girl in the shadow of the Eiffel Tower in the evening. A damn sight better than sharing a muddy foxhole with three smelly men while fascists lob artillery shells at you."

Ramón grinned. "Well, when you put it that way . . . Why are *you* here, Mikhail? You could be back in Russia sipping vodka along the Moscow River with a pretty female comrade."

Koltsov laughed. "Touché. I'm here because I'm a journalist, a war correspondent. To do my job, I have to be in the war."

Ramón shrugged. "And I'm a soldier. The same applies for me."

"So, tell me. How's it going at the front?"

"As well as expected, I suppose. The fascists are better funded and better equipped. I appreciate what the Soviet Union and our other allies have provided, but for every bullet or airplane you supply, the Germans supply two to Franco and the Nationalists."

"It might seem that way, but I assure you, Stalin is doing all he can," he lied. "Speaking of Comrade Stalin, his efforts to help the Spanish people are complicated by the presence of his enemies. There are many in Spain who profess to be communists but who actually are working against Comrade Stalin and, by extension, the Spanish Republic."

Ramón smiled. He knew where this was going. "I assume you're referring to POUM and the other Trotskyists."

Koltsov asked cautiously, "What are your opinions of POUM and the other counterrevolutionary members of Anzaña's government?"

"I'm no politician, but as long as they help us kill Franco's soldiers, I'm okay with them."

"Sure, but what about after the war?"

Ramón shrugged. "I guess we'll cross that bridge when we come to it."

"We may have to cross that bridge now. We've learned that some within the POUM, including many of its leaders, are actively collaborating with Franco. They're selling out the republic in the hope of taking power when the war is over. What the fools don't understand is, they are not just undermining Anzaña and true patriots like the PCE, they're helping the fascists win. Why do you think the war is going so poorly? It's not because of the cowardly soldiers or lack of material support, it's because of traitors. How else could we have lost Oviedo, Bilboa, and Málaga?"

"If that's true, we need to stop the Trotskyists before they do any more damage."

"I agree. Can we count on your support? To fight hard and keep your men on the true path?"

"Yes, Comrade Koltsov, you certainly can. If there is anything I can do for the party, you have only to ask."

"That's good to hear, Ramón. Your mother was right about you. You're a true patriot."

Two weeks later, Ramón was on the front lines north of Guadalajara when he got an order to meet with the colonel in charge of his sector. He was told his presence was required in Madrid. The next day he reported to his division headquarters and was shown into a room to wait. The room was furnished only with a table and a couple of chairs like an interview room—or an interrogation room. He was still wearing his dirty uniform and embarrassed to receive a senior officer in such a manner. When the door opened, it wasn't a Spanish officer who entered but a civilian. The man had pale skin, dark hair, and large oval face. He was distinctly Russian.

"Sergeant Mercader?"

Snapping to attention, Ramón replied, "Yes, sir." Whoever this man was, he had enough clout to have him pulled off the front lines.

Motioning to the table, the man said, "Please, relax. Have a seat. We're all friends here." The man spoke fluent Spanish with not a trace of an accent. Ramón sat nervously. "My name is Leonid. You've been recommended by a number of people as a man whose dedication to the party is unassailable."

"Thank you, sir." Ramón sat rigidly. Sweat was beginning to form on his brow.

Ramon was obviously nervous, so the Russian changed tacks. "You know, today is a beautiful day. It would be a shame to waste it indoors. Let's go out for a coffee—my treat." Leonid opened the door and motioned for Ramón to exit first. Once in the hallway, they walked downstairs at the rear of the building and out onto the street.

It was a warm spring day, and the bustle of the city was energizing. Ramón finally screwed up the courage to ask, "Sir, what is this about? I have my troops to attend to."

Leonid smiled, "They'll be fine . . . but I admire your dedication. Your name has been mentioned by people."

"People?"

"People here in Madrid, in Barcelona, and even in Moscow."

"Moscow?"

"Yes. Your mother has been a trusted . . . colleague . . . for many years."

Ramón instantly understood what was going on. Speaking softly, he said, "So, you are NKVD?"

"You're very astute. Your mother said you were. Yes, I am. We need your help."

"What can I do?" Ramón asked.

"We need someone, a Spaniard, to help us identify the Trotskyists who are undermining the Republican government. We need someone to befriend them, infiltrate their ranks, and identify them to us and the Spanish Ministry of Interior."

"Sir. Leonid. I am not at liberty to simply abandon my soldiers."

Leonid laughed, "My boy, let me take care of that."

The seriousness of what Leonid was asking started to dawn on Ramón. "Sir, as much as I want to help, I have no experience at this sort of thing."

"Don't worry, we'll train you. It's all arranged. Go back to your unit to collect your things. By the time you get there, your discharge papers will be waiting for you. Do you have a passport?"

"Yes, but it's a French passport—from my time in Paris."

Leonid beamed. "Perfect." Leonid and Ramón found a quiet café where they ordered espressos. They talked for almost two hours about life in general, not about the mission. Ramón believed they were just getting acquainted, but Leonid was continuing to assess the young man, and he liked what he saw. So far, the assessments of Orlov and Koltsov had been spot on.

While Ramón returned to his unit, Leonid went to the Soviet Embassy. Leonid was actually Nahum Isaakovich Eitingon. In Spain he used the Russified version of his name, Leonid Aleksandrovich Eitingon. He was an experienced and successful Russian intelligence officer. He had joined the first Soviet intelligence body, the Cheka, in 1920. Before coming to Spain, he ran deception operations against the Japanese, was deputy of the Department of Special Tasks, which

NKVD agent Nahum Eitingon

conducted sabotage and assassination operations, and was in charge of coordinating operations involving NKVD "illegals"—Soviet deep-cover spies. Now his job was to root out Trotskyists in Spain, and he needed Mercader's help.

As promised, Mercader's discharge was approved before he got back to the line. Eitingon immediately set about educating his young agent in the ways of espionage. Much of this took place in Spain, but he was also sent back to the Soviet Union for the more sensitive training.

Mercader wasn't the only one recruited. David Crook was a British communist and war correspondent for the *News Chronicle*. He was recruited by the NKVD to spy on the Trotskyists, specifically fellow British writer and journalist George Orwell. Upon arrival in Spain, Orwell joined POUM and therefore was a "proven" Trotskyist. Mercader was called on to train Crook on the surveillance techniques he'd use against Orwell. In June 1937 the Republican government finally yielded to Soviet and PCE pressure and declared POUM illegal. The POUM leaders were arrested, tortured, and executed.

In 1938, with the Trotskyists in Spain successfully neutralized, Eitingon was given a new task by Stalin himself—organize and implement a scheme to assassinate Leon Trotsky. Mercader was given a new task too—identify and infiltrate Trotskyists in Paris. Mercader moved back to Paris and enrolled at the Sorbonne. He was assigned a new NKVD handler, a mild-mannered Russian anthropologist named Mark Zborowski. Although he came across like a mousy bookworm, he was actually quite ruthless and was involved in the murders of several people deemed to be enemies of Stalin.

When Mercader arrived in Paris, Zborowski was finishing up his most recent operation targeting Leon Trotsky's son, Lev Sedov. Using the alias Etienne, he befriended Lev's wife, who recommended him for a position as her husband's secretary, and he quickly became an indispensable assistant. In February 1938 Sedov

NKVD agent Mark Zborowski (circa 1933)

suffered an appendicitis attack. Zborowski convinced Sedov to have his operation at a private clinic, information he immediately passed on to the NKVD. The operation was successful, but while recovering, Sedov became violently ill and died in great pain. While nothing was proved, all signs pointed to murder.

When he arrived in Paris, the dashing Mercader was directed to befriend Sylvia Ageloff, an unattractive Jewish American girl from Brooklyn and a confidante of Trotsky. Zborowski, having been part of the Trotskyist clique in Paris, provided Mercader with valuable insights on her. Before approaching her, he was given a whole new persona. He assumed the identity of Jacques Mornard and claimed to be the son of a Belgian diplomat.

* * *

Life in Mexico for the Trotskys was mostly pleasant. Famed artist Frida Kahlo and her husband, Mexican muralist Diego Rivera, were members of the Mexican Communist Party and lobbied the Mexican government to grant Trotsky asylum in late 1936. Kahlo and Rivera lived in Coyoacán, a town just outside Mexico City where they'd built a unique home with two sections joined by a bridge. Rivera's section was painted pink and white.

Kahlo's was painted blue and known locally as *La Casa Azul*, the Blue House. The Trotskys moved into the Blue House.

Frida Kahlo (1932)

While his living conditions were much improved, Trotsky's personal life was a continuous string of tragic events. Trotsky's two daughters from his first marriage were both dead. The younger daughter died of tuberculosis at the age of twenty-six. While visiting Trotsky in Turkey, his older daughter, Zinaida, and her son had their Soviet citizenship revoked. Not allowed to return home, they had no choice but to follow Trotsky into exile. She became depressed and committed suicide in 1933.

Leon and Natalia had two sons of their own and gave both of them her last name, Sedov, in an attempt to protect them from their father's enemies. It didn't work. Lev, the older brother, followed his father into exile, only to die under suspicious circumstances in Paris a month after Trotsky arrived in Mexico. Their younger son, Sergei, remained behind in the Soviet Union. He was working as an engineer when he was arrested. Refusing to denounce his father, he was sent to Siberia, where he died sometime in 1937.

Politically, things were also strained for Trotsky. Stalin's Purge had started in 1936 and was continuing unabated. There was another show trial in Moscow in January 1937 for twenty-one more of Trotsky's former supporters. As with the 1936 show trial, all were convicted. Thirteen were executed and the remaining eight were sent to labor camps, where they were later murdered. There wasn't much future in being a Trotskyist in the Soviet Union.

To counter Stalin's message, a Commission of Inquiry was set up in March 1937 to investigate the charges made against Trotsky and his now-dead comrades. The commission was led by American philosopher and psychologist John Dewey. The commission found the Soviet claims to be baseless and published its findings in a book titled *Not Guilty*.

Needing to seize the initiative, in 1938 Trotsky and his followers founded the Fourth International in Paris, a revolutionary socialist international organization whose stated goal was the overthrow of capitalism and the establishment of global socialism through revolution. It was to be an alternative to the Third International, also known as Comintern, which they described a puppet of Stalinism. This challenge did nothing to dull Stalin's anger, and he dispatched the NKVD to hector, harass, and discredit the organization and its members. Stalin at this point openly admitted allowing Trotsky to go into exile had been a mistake. It was a mistake he needed to correct. He needed Trotsky dead.

* * *

In Paris, Ramón Mercader, now going by the name Jacques Mornard, successfully met Sylvia Ageloff. They become friends and then lovers. With Zborowski to guide him, Mercader continued to groom Ageloff while playing the role of a Trotsky sympathizer. Slowly over time, he allowed Ageloff and her friends to "convince" him and he outwardly became a more ardent and dedicated devotee of Trotsky's brand of communism. Their patience paid off. In 1939 Mercader was contacted by a representative of the Bureau of the Fourth International.

* * *

In March 1939 there was a failed attempt to kill Trotsky. Details of the plot are not clear, and it is uncertain if Trotsky was even aware of it, but the impact in Moscow was immediate. Stalin now assigned the task of killing Trotsky to Pavel Sudoplatov of the NKVD, and failure was not an option. Stalin said, "If Trotsky is finished, the threat will be eliminated. Trotsky should be eliminated within a year."

NKVD agent Pavel Sudoplatov

Sudoplatov was coming off the successful assassination of a Ukrainian nationalist in Rotterdam. While the assassination was a success, the aftermath was a disaster. Sudoplatov gave the man a box of chocolates containing a bomb. When the bomb exploded, Sudoplatov walked to the railway station and jumped on a train for Paris. Unfortunately, his sudden disappearance was noticed by both the Dutch police and the Organization of Ukrainian Nationalists (OUN).

A photograph of Sudoplatov together with the dead man was distributed to every OUN unit with orders to kill him. Any spy with his name, affiliation, and photo splashed all over the world with orders to "shoot on sight" is not particularly effective. His career in the field effectively over, he returned to Moscow to be acting director of the Foreign Department of the NKVD. His predecessor had recently been purged by NKVD chief Nikolai Yezhov, and Sudoplatov almost joined him when fate stepped in and Yezhov himself was purged. Stalin "rehabilitated" Sudoplatov and put him in charge of killing Trotsky. He was under no illusions, however. If he didn't kill Trotsky, Stalin would probably kill him.

To increase his chances of success, Sudoplatov set up three independent NKVD networks tasked with assassinating Trotsky. Each would be isolated from the other two, as well as any NKVD networks being run out of Mexico or the United States. For one of the efforts, he turned to his trusted friend and fellow intelligence officer, Nahum Eitingon. Despite being responsible for the most recent failed attempt, Eitingon had a long track record of successes, including a string of kidnappings and assassinations in Spain and other Western countries. He was the perfect man for the job. Eitingon knew his former agent, Ramón Mercader, was already infiltrating Trotskyist groups in France, so he commandeered him for his assassination plot. It wasn't like he had anywhere to go. The Spanish Civil War ended in April 1939 with a Nationalist victory. If he returned home to Barcelona, he faced a Nationalist firing squad.

* * *

About the time General Francisco Franco was declaring victory in Spain for his Nationalist armies, Trotsky had a falling out with Frida Kahlo and Diego Rivera. During his stay at Kahlo's home, Trotsky and Kahlo engaged in a brief affair. This was not unusual for her—or her husband for that matter. Both were notorious for their sexual dalliances with multiple partners, and Rivera even had an affair with Kahlo's sister. Whatever the reason, the relationship between the Trotskys and their hosts had become strained. Trotsky, along with his wife and grandson, moved into a residence of their own on Avenida Viena in Coyoacán, a few blocks from Kahlo's Blue House.

* * *

On September 1 Nazi Germany invaded Poland, signaling the outbreak of World War II. On September 3 Britain and France declared war on Germany, followed soon after by Canada, Australia, New Zealand, and South Africa. Who didn't declare war on Germany was the Soviet Union. Nine days before the invasion, Germany and the Soviets signed the Molotov-Ribbentrop Pact, a nonaggression agreement that also secretly divided Poland between them. Communists the world over interpreted it as a total betrayal of communist principles. With this as the backdrop, Sylvia Ageloff returned home to Brooklyn. She had been in France for some time and missed her parents. With the outbreak of war, her parents were eager for her to be safely on the American side of the Atlantic.

For Mercader, America was a lot closer to his target than France, so he maneuvered to join her. This was not going to be easy. His Jacques Mornard false identity didn't come with a valid passport, and there wasn't enough time for the Russians to forge one. It was time to get creative. Mercader assumed the identity Frank Jacson, a French Canadian. He told Ageloff that he'd purchased forged documents to avoid military service, and she believed him. With this cover story in place, he could explain any number of discrepancies. Using the Jacson persona might get him into the United States, but he still needed a passport to get off the boat.

The NKVD came up with a solution. They had a passport belonging to a Canadian named Tony Babich. He had joined the Spanish Republican Army and was killed in action during the Spanish Civil War. They simply replaced Babich's name and photo with the name Frank Jacson and Mercader's photo. He was good to go.

A month after arriving in America, Mercader told Ageloff he wanted to move to Mexico City. He still needed entrée to the Trotskyists, so he asked Ageloff to come with him. She was in love with the dashing young man and readily agreed. They arrived in Mexico City in October 1939. Since Ageloff was known to the Trotskyists, Mercader, as Frank Jacson, gained access to Trotsky's home. He posed as a sympathizer and began to meet with Trotsky on occasion; Trotsky was justifiably paranoid and had bodyguards present at all times. Mercader made an effort to befriend Trotsky's guards and was called on to run errands for the household. He was slowly becoming accepted as part of the entourage, just as Nahum Eitingon had instructed.

* * *

Eitingon was but one of three NKVD operatives assigned to the mission to kill Trotsky. One of the others was Iosif Grigulevich. He and Eitingon were both in Spain at the same time working for NKVD General Alexander Orlov. Grigulevich organized hit squads that killed known or suspected Trotskyists, including POUM leader Andrés Nin. He too had a man on the inside, but his plan was much more direct than Eitingon's. He was just going to burst in and shoot up the place.

Grigulevich's "inside man" was Robert Sheldon Harte, an American communist who was recruited by the NKVD in New York and code-named Amur. He served on Trotsky's security detail. Harte provided the attackers with the complete layout of the house and would let the assassins in when the time came. Grigulevich planned to lead the raid himself, along with Mexican communist painter David Alfaro Siqueiros and Italian communist Vittorio Vidal, two men who had fought with the Republicans in the Spanish Civil War. The raiding party also included some of Siqueiros's former comrades from Spain and miners from a local union he was affiliated with.

The attack came on May 24, 1940. At around 4:00 a.m., the police guards outside the house were overpowered and tied up. Harte let the assailants in and directed them toward Trotsky's room. Trotsky himself provided the details of what happened next in an article published two weeks later. Trotsky was asleep in his bed when he was awakened by the rattle of gun fire. He had taken a sleeping pill before retiring and was in a fog when first roused. He initially mistook the gunfire for fireworks, but the noise was too close. Bullets started crashing through his bedroom windows and shattering the room around him. Natalia pushed him from the bed into the space between the bed

David Alfaro Siqueiros. Photo by Hécytor Garcia

Trotsky house in Coyoacán. Photo by Rod Waddington

and wall, and piled on top of him. Having regained his senses, Trotsky motioned for her to lie flat on the floor. The shooting continued for several minutes, and although they were covered in broken glass and chips of brick, paint, and concrete blasted from the walls, neither Trotsky nor his wife were hit.

When the shooting subsided, Trotsky's grandson, Seva, called out to him from a neighboring room. The attackers shot at the boy, and he dove under his bed. One assailant fired a burst into the bed. A bullet passed through the mattress and struck Seva in the big toe before burrowing into the floor. The attackers threw two incendiary bombs in the boy's bedroom before leaving. Seva bolted for one of the guards' rooms, leaving a trail of blood behind him. Natalia made her way to Seva's room. When she found it empty, she assumed he had been kidnapped.

The gunfire abated and was more distant. The attack was over, but the assailants were firing randomly to cover their retreat. Natalia smothered the flames in Seva's bedroom with a rug. Shell casings found in Trotsky's bedroom confirmed that at least one shooter had entered the room but missed. Grigulevich and his men assumed they were successful, but despite the hundreds of rounds fired, no one inside the house was killed.

Trotsky's traitorous bodyguard, Robert Sheldon Harte, left with the attackers. He was later found in a shallow grave with a bullet in his head. Trotsky insisted he was kidnapped and murdered, but years later, Nahum Eitingon admitted Harte was killed after expressing second thoughts. "During the operation it was revealed that Sheldon was a traitor. Even though he opened the gate to the compound, once in the room, neither the archive nor Trotsky himself was found. When the participants in the raid opened fire, Sheldon told them that had he been aware of all this, as an American he never would have agreed to participate in this raid. Such behavior served as the basis for deciding on the spot to liquidate him. He was killed by Mexicans."

After the failed attempt, the assailants fled the scene. Siqueiros was accused of being one of the conspirators and arrested. Pablo Neruda, a Chilean communist poet who was serving as the Chilean consul general in Mexico City, issued Siqueiros a Chilean visa. This allowed Siqueiros to get out of jail and leave Mexico for Chile. Neruda also helped Grigulevich and two other attackers escape the Mexican police. When criticized for his role, Neruda dismissed it as "sensationalist politico-literary harassment."

After the failed attack, Trotsky knew the NKVD would redouble its efforts. Only his death would save them from Stalin's wrath. Trotsky's followers raised money to increase his security. Exterior windows on the house were bricked up. On the roof, fortified guard stations resembling pill boxes were added. What they didn't do was reinvestigate the staff in an effort to identify infiltrators. Trotsky was convinced that Robert Sheldon Harte was a martyr, not a conspirator. Two weeks after the attack, Trotsky wrote a long article titled "Stalin Seeks My Death," in which he detailed the attack and dispelled rumors—Soviet misinformation, actually—that Trotsky had staged the attack himself to smear Stalin.

* * *

There were no more attempts on Trotsky's life for the next couple of months. The Chicago-style gangland attack was sensational and drew a great deal of attention to Trotsky—not exactly what Stalin had in mind. Sudoplatov was on the hot seat and needed to kill Trotsky before Stalin killed him. There was already one out, and the next batter at the plate was Nahum Eitingon. Since physical security was much improved, another frontal assault was out of the question. Eitingon assessed that a lone assassin would be more effective.

With Sylvia Ageloff's unwitting assistance, "Frank Jacson" became a regular fixture at the Trotsky home. Ageloff was now one of Trotsky's secretaries. She was trusted, so Frank was trusted. He was Sylvia's charming businessman boyfriend who performed the occasional service. He had a car and would take Sylvia and Natalia shopping. Alfred Rosmer was an American-born French communist and longtime friend of Trotsky. He and his wife, Maguerrite, spent several months in Mexico in 1939. When it was time for them to depart, it was Frank Jacson who drove them to their ship. Mercader had successfully infiltrated Trotsky's inner circle. Nahum Eitingon knew it now fell to Mercader to complete the mission.

On August 17, 1940, Mercader brought Trotsky an article on American Trotskyism for him to read. Three days later, he returned unannounced. Trotsky asked, "Frank, what are you doing here?"

"Comrade Trotsky. I brought another copy of that article on American Trotskyism I showed you the other day. This one is typed out and much easier to read. I'd like to get your opinion on it."

Trotsky took the paper and glanced at it. "Of course, Frank. Come with me to my study." Trotsky walked into the next room while Mercader, a raincoat draped over his arm, followed. Trotsky's back was to Mercader;

it was time to strike. He laid his raincoat on a table and removed an ice axe concealed in it. The ice axe was a mountain climbing tool with a short wooden handle. The head of the axe had an arched blade at one end and a sharp pick on the other. Gripping it with one hand, he raised the axe high in the air, closed his eyes and brought it down hard onto the old Bolshevik's head. The pointed pick struck Trotsky's skull, punching through his parietal bone and penetrating almost three inches into his brain. Trotsky let out long, mournful cry. Despite his injury, he fought back. He spat in Mercader's face and began struggling with him, biting his hand. The sixty-year-old Trotsky put up such a fight he broke Mercader's hand, and the commotion drew Trotsky's bodyguards. Bursting into the room they latched onto Mercader and started to beat him savagely. Only Trotsky's intervention saved him.

"No . . . don't . . . kill . . . him." Trotsky labored to speak. "We . . . need . . . answers." The men did as he said and restrained the bruised and bleeding assassin.

Ice axe used to kill Trotsky.
Photo by Jack Donaghy

* * *

Outside the Trotsky house, two cars waited. One was driven by Nahum Eitingon, the other by Caridad Mercader, the assassin's mother. They were there to ensure his escape. When Ramón didn't emerge from the house, they knew something had gone wrong. They fled the scene and left the country, leaving Mercader to the mercies of the Mexican authorities.

* * *

Trotsky was immediately taken to the hospital, where he was operated on. He lived for more than a day, but his injury was too great. His brain swelled, and he slipped into a coma. He died on August 21, 1940, of blood loss and shock. His last words were, "I will not survive this attack. Stalin has finally accomplished the task he attempted unsuccessfully before."

Stalin's most feared rival, Leon Trotsky, one of the original Bolsheviks, father of the Red Army, the proponent of Permanent Revolution, was finally dead.

* * *

Mercader was arrested but refused to provide his true identity. He identified himself as Jacques Mornard, the name he used when he first met Sylvia in Paris. When asked why he had killed Trotsky, Mercader claimed that he wanted to marry Ageloff and that Trotsky had forbidden it. A subsequent argument led him to want to kill Trotsky. Under the name Jacques Mornard, Mercader was convicted of murder and sentenced to twenty years in prison. His true name was not confirmed until decades later, through a U.S. counterespionage project.

Ageloff was arrested as an accomplice, but charges against her were eventually dropped. Even Frida Kahlo was brought in for questioning. As for Eitingon, he got away clean. He went on to help his old friend, Pavel Sudoplatov, run a network of Soviet spies inside the United States targeting American atomic secrets. Caridad Mercader escaped to the Soviet Union, where she and Ramón were awarded the Order of Lenin, Ramón's in absentia. Four years later, she obtained a permit to leave the USSR, but in violation of the terms of the agreement, she went to Mexico in an effort to get her son out of prison. Unbeknown to her, the NKVD was in the middle of an operation to free Ramón from prison. Caridad's presence in the country alerted Mexican authorities, who increased security around Ramón causing the NKVD to abandon the plan.

Ramón never forgave his mother for her meddling. As a result, he served almost the entire twenty years. He was released in 1960 and moved to Cuba, where the newly installed Fidel Castro welcomed him. In 1961 he moved to the Soviet Union, where he was personally awarded the country's highest honor, the Order of Lenin and Hero of the Soviet Union, by

Alexander Shelepin, the head of the NKVD successor organization, the KGB. Mercader died of lung cancer in 1978. His last words were, "I hear it always. I hear the scream. I know he's waiting for me on the other side."

The Aftermath

Stalin finally eliminated his greatest rival, but he soon found himself facing an even greater threat—Nazi Germany. Ten months after Trotsky's death, Germany and its allies invaded the Soviet Union, initiating four years of fighting and destruction on a scale never seen before or since. Instead of the existential threat posed by Trotsky and his adherents, Stalin faced the specter of total national obliteration.

The assassination of Trotsky did not put an end to Trotskyism. His Fourth International continued on, but the war did more damage to it than Stalin. Many of its European leaders were wiped out during the war by the Nazis, who viewed all communists as enemies. Trotskyism survived the war, but afterward became marginalized by the emergence of an even more powerful Soviet Union, replete with a host of new client states in Eastern Europe. Trotsky was the proponent of "permanent revolution." He believed the only way a workers' state would survive was if the revolution spread to neighboring states. Before the war, Stalin favored "socialism in one country," as in the Soviet Union. In a bit of irony, Adolf Hitler did more to push the Soviet Union toward Trotsky's "permanent revolution" than Trotsky ever did.

It did not end well for many of the people involved in the various plots to kill Trotsky and his followers. Mercader spent twenty years in prison. Vladimir Antonov-Ovseyenko, the Soviet consul general in Barcelona, was arrested in 1937 and shot in 1938. Mikhail Koltsov, the journalist and NKVD agent, returned to Moscow, where he foolishly started an affair with the wife of NKVD head Nikolai Yezhov. After Yezhov was removed, Koltsov was arrested and executed along with 346 "enemies of the people." Colonel Alexander Mikhailovich Orlov, the NKVD rezident in Madrid, fearing he was about to be purged, defected to the United States, where he lived until his death in 1973. In a bit of irony, he had sent

Trotsky an unsigned letter warning him that an NKVD agent named Mark and fitting Zborowski's description had infiltrated their Paris organization. One of Trotsky's confidants convinced him it was an NKVD provocation.

Lt. General Pavel Sudoplatov, the man Stalin personally put in charge of killing Trotsky, had a successful career—up until the point his boss, Lavrentiy Beria, was deposed. Sudoplatov was arrested and charged as one of Beria's collaborators. He feigned insanity to avoid being executed alongside Beria in 1953. However, he was arrested and tried in 1958 and sentenced to fifteen years in prison. He served the full term and was released in 1968. He wrote his autobiography, *Special Tasks*, in 1994 before passing away two years later at the age of 89.

Nahum Eitingon, the mastermind of the successful plot, returned to Moscow and became a major general in the State Security apparatus but in 1951 was implicated along with his sister in the Doctors' Plot, an alleged Zionist attempt to seize power in the Soviet Union. After two years in prison with no trial or charge, he was released by KGB Director Beria after Stalin's death in 1953. When Beria was arrested and executed only three months later, Eitingon was rearrested, this time for being one of Beria's supporters. He spent another four years in jail before finally being tried and convicted of "conspiracy against the regime." He was sentenced to twelve years in prison and stripped of all his ranks and awards. After Nikita Khrushchev was ousted in 1964, Eitingon was released from prison and spent the rest of his career working as a translator. He died in 1981 at the age of 81.

Chapter 8

The Czechoslovak Resistance and Reinhard Heydrich

—Some Guys Just Need to Be Killed

It was a cold, damp night on December 27, 1941. That was bad enough, but the propeller blast from the four 1,600 horsepower Bristol Hercules XVI engines made the men's leather and sheepskin flight suits feel like summer linen shirts. Already bowed by their tightly cinched parachute harnesses, they plodded toward the Handley Page Halifax Mk. II bomber that would serve as their chariot for the evening. These men were not part of the flight crew; they were the payload. The Halifax wouldn't be dropping bombs on Hamburg or Berlin; it would be dropping commandos into Czechoslovakia—or what used to be Czechoslovakia before the Nazis effectively annexed it into the Reich.

Halifax bomber

The ground crew loaded their supply canisters into the airplane before helping the commandos up the narrow aluminum ladder. A makeshift passenger compartment fitted into the massive bomb bay would be their home for the next four hours. The men scrambled in, happy to be out

224

of the wind. It was going to be a long, cold, noisy night; eventually the noise would give way to absolute quiet as they drifted down silently to the Czech countryside. First, they had to get past Germany alive.

Their route took them east over the North Sea before crossing the coastline between Bremen and Hamburg, keeping them far from Germany's industrial Ruhr Valley, which was a maze of searchlights and anti-aircraft artillery. If the airplane developed mechanical trouble over the North Sea, it meant a plunge into its frigid waters. Their biggest concern was running into German night fighters; maybe a Dornier Do 217 from Nachtjagdgeschwader 1 scrambling out of Venlo, the Netherlands, or a Messerschmitt Bf 110 from Nachtjagdgeschwader 5 flying out of Döberitz. A lone airplane, even if spotted on German radar, would be assumed to be a reconnaissance flight, hardly worth pursuing. The night fighters were more interested in large formations of British bombers headed for Germany's industrial heartland, although the anti-aircraft guns might take a few pot shots if it was a slow night.

The Halifax was from the No. 138 Squadron of the Royal Air Force (RAF) stationed in Tangmere in southern England. The beast lumbered down the runway and lifted gracefully into the air. The nine men were a lot lighter than the six metric tons of bombs the plane normally carried, but the extra fuel required to make the nearly 3,200-kilometer roundtrip made up for some of that. The nine men inside were not British commandos—they were Czechoslovak. The men were selected from the Czechoslovak army-in-exile and trained by British commandos from the storied Special Operations Element—the SOE—to conduct missions deep in Nazi-controlled territory.

There were three different units on this flight. Operation Silver A consisted of three men—Alfréd Bartoš, Josef Valčík, and Jiří Potuček—who were to establish liaison with Czechoslovak resistance units near Kolin, a city some forty miles east of Prague. The four men of Silver B were to perform a similar mission further south. The final pair of men was Jozef Gabčík and Jan Kubiš of Operation Anthropoid. They were to be dropped near Pilsen, sixty miles southwest of the capital. Their mission was to kill Reinhard Tristan Eugen Heydrich, the deputy protector of Bohemia and Moravia and the director of the Reich Main Security Office, the parent organization of the dreaded Gestapo.

Warrant Officer Josef Gabčik

The men sat in silence. It was nearly impossible to talk over the noise of the engines anyway. Finally, a red light flashed above their heads. It was nearing time to jump. Jozef Gabčík and Jan Kubiš were up first. One of the crewmen on the airplane motioned them to stand up and double-checked each man's parachute to make sure everything was connected properly. He then signaled them to connect the static lines of their parachute to the metal cable that ran the length of the compartment. A parachute-equipped canister containing the men's guns, papers, clothing, and other supplies was also connected to the same cable. The crewman then pulled a lever, and the rearmost of the airplane's

Staff Sergeant Jan Kubiš

four bomb bay doors opened. There was a sudden rush of cold as the frigid night air invaded their space. The crewman was focused on the flashing light. When it turned from red to green, he kicked their container and it disappeared through the bomb bay door. He yelled over the noise, "All right, gentlemen. Your turn. Good luck and God speed." Jozef Gabčík gave the man a quick salute, crossed his arms across his chest, and stepped through the hole in the floor. Right behind him, Jan Kubiš stepped up.

"Buy me a beer when I get back." The crewman gave him a thumbs up as Kubiš stepped into the abyss.

When Jan jumped, the slipstream of the massive bomber ripped him away instantly. The static line, still attached to the airplane, yanked tight and pulled the tightly packed parachute from its bag. The billowing silk caught the air after a moment and inflated, and his rapid downward descent stopped with a snap. He turned to where the Halifax had once been. There was only inky blackness, with the distant noise of the four massive engines droning on in the night. In a few seconds, all was quiet. They were truly alone.

He directed his attention downward. He spotted Jozef's dark parachute drifting below him. He strained to pick out the chute of their canister, but beyond Jozef was only inky blackness. He muttered to himself, "I hope Jozef has eyes on it."

Jan drifted on for several minutes. The bomber was flying at an altitude of over three thousand meters when they jumped, in the hope that those on the ground would not hear its engines or would at least assume it was either a German airplane or was on its way to a distant target. There was only a sliver of a moon; it gave him enough light to make out the ground rapidly rising up to greet him. He prepared for his landing. When his feet hit, he rolled onto his right shoulder and threw his feet over his left, allowing him to dissipate the energy of the fall harmlessly. He immediately popped to his feet and gathered in his parachute. As he did, he surveyed his surroundings. He was in an empty field—a pasture, probably. A dog was barking off in the distance. About a hundred meters away, Jozef was reeling in his parachute. Jozef gave Jan a thumbs up. Jan repeated the gesture; both men were uninjured.

Jozef ran over to the hedgerow that marked the border of the field. He found an old badger den and stuffed his parachute inside. He waved for Jan, who trotted over and crammed his parachute in on top of it. Both men then collected rocks and dirt to bury them. Jan asked in a whisper, "Did you see where the canister landed?"

Pointing to the west, Jozef replied, "Yes, I think it's in the next field, through those trees."

Both men started jogging west. When they reached the tree line, they found where a dirt path pierced the foliage. It was dark under the trees, so they walked cautiously until they encountered another open pasture. The canister was to their right, standing upright. Its parachute was caught on a pine tree. Jozef cut loose the harness straps to free the canister, while Jan tugged the parachute canopy from the tree. Within seconds it was free, and they dragged the canister into the narrow wood. Jozef opened it to inspect the contents. Inside were two small suitcases of clothes. The suitcases and their contents were all older and made in Czechoslovakia, requisitioned by the SOE from refugees. There was also a British Sten 9 mm submachine gun and a modified anti-tank grenade. Each man also had a Colt Model 1903 .380 ACP semiautomatic pistol and a box of ammunition. The men had forged identity papers, German work permits and transit passes, a few thousand Reichsmarks in cash, and "pocket litter"—an assortment of business cards, matchbooks from local pubs, and other items commonly found in a man's wallet. They stripped off their flight suits and shoved them and the parachute into the canister before burying it in the woods. They placed the submachine gun and grenade in their luggage, tucked the pistols into their coat pockets, and started walking.

After reaching a road, they stopped to rest. They took a last sip of water from their canteens before tossing them in the weeds. There was no explanation as to why a Czechoslovak workman would have a British military canteen. The plan was to go to Pilsen and meet up with their resistance contacts after they figured out where they were. They had no idea if they were north, south, east, or west of Pilsen, so they continued walking. The road was deserted—no people, no cars, no carts. It was a little after 3 a.m. Finally, they reached a crossroads. There was a sign that read, "Nehvizdy 2 KM."

Jozef said, "Nehvizdy? Where the hell is that? I didn't see that on the maps."

Jan was a Czech and more familiar with that part of the country. "Jesus Christ! They missed our drop zone."

"By how much?"

"About 120 kilometers. We're about fifty kilometers east of Prague."

"East! We're supposed to be west!"

"I know. We need to start moving west. We'll have to go through Prague. After morning breaks, we might catch a ride with a farmer. Once in Prague, we can probably take a train or an autobus. Either way, we'll not be meeting our colleagues right away."

The Halifax bomber that delivered them had experienced navigation problems. All three commando teams landed far from their intended drop zones. But such was war. No plan survives first contact with the enemy, or in this case, the ground.

* * *

Czechoslovakia was the first country to be ground up by the Nazi war machine, even before there was a war. In March 1938 German Chancellor Adolf Hitler engineered the German annexation of Austria without firing a shot. Then he set his sights on Czechoslovakia. The mountainous region along its border with Germany had defined the division between Czech lands and those of their Germanic neighbors since the early Middle Ages. But by 1938 this region, which Hitler now called the Sudetenland, was home to about three million people, most of whom spoke German. Hitler, still high on his success in Austria, wanted to incorporate these German-speaking peoples and their land into the Third Reich. On September 17, 1938, Germany started a low-intensity but undeclared war against Czechoslovakia. In an attempt to appease Hitler and prevent another war in Europe, Great Britain and France asked Czechoslovakia to cede the Sudetenland to Germany. The Czechoslovaks refused. The land in question contained significant border fortifications and was critical to the country's overall defense. Hitler's forces invaded dozens of border counties and while repulsed from most, managed to conquer two districts. Sensing an opportunity, Poland and Hungary also moved to take slices of Czechoslovakia for themselves. Poland attacked on September 23 but was repulsed. Hungary moved its forces to the border but didn't attack.

The European powers called an emergency meeting to discuss the crisis, without inviting Czechoslovakia. The meeting took place September 29–30 in Munich, Germany, and the result was Hitler getting everything he wanted. Czechoslovak President Edvard Beneš was facing military pressure from Czechoslovakia's neighbors and diplomatic pressure from its "friends" in London and Paris. Despite earlier promises, Britain and France said they would remain neutral in the event of a war between

Germany and Czechoslovakia. Beneš was in a corner. Prague agreed to cede the Sudetenland to Germany. The next day, it agreed to Poland's territorial demands as well. Beneš resigned under German pressure and was replaced by Emil Hácha, a Nazi puppet.

A diminished Czechoslovakia creaked along until March 1939, when the First Slovak Republic, a Nazi client state, announced its independence. Czechoslovakia was cleaved in half.

Czechoslovak President Edvard Beneš

The next day, Germany moved to occupy the Czech half. Hitler claimed the country was breaking itself apart and he was only trying to restore order. Hitler declared it the Protectorate of Bohemia and Moravia and placed it under German control. Czechoslovakia was no more.

It wasn't just the land and the people Hitler wanted; it was the Czechoslovak arms. When the Germans took over, they gained over two thousand field artillery pieces, 469 tanks, five hundred anti-aircraft artillery with three million rounds of ammunition, some forty-three thousand machine guns, one million rifles, 114,000 pistols, and a billion rounds of ammunition.

Beneš, now in exile in Britain, watched from afar as his country dissolved. When World War II broke out in September 1939, he established a Czechoslovak government-in-exile. He just needed the rest of the world to recognize it. The problem came from the French more than the British. Since there was a rump Slovak state in Bratislava, France questioned whether Beneš actually spoke for all the Czechoslovak people. The French did, however, allow Beneš to reconstitute the Czechoslovak Army on French soil. Hitler provided the impetus to recognize the government-in-exile by invading France. The Czechoslovak Army fought alongside the French in the Battle of France. When Germany won, British Prime Minister Neville Chamberlain was replaced by Winston Churchill. With the French now a government-in-exile as well, Churchill was not particularly concerned about French opinions as to whether Beneš represented all Czechoslovaks. He wasted no time recognizing Beneš as the leader of the official Czechoslovak government-in-exile.

* * *

Reinhard Tristan Eugen Heydrich was a man with an unusual background. He was born in 1904 in Halle, Germany, the son of a composer and opera singer. His grandfather was the director of the Dresden Royal Conservatory. His father founded the Halle Conservatory of Music, Theater, and Teaching. His father was also a German nationalist and enforced patriotism in his sons. Reinhard was musical, academic, and athletic. He was a very good violin player and excelled in science. He was also an expert swimmer and fencer who engaged his brother in mock duels. After World War I, there were clashes in Halle between communists and anti-communists. At the age of fifteen, Reinhard joined a paramilitary Freikorps unit to fight the communists. The ensu-

Cadet Reinhard Heydrich

ing postwar hyperinflation of the Weimar Republic hit his family hard, so in 1922 he joined the German Navy, the Reichsmarine, for the security and the pension.

By all accounts, he did well in the navy and by 1928 was promoted to sub-lieutenant. Arrogant and ambitious, he was notorious for his womanizing. In December 1930 he became involved with Lina von Osten. Lina and her family were Nazi supporters, and she had attended her first Nazi rally the year before. They soon announced their engagement, but there was a problem: Heydrich was already engaged to another woman. When this came to the attention of Admiral Erich Raeder, Heydrich was charged with "conduct unbecoming an officer and a gentleman" and kicked out of the navy in April 1931.

After his formal discharge on May 30, 1931, Heydrich joined the Nazi Party and six weeks later the Schutzstaffel (SS), then an internal party militia. Nazi leader Heinrich Himmler was setting up a counterintelligence division with the SS, and Heydrich was advised to apply. He travelled to Munich for an interview with Himmler. The Nazi leader was so impressed, he hired Heydrich on the spot. The pay was low, but Lina's family supported the Nazi movement, and Heydrich was drawn to its revolutionary and militaristic nature. He started his new job on August 1 and quickly recruited a network of spies and informers to obtain information on political rivals he could use for blackmail and intimidation. In December 1931 Reinhard and Lina married, and he was promoted to the rank of SS-*Sturmbannführer*, equivalent to a major. In 1932 he was made chief of the Nazi security service—the *Sicherheitsdienst* (SD).

The year 1933 proved a pivotal one. Adolf Hitler became Chancellor of Germany and named himself the country's *Führer und Reichskanzler* (leader and chancellor). Heydrich and some of his men from the SD stormed police headquarters in Munich and simply took over the organization by intimidation. Himmler became chief of Police and Heydrich became commander of the Political Police. Hermann Göring founded the Gestapo as a Prussian police force before transferring authority over it to Himmler the following year. Himmler

SS Obergruppenführer Reinhard Heydrich

named Heydrich the head of the Gestapo in April 1934, and it went from a regional police force to an SS instrument of terror. Two months later, the SD—which Heydrich still ran—was declared the official Nazi intelligence service. In just three years, Reinhard Heydrich went from cashiered and disgraced sailor to the head of the country's secret police.

Himmler and Heydrich had greatly increased their power but were faced with a rival—Ernst Röhm. Röhm was one of the founders of the Nazi Party, and he controlled the Sturmabteilung (SA), the party's three-million-man militia. To Hitler, now chancellor of Germany, Röhm and his people were political threats. On Hitler's orders, Heydrich, Himmler, Göring, and another Nazi official, Viktor Lutze, drew up a list of people to be eliminated. On June 30, 1934, Heydrich's Gestapo began arresting people en masse. It would become known as the Night of the Long Knives. Röhm was summarily executed and more than two hundred others were killed as well. Lutze took over the SA and converted it to a sports and training organization. With the SA marginalized, Heydrich increased the Gestapo's power even more. A reorganization of all German police made Himmler the chief of German Police, and Heydrich was named the head of the Security Police (SiPo)—comprised of the Gestapo and the Criminal Police (Kripo). Since he was also the head of the SD, at the age of thirty-two, Reinhard Heydrich was one of the most powerful men in all of Germany.

In early 1938 Hitler was pushing for a merger with Austria, but its chancellor was resisting. Heydrich used the Gestapo to put pressure on the Austrian chancellor by organizing Nazi demonstrations and distributing prounification propaganda. Two months later, Hitler announced the *Anschluss*: the annexation of Austria into his Third Reich. By the end of the year, Hitler's attention had turned to the Jews. At his direction, Heydrich and others organized a pogrom against Jews throughout Germany on the night of November 9, 1938. Heydrich coordinated the use of the SS, Gestapo, SD, uniformed police, SA, and even fire departments. He granted permission for the destruction of Jewish businesses and synagogues. He also ordered the arrest of as many Jews—especially affluent Jews—as could be accommodated in detention centers. Over the next few days, over twenty thousand Jews were sent to concentration camps. Because of all the smashed windows on Jewish businesses and synagogues, the pogrom would go down in history as Kristallnacht—the Night of Broken Glass. It was the start of the Holocaust.

In September 1939 the SD and SiPo (including the Gestapo) were folded into the new Reich Main Security Office, with Heydrich as its chief. With the outbreak of war that same month, Heydrich took on new responsibilities, including the Nacht und Nebel (Night and Fog) decree under which people determined to be a threat to German security were discreetly arrested "under the cover of night and fog"—no notification, no charges, no trials. They simply disappeared without a trace.

After the invasion of Poland, Heydrich created a Gestapo unit to oversee the ethnic cleansing of Poles. With Operation Tannenberg and Intelligenzaktion, some one hundred thousand people were murdered, including over sixty-one thousand scholars, clergy, former military officers, and other members of the Polish intelligentsia. He also formed Einsatzgruppen (task forces) to follow Germany's invading armies, round up Jews, and put them in ghettos. These units later followed the troops into Russia and summarily executed more than two million people. Jews in Bohemia and Moravia were deported to ghettos in Riga and Minsk from which very few returned. Reinhard Heydrich was, by any objective measure, a monster. This was the man who, on September 27, 1941, was named deputy Reich protector of the Protectorate of Bohemia and Moravia.

* * *

The Czechoslovak government-in-exile did not have a set location in London. It had offices scattered throughout the city, with the largest in Fursecroft, a building near Kensington Gardens. Edvard Beneš was worried about the government-in-exile's position vis-à-vis the other allies. On June 22, 1941, Germany launched Operation Barbarossa, the invasion of the Soviet Union. By August 25 the Germans were less than fifty kilometers from Leningrad. By September they had cap-

František Moravec, the head of the Czechoslovak intelligence service

tured Kiev and were driving for Moscow. Prague was even further behind enemy lines. Edvard Beneš called a meeting with František Moravec, the head of the Czechoslovak intelligence service.

"František, I'm glad you're here. We have something important to discuss."

"Of course, Mr. President."

"Let's not stand on formality. Just call me Edvard. The war isn't going well for our side. The Nazis conquer more land and destroy more Russian armies every day. All the while, our homeland grows further and further away from free lands."

František chuckled, "I wouldn't consider the Soviet Union a free land, but I understand your meaning."

"I am concerned that the people of Czechoslovakia are becoming too accustomed to living under the Nazi boot. There's been active resistance in Poland, Greece, Yugoslavia, France, and the Netherlands after their defeats on the battlefield. However, Czechoslovakia has done little. Slovakia has openly sided with the Nazis, and our Czech countrymen have done little to thwart the Nazis. If anything, they are helping by producing war materials for them. At this rate, even if the Allies do eventually win the war, what reason would they have to reestablish a Czechoslovakian state? What have we done to earn it?"

František replied, "That is not entirely fair, Edvard. We have produced plenty of intelligence from our networks in the country. MI6 confided that they are essentially blind in eastern Germany. Were it not for our people, they'd have no insight on the German war industry there."

"You and I both know that intelligence gathering is well and good, but it does not stick in one's mind."

"You mean it doesn't make headlines."

Edvard replied, "Don't sound so crass. We need more than the politicians on our side; we need the public. We need to show them we're deserving of their help. We need to be more proactive. We need to make it politically untenable for them to again—"

"Betray us?"

"Well, yes. Churchill is no Neville Chamberlain, but his primary concern is not the future of a Czechoslovakian state. We need to do something to show the British that we are Allies too. We need to do something that will inspire the Czechoslovak people to resist."

František stroked his chin. "I have an idea. It'll be bold. It'll make headlines, even in Berlin. And I'm confident our British hosts will approve. An assassination."

Edvard chuckled, "Who? Hitler?"

"I wish. That would be too difficult. I've been thinking about this for some time. I was initially going to suggest Karl Hermann Frank."

Beneš snorted, "I would agree with that. He's a traitor. To think that a man I worked with in the Czechoslovak Parliament would become an SS-*Gruppenführer* and be appointed by Hitler as the secretary of state for their Reich Protectorate . . . " He turned to František and smiled. "It would send a message to eliminate the most senior Sudeten German in the government."

"That was my thinking too, initially, but I have reconsidered."

"Oh? Why?"

"Frank is not well known outside of Czechoslovakia. But the *Stellvertretender Reichsprotektor* certainly is."

Beneš was taken aback. "Heydrich? You want to kill Reinhard Heydrich, the director of the Reich Main Security Office?"

"Yes. He is in Prague. We can get to him. If killing the head of the Gestapo doesn't get the Allies' attention, nothing will."

"That would certainly get the attention of Churchill."

"And Hitler and Stalin."

"František, can you pull it off?"

"Not only can we, we must."

"How would you go about it?"

"We have two thousand Czechoslovak soldiers in Britain. We would select two men, one Czech and one Slovak, to represent our unified country."

"Only two?"

"Yes. Less chance of compromise. The British SOE can train them on commando tactics, and the RAF can insert them into Czechoslovakia. They'll contact local resistance units for support. Once in Prague, they will find Heydrich, gather intelligence on his movements and security. Then they strike."

"It would be a suicide mission."

"Perhaps. But the men would know what they're getting into. I'm sure we'd have no shortage of volunteers."

Beneš drew a deep breath. "All right. Let's proceed."

The next day, Moravec met with Brigadier Colin Gubbins, the director of operations at the SOE. He was in charge of the Czech and Polish sections.

Entering Gubbins's office, Moravec gave a slight bow. "Brigadier Gubbins, thank you for meeting me on such short notice."

"Certainly, Mr. Moravec. What can I do for you?"

"We want to propose a resistance action in Prague, one that will harm German command and control, as well as their morale."

Gubbins smiled ever so slightly. The Czechs had been good sources of intelligence, but as yet had taken little direct action against the Germans. "I see. And what did you have in mind?"

"We propose to infiltrate two Czech soldiers into the country outside Prague. There they will make contact with local resistance units who will provide logistics and support for their military mission."

"Which would be what, exactly?"

"Locate and kill Reinhard Heydrich."

Gubbins sat quietly as he digested what he'd just heard. "You propose to assassinate Heydrich, the director of the Reich Main Security Office."

"And the acting protector of Bohemia and Moravia."

"You mean deputy protector, don't you? Konstantin von Neurath is the protector."

"Do you really think that Heydrich takes orders from Konstantin von Neurath? He's a diplomat."

Gubbins smirked. "No, I don't. Heydrich only takes orders from Hitler and Himmler . . . and maybe Göring . . . if he's feeling generous."

"Well, is the target worthy of the effort?"

"Absolutely! Except for the men just mentioned, there is no more worthy a target. Heydrich is Hitler's favorite boy. He is the prototypical Nazi *Wunderkind*. Eliminating that inhuman bastard would poke a rather large hole in the balloon of Nazi's Aryan superiority theory."

"I want to select a group of men from our forces here, have your men train them, and then select the best. But there must be a Czech and a Slav on the mission."

"Yes, of course. Politics what they are. I'll approve it, but we must keep this hush-hush. I don't want word of this leaking. There are spies everywhere. One whiff and they'll pull him back to Berlin. Who in your organization is aware of your plan?"

"Just myself and President Beneš."

"Good. Tell no one else. I worry about Russian spies as much as German ones. On our end, no one will be privy to this beyond my office and the trainers. We'll have to assign it a code name."

"What do you have in mind?"

Gubbins mulled it over for a moment. "Anthropoid. From the Greek, meaning 'having the form of a human.' Heydrich looks like a man but is, in fact, a monster."

Moravec chuckled. "Very approriate and creative."

"The benefit of a classical education." Pouring two whiskeys from his crystal decanter, Gubbins lifted his glass. "To Operation Anthropoid."

* * *

By October 20 František Moravec had gleaned two dozen prospects from the ranks of the exiled Czechoslovak troops. These men were sent to an SOE training center at Arisaig on the west coast of Scotland. The men were put through a rigorous training program while the SOE prepared false German identity and travel documents. Cecil Clarke, an SOE weapons expert, developed a special bomb that was small enough to be thrown but powerful enough to penetrate Heydrich's armored car. Soon the two primary candidates were selected: Warrant Officer Jozef Gabčík, a Slovak, and Staff Sergeant Karel Svoboda, a Czech.

Jozef Gabčík was born in 1912 in the village of Poluvsie in northwest Slovakia, where he worked as a farrier and a blacksmith. He later took a job at a military chemical plant in Žilina before transferring to an army gas storage facility in Trenčín. He didn't accept the new Nazi-aligned

Slovak client state that emerged after the breakup of Czechoslovakia. When the German Wehrmacht took over the gas facility in June 1939, Gabčík sabotaged it and fled to Poland.

Once in Poland, he joined the Czechoslovak Legion, an expatriate military unit being organized to support the Poles. He was transferred to France, where he entered the First Regiment of the French Foreign Legion. Three weeks after Germany invaded Poland, he was drafted into the First Infantry Regiment of the First Czechoslovak Infantry Division in Adge, France. He was promoted to sergeant in December 1939 and was fighting the Germans during the Battle of France by the spring of the following year. After France surrendered, Gabčík evacuated to Great Britain, where he trained as a paratrooper at Cholmondeley Castle in Cheshire. Now a staff sergeant, Jozef was itching to get back into the fight and volunteered without even being told the target. Things were progressing apace when Svoboda was injured in training and had to be replaced.

British Major Alfgar Hesketh-Prichard had just been nominated to head the SOE's Czech section, and he was in charge of the training. "Gabčík, as I am sure you are aware, Staff Sergeant Svoboda sustained a head injury this morning in training."

"Yes, sir. I am aware. Is he going to be alright?"

"The doctors assure me he will . . . in time. But he has been scrubbed from this mission, and we need to select a replacement."

"How will that affect our mission? Our training was almost complete."

"There will be a delay, I'm afraid. We need to get a new man up to speed, and then there is a problem with documents. We will need to have the forgers come up with new ones for him and, I suppose, you too. New dates, forms, and whatnot."

"I understand, sir. Who did you have in mind to replace him?"

"There are several candidates."

"If I may be so bold as to make a suggestion?" The major nodded his consent. "I'd like to recommend Sergeant Jan Kubiš."

"I know him. He's on my short list. You two are mates, are you not?"

"Yes, sir. We both fought in France. Jan earned the Crois de Guerre. He's a fine soldier, and I trust him."

"You speak for him, do you?"

"No, sir. I would not presume, but he'd do it in a minute. He wants to kill Germans as much as I do."

"All right. Send him over."

Kubiš jumped at the opportunity.

Jan Kubiš was born in Dolní Vilémovice, Moravia, where he was a Boy Scout and a member of Orel, a Catholic athletic and youth organization. He was conscripted into the Czechoslovak Army in 1935, serving in an infantry regiment. He was a platoon sergeant during the Czechoslovak mobilization of 1938 and served as a deputy commander of a platoon manning border defenses when the Munich Agreement was signed. After the Sudetenland was ceded to Germany, the army was demobilized, and he was discharged. In June 1939 he was working in a brick factory when he fled Czechoslovakia to Poland to join a Czechoslovak military unit forming there. He was subsequently transferred to Algiers where, like Gabčík, he joined the French Foreign Legion. He fought the Germans in France and fled to Britain after the German victory. He, too, was eager to get back into the war.

* * *

Jan and Jozef had been too keyed up to sleep the night before their insertion. The noise and cold of the Halifax bomber made sleeping during the four-hour flight virtually impossible. Now they were on the ground in their home country for the first time in two years, and they were about to fall asleep where they stood. Jozef checked his watch. "It's 0330 hours. If anyone catches us on the road at this hour, we won't be able to explain it."

Jan pointed to the south. "Well, Nehvizdy is two kilometers that way. I suggest we walk until we reach the outskirts of the village and then find somewhere to get a couple hours sleep." He rubbed his arms and blew into his hands. "Preferably someplace indoors, a barn perhaps."

"Sounds good." The two men walked south until they found a small farm. The house was dark, and there were a couple of outbuildings. One looked to be a small hay barn. Each man managed to get an hour of sleep while the other stood watch. The light of a lamp in a window of the house meant its owner was awake. Time to move on.

Once in Nehvizdy, the men bought a bus ticket to Prague. Fortunately, the clerk didn't question their story of being two workers from Hradrec Králove looking for work in the capital. Once in Prague, they checked into a cheap hotel in the seedy side of town to get some desperately needed sleep. Their plan, of course, took them to Prague, but they had to make contact with their colleagues in the underground, and they were in Pilsen. They took the afternoon train to Pilsen. Although a day behind schedule, they had plenty of time. They finally reached their resistance contact in Pilsen. He, in turn, passed them along to other resistance members in Prague, where planning for the assassination of Heydrich could continue.

Kubiš and Gabčík began collecting information on Heydrich's movements. They identified his house, his office, and the places he frequented. They learned from their contacts in the resistance that Heydrich took the train to Berlin on a fairly regular basis. Jan proposed attacking him there. "If we could catch him on the train, he would have limited avenues of escape. He would be in a first-class compartment with, at most, three bodyguards."

"Yes, if we buy first-class tickets, with luck we'd be in the same car as him. We could simply walk up, open the compartment door and machine gun everyone inside. Then we jump off the train before anyone realizes what's going on. Simple."

Jan nodded. "I like simple. Complex plans have too many chances to go wrong. Before we commit to it, we should buy a ticket on the first train heading to Germany to observe things firsthand."

"Agreed."

The men immediately discovered holes in their plan. The train station was crawling with German soldiers. The invasion of the Soviet

Union was in full swing, and troops were being moved east as fast as the Wehrmacht could load them on trains. This was not the biggest problem though. First, they learned that two first-class cars were reserved for German officials and senior military personnel only. The best they could manage was second class, which was still filled with a lot of lower level officers. The second, and most serious problem, was the Kriminalpolizei, the Criminal Police. They were searching random civilians boarding the trains. Even if they could get second-class seats and make their way past the scores of soldiers and officers in the two or three train cars between them and their quarry, they needed their weapons to kill Heydrich, and there was no guarantee they wouldn't be searched and found out in the station. They had to come up with another plan.

Kubiš and Gabčík continued their surveillance of Heydrich to identify a time and location for the attack, with no luck. It had been three months since Kubiš and Gabčík parachuted in on that cold December night. Both they and their bosses in London were becoming frustrated. Fate intervened on March 28, 1942, when a sabotage team codenamed Out Distance parachuted into Czechoslovakia.

Lt. Adolf Opálka

Out Distance was made up of three men: its commander, Lt. Adolf Opálka, and two Czechoslovak soldiers, Karel Čurda and Ivan Kolarík. Their mission was to sabotage gasworks in Prague, provide clandestine radios to the resistance, and help British bombers navigate to the Škoda Works—a major producer of tanks and artillery for the Nazis. Unfortunately, just like the Anthropoid team, they landed miles from their intended drop zone. Having lost most of their gear and being chased by the Gestapo, they split up. Kolarík lasted only three days. When his cover was blown, he committed suicide on April 1 in a futile

Karel Čurda

attempt to protect his family. Opálka and Čurda went to Prague to join Operation Anthropoid.

They met in a Prague safehouse belonging to a family named Moravec (unrelated to Czech intel chief, František Moravec). Kubiš and Gabčík were already there when Adolf Opálka and Karel Čurda arrived. The men were acquainted with each other from SOE training in Scotland. Jozef shook Adolf's hand. "Lieutenant Opálka, it is good to see you again." Turning to Čurda, he added, "Karel, you look well."

Adolf replied, "Please, let's drop the formalities. We need to get in the habit of calling each other by our first names to avoid any slip-ups in public. So, what's the status of your operation?"

Jozef got serious. "First, about this safe house. The Moravec family has been very generous, but you need to be aware of the situation. Only the mother, Marie, and her son, Ata, are aware of us. Her husband, Alois, is not. We only use this place during the day when he's at work. You cannot come here early in the morning or in the evening. Do you understand?"

"We understand."

"I assume London wants to know why we haven't acted yet."

Adolf assumed a markedly diplomatic tone. "Well, there have been some questions as to your progress."

Jozef smiled. "I'm sure. Heydrich has been surprisingly effective. Within a week of his arrival last year, he declared martial law and promptly executed over 140 people to send a message. Resistance members awaiting trial, mostly. Since then, he has arrested thousands more and executed several hundred. Those not killed were sent to Mauthausen concentration camp. God only knows what happened to them there. Prime Minister Eliáš is among them. People call Heydrich 'the Butcher of Prague.'"

"So we've heard."

"But he also rewards those who fall in line. He raised wages to the same level as those of German workers. He provides food rations and free shoes. He has increased pensions and even gave the workers Saturdays off. He also clamped down on the black marketeers who rob the people. When you balance this against the execution and deportation of any who resist him, you understand why the people remain peaceful and military production has increased. He is a cruel man, but he's also a smart one."

Adolf drew a deep breath. "That makes your mission all the more important, that and—"

"And what?"

"British intelligence sources have reported that Heydrich called a meeting in January, in Wannsee, outside Berlin. We don't know everyone who attended, but it included SS-Gruppenführer Otto Hofmann, the head of the SS Race and Settlement Main Office; Heinrich Müller, head of the Gestapo; Oberführer Schöngarth, the commander of the Political Police and the SD; and others from the Chancellery, Interior and other ministries. At this meeting, they decided on what they called *Endlösung der Judenfrage*, the final solution to the Jewish question. We don't have all the details, but it essentially laid out their plans to murder all the Jews in Europe."

Jozef was stunned. "Oh my God! I knew Heydrich was a bastard, but I had no idea—"

"So you see, it's imperative that we complete this mission."

Jan interjected, "We've been working. We have a great amount of information on his movements and patterns. We were planning to kill him on the train to Berlin, but his security was too good. We couldn't have done it with only two men."

Adolf smiled. "Well, there are five of us now. We just need to find Ivan Kolarík."

Jan was suddenly morose. "Four will have to do. Ivan is dead. He was about to be captured by the Gestapo and killed himself. His family was arrested. That's all we know."

A grim-faced Adolf replied, "Well, then four will have to do."

Jozef said, "We have identified another opportunity to get to Heydrich. I wasn't sure how we might do it just the two of us, but now that you're here, it should be achievable."

"What do you have in mind?"

Jozef spread out a map of Prague on the kitchen table. Pointing to the map, he said, "This is where Heydrich lives, Paneské Brežany. He lives in an estate the Nazis confiscated from Ferdinand Bloch-Bauer, a wealthy Jewish businessman. Heydrich's office is here, in Prague Castle. Every day he has to transit this road here. This two-hundred-meter section just south of the estate is heavily wooded and fairly well traveled . . . during the day."

Adolf smiled. "But not at night?"

"No. The area is very quiet. Plus, the military restricts the area around the estate to protect Heydrich. He's the only one who regularly uses the road after dark. The security details tend to stick to the roads. We've never seen them in the woods."

"So, if we moved through the woods, we could ambush him on the road."

Jozef nodded. "That was my plan, but I needed more men. I figure two men attack the car and one each at either end of the woods to keep any German troops from coming to his aid. After the attack, we slip through the woods to the west and escape in the confusion. Across this field is another road. We leave a car there and drive back to Prague."

Adolf pored over the map. "This plan has merit. How often does Heydrich drive home after dark?"

Jan answered, "At least three or four times a week. He tends to go to work late in the morning and come home in the evening. If he comes in after 1030 hours, he'll probably be working late. That would be our signal to go ahead with the attack."

Adolf turned to Čurda and asked, "Karel, you up for a little action?"

He shrugged, "That's why we came, isn't it?"

"Well, as the senior officer here, I say we proceed."

The next day Adolf and Jozef drove up to Paneské Brežany to get the lay of the land. The woods were thick enough to offer plenty of cover, but not so thick they couldn't escape through them quickly. Near the middle, they found a spot where two large trees encroached on the road. Jozef pointed them out and said, "If we stretch a thick cable across here, he'd have no choice but to stop. When he does, we open up on him. He'll be dead before he knows what happened."

Adolf grinned. "I agree. Let's do it. Tomorrow we start watching for his arrival. The first day he arrives after 1030 hours, we attack that night. Now, let's go back and brief the others. I want a weapons check tonight."

Two days later, Jan Kubiš was reading a newspaper in the square opposite the entrance to Prague Castle when Heydrich's armored Mercedes 320 Cabriolet rumbled by. The top was down with Heydrich in the back seat. Jan checked his watch. It was 10:50.

That night, the four men collected their gear and drove north. Leaving their car on the country road about a kilometer west of the woods, they waited until darkness to cross the field and enter the woods. German soldiers were positioned at the north end of the woods where Havni Road crossed Na Pískách at the southern corner of the estate's grounds. Two other soldiers stood guard near the south end of the woods. They were bored and spent their time talking and smoking cigarettes.

The four commandos crept silently through the woods until they reached the road. Karel Čurda moved south and stopped about fifty meters from the edge of the trees. Jan Kubiš moved north until he was about fifty meters from the crossroads. Adolf Opálka and Jozef Gabčík made their way to the midpoint of the small forest where the two large trees loomed near the road. Jozef stretched a length of thick cable across the road and secured it to the trees. Jozef made sure his Sten submachine gun had a round chambered. Adolf double-checked the heft of the bomb. He wanted to lob it directly into the car if possible.

The men slipped back into the trees to wait. As the night dragged on, Jozef repeatedly checked his watch. One hour. Two hours. Three hours. As the time neared 2300 hours, Adolf crept across the road to Jozef and whispered, "Is he normally this late?"

Jozef shook his head. "No. He is always home by 2200."

"I think we need to abort. Do you concur?"

"Yes. I think we missed him."

"Okay, get Jan. I'll get Karel. We'll meet at the safehouse tomorrow to determine what to do next."

* * *

All the men were disappointed about their failure. No one knew what went wrong; it was clear Heydrich's pattern was not as routine as they'd thought. They could go back and try again, but they risked being detected. Strangers in a small village are quickly noticed. They needed the anonymity of a large city.

Lt. Adolf Opálka arrived at the safehouse with a new man in tow. Jozef Gabčík was concerned until he saw who it was. "Josef Valčík! What are you doing here?"

Lt. Joseph Valčik

Opálka smirked. "I see you already know each other. Valčík was part of—"

"Silver A. We came in on the same insertion flight."

Jan Kubíš asked, "Did you make your drop zone? We were off by 120 kilometers."

Valčík shook his head. "We weren't even that close. Damn British. Well, we're here now. Adolf told me the target is Heydrich. I'd be honored to put a bullet into the brain of that son of a bitch."

Adolf interrupted, "We all would, but back to work. Gentlemen, what's our Plan B?"

Jan stepped forward. "I have a suggestion. Heydrich always comes south on Kirchmayerova Trída and then west on Holešovičkách before crossing the river and heading to the castle. The turn from Kirchmayerova onto Holešovičkách is very, very tight. His driver has to slow down almost to a stop to keep that big Mercedes on the road. I've seen it several times."

Valčík studied the map. "Interesting. A moving target that has to stop."

"And another thing. Now that the weather is nice, he's been traveling with the top of his car down."

Adolf smiled. "What's the point of an armored vehicle if you are going to ride in the open?"

Jan continued. "He's arrogant. He wants to show the world that he's in charge, that he has nothing to fear here."

Jozef sneered, "Arrogant . . . and stupid."

Lt. Opálka took charge. "The way I see it, we can do this with fewer men than the ambush in the woods. There is a tram station near the curve. This will give us an excuse to be loitering. When he slows for the curve, one man opens up with the machine gun, and the other throws the bomb. If we get the bomb into the car . . . " He dragged his finger across his throat.

Jozef stood erect. "I insist that Sergeant Kubiš and I be the two men to make the attack. Operation Anthropoid was our mission. We should be allowed to complete it."

Jan chimed in, "Aye, sir."

Opálka nodded. "Granted. But we need another man. If you're at the tram stop, you won't see him coming, especially if there is a tram there. We need someone to alert you."

Valčík stood up. "I volunteer, sir. I've missed everything so far. I want to do my part."

Turning to Čurda, Opálka asked, "Any objections?" Čurda shrugged and shook his head. "All right, it's yours. Set up about a hundred meters to the north. Make sure Grabčík and Kubiš can see you."

"When the car approaches, I'll take off my hat. That'll be my signal."

Jozef said, "I'll stand over here with the Sten. As the car turns, I should have a direct line of fire at Heydrich. Jan, you stand of the other side and throw your bomb. As soon as it detonates, the people at the tram stop will panic. We use them to cover our escape."

Lt. Opálka stared at the map. "Tomorrow. We will go tomorrow."

* * *

Wednesday, May 27, 1942, was a warm, sunny day. At 1030 hours, Schutzstaffel Obergruppenführer Reinhard Heydrich climbed into his green Mercedes for his drive to work. The man behind the wheel was

SS Oberscharführer Johannes Klein. As was his custom on warm days, the top of the armored car was down. As they drove through the woods south of his estate, he was reading some reports that had been delivered to his home that morning. Production of artillery pieces at the Škoda plant was up. Berlin would be pleased. There was also a letter from Himmler. He and the Führer were so pleased with his pacification of the Czechs, they were contemplating sending him to France to deal with the resistance there—another opportunity to prove his loyalty to the Reich. At thirty-eight years old, he was already one of the most powerful men in the Third Reich. Only Hitler, Himmler, and Göring could be considered true superiors. Joseph Goebbels was just a mouthpiece, and Martin Bormann was a glorified secretary. If Hitler needed something done, he turned to Heydrich—Himmler's Evil Genius, the Butcher of Prague, the Man with the Iron Heart.

Josef Valčík nervously eyed traffic on Kichmayerova třída to his north. He was trying not to stare, but he dared not risk missing Heydrich's approach. Then the green behemoth came rumbling into view. In the back seat he could clearly make out Heydrich in his sharp SS uniform. Turning toward his colleagues, he made sure they were watching him before taking off his hat. The operation was a "go."

By the tram stop, Gabčík and Kubiš looked at each other and nodded. Gabčík had the Sten submachine gun hidden under his raincoat. Kubiš had his bomb concealed in leather briefcase. As the big Mercedes slowed to make the tight turn onto V Holešovičkách, Gabčík dropped his raincoat, raised his weapon, and pulled the trigger. Nothing happened. The gun had jammed!

As his car passed Gabčík, Heydrich saw the submachine gun in his hands. Rather than ordering his driver to speed on, he stood up in the back of the car, drew his Luger pistol from its holster, and yelled at Klein. "Stop the car!"

Klein mashed on the brakes. "Yes, sir. What is it?" Klein turned toward Gabčík, who was desperately trying to clear the jam. Neither Klein nor Heydrich noticed the man directly in front of their car with a briefcase.

Kubiš threw the briefcase with the bomb inside, but his throw was off. Rather than land inside the car, it exploded against the right rear wheel of the armored Mercedes. But, unlike the Sten, Cecil Clarke's bomb worked as designed. Its fragments ripped through the fender of the car, taking

Heidrich's car after the attack

with them shreds of the car's upholstery. Several of the fragments tore into Heydrich's body, breaking a rib and injuring his diaphragm, spleen, and lung.

Kubiš was wounded in the face by shrapnel, as were a few passengers getting off the tram stopped across the street. Heydrich and Klein jumped out of the car with pistols raised. Klein ran toward the stunned Kubiš, while Heydrich, apparently unaware of his injuries, went after Gabčík, who was still holding the useless Sten.

Kubiš recovered his senses, jumped on his bicycle, and pedaled toward the panicked passengers pouring off the tram. He cleared a path by firing his Colt M1903 pistol into the air to scatter the bystanders. Klein took aim at Kubiš with his Luger, but he was still disoriented by the bomb blast. He accidently hit the magazine release, which caused the gun to jam. Kubiš got away.

Heydrich stumbled toward Gabčík. The Slovak commando dropped the Sten and ran for his bicycle. Heydrich started firing at him with his Luger. Gabčík took refuge behind a telegraph pole and returned fire with his Colt. Heydrich now sought cover and slid behind the stalled tram. His injuries finally caught up to him. Heydrich doubled over and stumbled to the side of the road. He collapsed against a railing, barely holding himself up. Klein had given up trying to catch Kubiš and came back to help his boss. As Gabčík started to run, Heydrich pointed at him. "Get that bastard!" Klein set off after Gabčík as Heydrich staggered back to his car and collapsed against the hood.

Gabčík ran into a butcher shop owned by a Herr Brauer. It was no safe haven. Brauer was a Nazi sympathizer and his brother worked for the Gestapo. "Help me, sir! Please. A Nazi soldier is trying to kill me!"

Brauer said nothing. Instead he ran out the door of his shop and starting jumping up and down while pointing to the door. "In here! The man is in here! Come quick!"

Klein sprinted toward the shop. His gun was in his hand, but it was still jammed. As he ran headlong into the butcher shop, he collided with Gabčík. His Colt in his hand, Gabčík shot Klein twice in the leg. He fled the shop, jumped on a tram, and headed for a safehouse. Gabčík and Kubiš fled the scene believing they'd failed yet again to kill the Blonde Butcher.

While Klein chased after Gabčík, a local woman and an off-duty policeman tried to help Heydrich. They flagged down a delivery van. They put him in the cab; the bumping of the truck caused him serious pain, so they moved him to the back. He lay on his stomach as the van drove him up the street to Bulovka Hospital. Once there, Dr. Slanina packed his chest wound while Dr. Diek, the chief of surgery, tried to remove the splinters of shrapnel. Professor Hollbaum, the chairman of surgery at Charles University, was called in to operate on Heydrich, with Diek and Slanina assisting. They managed to reinflate his collapsed left lung, stitched his torn diaphragm, and removed part of a broken rib. Heydrich's spleen was damaged by a grenade fragment, with pieces of upholstery blown into his body by the blast. It couldn't be saved, so they performed a splenectomy.

When Heinrich Himmler learned of the attack, he dispatched his personal physician, Dr. Karl Gebhardt, who arrived from Berlin that evening. The next day, all local physicians were dismissed and SS doctors took over his care. Fearing infection, Hitler's personal physician, Dr. Theodor Morell, suggested giving Heydrich sulfanilamide, a new antibacterial drug. Gebhardt believed Heydrich was on the mend and declined. He developed a fever and was in significant pain, but his recovery appeared to be progressing normally. On June 2 Himmler visited Heydrich in the hospital. During the visit, a fatalistic Heydrich quoted a line from one of his father's operas. "The world is just a barrel-organ which the Lord God turns himself. We all have to dance to the tune which is already on the drum."

The next day, Heydrich was sitting up eating lunch when he suddenly collapsed. He went into shock before slipping into a coma. He died the next day without regaining consciousness. He had died of sepsis.

* * *

Hitler's response to Heydrich's assassination was swift. As retribution, he wanted to execute ten thousand Czechs, but Himmler objected. He feared such indiscriminate slaughter would negatively impact military industrial output in the region. Hitler also blamed Heydrich and his arrogance, noting, "Such heroic gestures as driving in an open, unarmored vehicle or walking about the streets unguarded are just damned stupidity, which serves the Fatherland not one whit. That a man as irreplaceable as Heydrich should expose himself to unnecessary danger, I can only condemn as stupid and idiotic." That, however, would not stop him from punishing the Czechs. More than thirteen thousand people were arrested and upwards of five thousand murdered by the Nazis. Among those killed were Jan Kubiš's girlfriend and Adolf Opálaks's aunt and father.

The Nazis wanted still more revenge. German intelligence falsely linked the commandos to the village of Lidice, northwest of Prague, and suggested the assassins were hiding there. On June 9, 1942, the Nazis committed the Lidice Massacre, in which 199 men over the age of fifteen were executed, 195 women were sent to Ravensbrück concentration camp, and 95 children were taken prisoner. Of the children, eight were adopted by German families; eighty-one others were sent to Chelmno extermination camp, where they were gassed to death. Lidice was burned and the ruins leveled with explosives. Two weeks later, in another village, Ležáky, a radio transmitter from the Silver A team was discovered. The Nazis murdered all the men and women in the village and burned it to the ground. Of the thirteen children seized, two were selected for "Germanization" while the rest were sent to Chelmno and gassed.

The assassins were not in Lidice or Ležáky, and the Gestapo had no leads. So far, the Operation Anthropoid team had evaded capture. Right after the attack, the commandos took shelter with two families in Prague before hiding in the Karel Boromejsky Church, also known as the Sts. Cyril and Methodius Cathedral. The Nazis issued a June 18 deadline. If they were not captured by then, they promised many more Czechs would die. To add a carrot to the stick, the Nazis also offered a reward of 1 million Reichsmarks for information on the team's whereabouts. The bounty proved the fatal blow. Tempted by greed, Karel Čurda, the saboteur from the Out Distance team, turned himself in to the Gestapo. In exchange for the bounty, he provided the names of the commandos' local contacts.

Čurda gave up several safe houses—homes of people who risked their lives to safeguard his. On Jun 17 at 5:00 a.m., the Gestapo raided the Moravec home. The family stood in the hall as the Gestapo searched the apartment. Marie Moravec stood calmly as the men traipsed in and out of her home. Her furniture and possessions were smashed. Stopping an officer, she asked, "Excuse me, sir. May I go to the toilet? It is just at the end of the hall."

He sneered at her but said, "I'll allow it." He motioned to a soldier. "Watch her."

"Thank you, sir." She glanced at her son, Ata, as she walked by. Her husband, Alois, was frozen with fear and confusion. He had no clue why they were there, but then, they didn't really need a reason.

Marie walked into the bathroom and closed the door behind her. She took out the cyanide capsule hidden in the hem of her skirt. She paused briefly, looking at herself in the mirror one last time before placing the capsule on her tongue. She whispered, "I am sorry, Alois," and bit down. The bitter taste of the cyanide and the faint smell of almonds were her last two sensations. She collapsed on the floor, dead.

The thud of her body falling on the tiled surface drew the soldiers' attention. When the guard opened the door, she was foaming at the mouth, but her blank eyes told him she was dead. The officer-in-charge was furious. "You imbeciles! All you had to do was watch three people! And you couldn't even manage to do that without screwing it up? I should have you transferred to Russia."

"I'm sorry, Obersturmführer. I just let her go to the toilet. She was searched but must have had the poison concealed on her person," the young officer pleaded.

"Take the other two to headquarters. Search them thoroughly first! Take the woman's corpse too. If you fuck that up, you'll be the one facing interrogation!"

Alois and his son, Ata, were taken to Petschek Palace, a large building the Gestapo had commandeered as its local headquarters. Alois was tortured. He would certainly have talked—if he knew anything. He was unaware that his wife and son were part of the resistance. The seventeen-year-old Ata was also tortured, but bravely refused to talk. The Gestapo plied him with brandy and when he was drunk, they continued the questioning. "Where are the terrorists that you and your family aided? Your mother killing herself has proven your family's complicity. Innocent people don't do that."

"I don't know what you are talking about. And if I did, I wouldn't tell you." The Gestapo man slapped Ata hard across the face and blood flew from his mouth.

"Perhaps this will change your attitude." He motioned to the soldier manning the door. A few moments later, a soldier entered holding a fish tank. He placed it on the wooden table in front of Ata. Inside was Marie's severed head. Ata Moravec winced and tried to turn away. The interrogator stood behind him, grabbed his face with both hands, and made him look at his mother's bloody head. "If you don't tell me what I want, your father's head will be sitting next to your mother's. Need I remind you that we also have your fiancée and your uncle in custody?" Turning to the soldier, he quipped, "We may need a bigger fish tank."

"Okay, okay. I'll tell you. The men are hiding in a church."

"Which church?"

"Sts. Cyril and Methodius."

* * *

The next morning, June 18, 1942, the Czechoslovak commandos were eating a breakfast of tea, bread, and cheese in the crypt under Sts. Cyril and Methodius Cathedral, about a kilometer southeast of Reinhard Heydrich's office in Prague. Their group had grown, adding three more orphaned commandos. Jaroslav Švarc was injured when he parachuted in and lost contact with the rest of his team in early April. Josef Bublík and Jan Hruby were part of the Operation Bioscop sabotage team but lost their equipment. All three men had made contact with Adolf Opálka in Prague.

Two of the men, Opálka and Bublík, were in the prayer loft to keep an eye on the street below. Suddenly, the people walking on the street started to scurry away. Opálka quickly learned why. A German armored car screeched to a halt in front of the church. Behind it were trucks full of SS soldiers under the command of Waffenn-SS Gruppenführer Karl von Treuenfeld, Reinhard Heydrich's deputy. In total, he brought 750 troops to deal with the commandos.

The commandos scrambled for their weapons. They were horribly outmanned—7 versus 750—and equally outgunned. The commandos were armed only with pistols, while the SS had machine guns and hand grenades. Despite this, the commandos put up a valiant defense. Opálka and Bublík, commanding the high ground in the prayer loft, held the Nazis at bay until they were overwhelmed and killed. The men in the crypt held out longer. The basement crypt was built like a pillbox. Attempts to force entry into the crypt failed, even after tear gas was used in an attempt to make the

Window of the Church of Saints Cyril and Methodius in Prague, where Reinhard's attackers were cornered

commandos quit their bunker. Finally, the Prague fire department was brought in to use its hoses to flood the crypt. After a two-hour siege, the SS finally forced their way into the crypt only to discover all the commandos, save one, had killed themselves rather than surrender. Jan Kubiš was found severely wounded and unconscious. He died before he could be questioned. All the commandos were dead. The traitor, Čruda, confirmed their identities.

Bishop Gorazd of Prague took blame for the actions in the church in an attempt to minimize German reprisals against his parishioners. It didn't work. He was arrested on June 27 and tortured. The Nazis then arrested all the priests at the church, along with the lay leaders. On September 4, they were all taken to the Kobylisy Shooting Range outside Prague and shot. They were only a few of the over 550 people executed there after Heydrich's assassination.

Karel Čruda did not escape justice in the end. He married a German woman and continued to collaborate with the Gestapo until the end of the war. His treason was not forgotten, and after the war, he was tracked down and arrested. During his trial, he was asked how he could betray his fellow soldiers. His response was, "I think you would have done the same for one million marks." He was found guilty of treason and hanged on April 29, 1947.

The Aftermath

Few would argue that Reinhard Heydrich didn't deserve to die. He was a man of exceptional cruelty with no regard for human life. From his involvement in the Night of the Long Knives, Kristallnacht; the *Nacht und Nebel* (Night and Fog) murders; the establishment of the death camps; the ethnic cleansing of the Poles; the organization of Einsatzgruppen, who followed the Wehrmacht troops and murdered millions of Jews; to his formalization of the Final Solution of the Jewish Question at the Wannsee Conference, Heydrich was personally responsible for millions of deaths. Had he survived the war, he most assuredly would have been tried at Nuremburg and executed for his uncountable crimes against humanity.

But did his death achieve the goals the Czechoslovak government-in-exile was seeking? That is a more difficult question to answer. For the Czechoslovakia government-in-exile, the mission was considered a success in that Heydrich was killed and, more importantly, it demonstrated to the British and the other Allies that Czechoslovakia was still a functioning political entity and an effective member of the alliance. It went a long way to ensuring that Czechoslovakia would remain a country after the war rather than being broken up and distributed among its neighbors. However, it came at a horrible cost in lives. The scale of the German reprisals shocked even hardened strategists. That may well explain why Operation Anthropoid was the only successful government-executed assassination of a high-level Nazi.

The brutal treatment of the Czechoslovak people at the hands of the Germans, especially after the assassination of Heydrich, helped gain support for the forceable expulsion of ethnic Germans from historical Czechoslovak lands after the war. There were many justifications provided for this—the desire to create an ethnically homogeneous country, the view that a German minority would be disruptive, and punishment for German atrocities. Whatever the reason, the officially sanctioned expulsion of German civilians from Czechoslovak lands was at times brutal. When the war ended, there were an estimated 4.5 million Germans in Bohemia and Moravia, many of whom were refugees from Poland and Slovakia. From May to August 1945, seven hundred thousand to eight hundred thousand ethnic Germans were forcefully expelled from Czechoslovakia in what were called "wild expulsions." Hundreds were killed by vengeful Czechoslovaks. The policy was later formalized under the Potsdam agreements, and from January to October 1946, about three million Germans were expelled to the American and Russian zones of a partitioned Germany. While the actual numbers are disputed, estimates of the number of German civilians who died during the expulsions ranged from 15,000 to 273,000 people.

One of Edvard Beneš's objectives was to maintain the geographical integrity of Czechoslovakia, and in this he was largely successful. The Sudetenland, the border regions ceded to Germany as a result of the infamous Munich Agreement of 1938, were returned to Czechoslovakia with its ethnic German population deported. Areas ceded to Poland and Hungary were also returned. The one exception was Carpathian

Ruthenia, a region on the extreme eastern end of the country. The USSR occupied that land, and Stalin wanted to annex it into the Ukrainian Soviet Socialist Republic. Not being in a position to argue, Czechoslovakia formally ceded it to the USSR in 1945.

The goal Beneš did not achieve was the reestablishment of a liberal democratic government. Czechoslovakia was firmly inside the Soviet-controlled zone of Europe when the war ended. Beneš was president of a reunited Czechoslovakia and was willing to work with the Soviets. In the 1946 parliamentary election, the Communist Party of Czechoslovakia won in the Czech areas while in Slovakia, the conservative Democratic Party won 62 percent of the vote. Beneš invited the communists, with 38 percent of the total vote, to form a government. This only lasted until February 1948, when the communists took over the whole country in a coup d'état. Beneš was forced out in June. His health already failing, Beneš was devastated to see everything he'd worked for washed away by a communist flood. Edvard Beneš, the man who worked so hard for Czechoslovakia's survival during the darkest days of World War II, died at his home on September 3, 1948, just seven months after the death of the liberal democratic government.

Czechoslovakia finally regained its freedom in 1989 after a bloodless revolution—the Velvet Revolution. The country changed its name to the Czech and Slovak Federative Republic, but there were ongoing tensions between the Czech and Slovak halves. In July 1992 the Slovak parliament voted for a declaration of independence, and the leaders agreed to dissolve Czechoslovakia as of December 31, 1992. Like their escape from Soviet dominance, the dissolution was entirely peaceful—the Velvet Divorce. Beneš's dream of a free and democratic Czechoslovakia was simply not to be.

Chapter 9

Nathuram Godse and Mahatma Gandhi

—Killing the Popular Guy Usually Doesn't Work Out for You

On January 13, 1948, Mahatma Gandhi announced a "hunger strike until death." It certainly wasn't his first, but it would be his last. This one was to protest the Indian government's decision to withhold monies due their neighbor and rival, Pakistan, per the partition agreement that dictated the terms of the dissolution of British India. Gandhi was India's most famous and most revered figure, and the person most responsible for India finally throwing off the shackles of the British Raj, the British colonial government dating back to 1858. Gandhi was born Mohandas Karamchand Gandhi in 1869 in Porbandar, India. After going to law school in London, he worked most of his life for human rights and freedom—first in South Africa and then in India. Mahatma was an honorific meaning

Mahatma Ghandi (1931)

"venerable" and a name he'd been using for thirty-four years. Now seventy-eight years old, he was trying to make peace between warring India and Pakistan, but not everyone agreed with his goals or his methods.

Nathuram Godse was waiting impatiently for his friend and fellow Hindu nationalist Narayan Apte to arrive. Apte had served in the British military during World War II but now was a teacher and managed a small newspaper on the side. The two men were together when they learned of the hunger strike. It was the final straw. India and Pakistan had gone through a bloody and violent separation less than a year before. Between ten and twenty million people were displaced and nearly two million killed in the ensuing chaos. Just a few weeks after its independence, Pakistan invaded India in an effort to wrest the princely state of Jammu and Kashmir from its neighbor. As a result, India withheld final monies due Pakistan under the conditions of the partition. Gandhi insisted the Indian government give Pakistan the money. To many Hindu nationalists, like Godse and Apte, this was a betrayal of Gandhi's own people.

As Apte approached, Godse grabbed him by the sleeve and led him into a dank alleyway just off the crowded New Delhi street. The air was thick with the smell of pungent spices, garbage, automobile exhaust, and raw sewage. "Did you get it, Narayan?"

Apte cautiously looked over his shoulder before reaching into his jacket and removing a small semiautomatic pistol from his waistband. "Yes. It's a Beretta. Model 1934, just like you asked for. Personally, I think we should have purchased a Webley. Revolvers are more reliable."

"But also harder to conceal. No, the Beretta will do nicely. Its .380 caliber ammunition is sufficient for the task, and it holds what? Seven bullets?"

"Eight if you have one in the chamber."

"What else did you find?"

Apte smiled. "I acquired two British hand grenades."

"Really? From where?"

"Digambar. He has friends in the military. It wasn't difficult."

Godse inquired, "Did they ask you why he wanted them?"

"No. They knew better. They're loyal RSS members. They just came off the line in Kashmir. They have no love for those supporting our enemies." RSS stood for Rashtriya Swayamsevak Sangh, the National Volunteer Organization, a militant Hindu nationalist organization.

"Okay, good. Where are they?"

"I hid them at my mother's house. If I get caught with a gun, I'll explain it's for self-defense. They'd believe that after all the riots. But hand grenades? That'd be a tough sell."

Godse laughed. "I'd think so." Suddenly more serious, he asked, "Narayan, do you think the government will acquiesce to Gandhi's demands over the funding?"

"I certainly hope not, but I have no confidence. Gandhi has too much influence among the people. They cannot afford to anger them."

Godse grimaced. "It's not right that one unelected man has so much power. He ignores the well-being of his own people while bending over backward to appease the Muslims."

Apte nodded. "Pakistan is an abomination. Gandhi speaks out against Hindu nationalism in a Hindu nation while Jinnah and the Muslim League openly declare Pakistan an Islamic State. We have to respect the Muslims, but they don't have to respect us. We should declare ourselves a Hindu nation, regardless of what Gandhi says."

"I agree. We're on the path to do just that."

"Nathuram, we need to speak to the others. We need to learn all about Gandhi's comings and goings. We need to track his movements, identify his entourage, his bodyguards. We need to know when and where to strike."

* * *

India had a complicated history. The British established their rule, the British Raj, over India in 1858, but they were not alone. The French and Portuguese also had enclaves on the Indian Subcontinent, and there were a number of independent princely states that were, more or less, subservient to the British Crown. The area was vast and included the modern-day countries of India, Pakistan, Bangladesh, Sri Lanka, Burma—some 390 million souls.

During World War II, the Indian National Congress, or Congress Party, led by Gandhi and Jawaharlal Nehru, offered its support to the British against the Germans in exchange for independence after the war. When the British rejected the proposal, without consulting Nehru, Gandhi publicly demanded the British leave India in his "Quit India" speech. This landed him, Nehru, and most of the Congress Party's working committee in prison until near the end of the war. In the meantime, the Muslim League, led by Muhammad Ali Jinnah, took advantage of the power vacuum and expanded its influence.

Prime Minister Jawaharlal Nehru (1947)

Gandhi's nonviolent protests and civil disobedience picked up again after the war. Sectarian tensions increased, and Great Britain, broke and exhausted by World War II, threw up its hands. India would finally get its independence in 1948. The Hindu-Muslim rivalry only got worse. There were violent riots throughout the country, and thousands died. The British were ill-equipped to deal with it, so they moved up the independence date. In June 1947, various nationalist leaders representing the Congress Party, the Muslim League, the Untouchable community, and the Sikhs agreed to partition the country along religious lines. Gandhi's vision of a united, multiethnic, and multireligious India was officially dead.

The creation of Pakistan from the Muslim-majority eastern and western reaches of Greater India left millions of people—Hindus, Sikhs, and Muslims alike—on the wrong side of the new national boundaries. While estimates vary, upwards of twenty million people moved from India to Pakistan or Pakistan to India. The mass migration was accompanied by extreme sectarian violence that neither fledgling government was prepared to handle. There are no exact figures, but estimates of the dead run as high as two million people. The worst of the violence occurred in Punjab, a region split in the partition. Almost no Muslims survived in East Punjab, and virtually no Sikh or Hindu was left alive in West Punjab. India and Pakistan were irrevocably separated.

* * *

Nathuram Vinayak Godse had a very unusual childhood. His father, Vinayak Godse, worked for the post office. Nathuram was born in Baramati near Bombay. At birth, he was named Ramachandra after the seventh avatar of Vishnu, a major deity in Hinduism. Prior to his birth, his parents had four children—three boys and a girl. All three boys died in infancy. His parents feared they were the subject of a curse that targeted their male children. To protect young Ramachandra,

Nathuram Godse

they raised him as a girl for the first few years of his life. He was even made to wear a *nath*, or girl's nose ring. Because of this, he earned the nickname "Nathuram," which means "ram with a nose ring." It wasn't until his younger brother was born that his parents were convinced the "curse" had been lifted and finally start raising him as a boy.

He attended local school in Baramati and then was sent to live with his aunt in Pune to study at an English-language school. Godse lost interest in education and dropped out of high school in the mid-1920s. He became very active in Hindu nationalist groups, including the RSS and the Hindu Mahasabha, a Hinduist political party. Hindu Mahasabha's stated mission was to protect the rights of Hindus, and it was formed in response to the creation of the All India Muslim League.

Despite not finishing high school, Godse was quite learned. He worked as an editor and journalist, wrote articles for various newspapers, and translated Hindi-language books into English. After having a falling out with a leader of the RSS over credit for a translation, in 1942 he started his own political organization, Hindu Rashtra Dal, but still maintained his membership in RSS and Hindu Mahasabha. Through it all, Godse described himself as a great admirer of Mahatma Gandhi for his lifelong fight against the British colonialists and the great personal sacrifices he made in pursuit of it. Godse, like most Indians, grew up considering Gandhi a national hero.

* * *

Gandhi's January 1948 hunger strike to compel the Indian government to release funds to Pakistan was the last straw for Godse and his nationalist cohorts. Given that India and Pakistan were engaged in a border war over Jammu and Kashmir at the time, to them this was the moral equivalent of a British politician insisting Churchill send money to Hitler during the Blitz. It was the latest in a series of statements and missteps from Gandhi they believed undermined Hindus.

In 1942 when Gandhi's "Quit India" campaign resulted in him and most of the senior Congress Party officials being locked up by the British, this provided substantial political advantage for the rival Muslim League. Muhammad Ali Jinnah, the head of the Muslim League, was an ally of Gandhi and Nehru when it came to the opposition of British rule, but they differed dramatically on the question of partition. Jinnah had long advocated forming an independent Islamic nation from India's Muslim majority regions in the east and west. With Gandhi and Nehru in jail, Jinnah alone had the ear of the British authorities. When the time came, he won the debate.

Godse and the other Hindu nationalists blamed Gandhi and the Congress Party for not acting to stop the slaughter of Hindu and Sikh minorities in West and East Pakistan. Gandhi in particular was faulted for not vigorously protesting the atrocities but instead resorting to fasts.

After the partition, there were calls within Pakistan to declare it an Islamic nation. Likewise, there was a push among Hindu nationalists for

India to proclaim itself a Hindu nation. Gandhi, though a Hindu himself, opposed this. He wanted India to remain secular and multicultural. Demographic realities were also a factor. Even after the partition, India had thirty-five million Muslim citizens within its borders. Add to that almost seven million Sikhs and over eight million Christians, and India already was a multireligious entity in both fact and name. In an attempt to appeal to Muslims, Gandhi publicly read verses from the Koran in Hindu temples despite protests from the congregants who considered it sacrilegious. Even secular Hindus criticized Gandhi's deference to the Muslims, noting he never read passages from the Gita in a mosque "in the teeth of Muslim opposition."

When the Indian government reversed its decision to withhold final payment to Pakistan per Gandhi's urging, many nationalists thought this was proof Gandhi had too much sway over the government, to the detriment of the public at large. Given his history, his moral standing, and the respect and admiration he garnered from Indians at all levels, the Hindu nationalists were convinced this would remain the case as long as he lived. Though he was the most admired man in India and much of the world, if the country was ever going to be responsive to its people, Mahatma Gandhi had to die. India would never become a Hindu state while he lived.

* * *

Nathuram Godse and Narayan Apte were part of a small group of men determined to carry out their plot. Vinayak Savarkar was another RSS member and a lawyer from Mumbai. At sixty-five, he was the oldest member of the group and the most educated. He had a long history of Hindu activism and had been the president of Hindu Mahasabha during the war.

Others included Gopal Godse, Nathuram's

Vinayak Savarkar

brother nine years his junior. He was an RSS member and worked with the Hindu Mahasabha. He joined the military during the war and served in Iraq and Iran. After the war he opened a shop and got married, but witnessing the riots during partition made him very nationalistic. Digambar Badge was a weapons merchant. Shankar Kistayya pulled a rickshaw and worked for Badge as a domestic servant. Dattatraya Parchure worked for the medical service. Vishnu Karkare had been an orphan on the streets and now did odd jobs at hotels.

Group photo of accused of Mahatma Gandhi assassination. Standing: Shankar Kistayya, Gopal Godse, Madanlal Pahwa, Digambar Badge Seated: Narayan Apte, Vinayak D. Savarkar, Nathuram Godse, Vishnu Karkare

Madanlal Pahwa was an unemployed former British soldier. He lived in West Punjab before migrating to India during the partition. This odd collection of men had one thing in common—they were all militant Hindu nationalists.

They met on January 17 at an empty flat in New Delhi to come up with a plan. Savarkar called the meeting to order. "All right, gentlemen. As you all know by now, the parliament backed down and agreed to give money to Pakistan. Can you believe it? In the middle of a war, these Congress Party fools give money to the ones we're fighting! Cowards and traitors, every one of them!"

Pahwa added, "They're afraid that if Gandhi dies, they'll be blamed for it."

Karkare asked, "How? He's starving himself. They didn't make him do it."

Nathuram Godse smirked. "Do you think the people will make that distinction? If their beloved Mahatma dies, someone must take blame, and politicians don't have the backbone. That is why it falls to us."

Apte nodded. "Nathuram is correct. The only ones who can save India are those willing to risk their lives for it."

Giving a salute to his fellow ex-soldier, Pahwa added, "Narayan speaks the truth. Anyone can wear a uniform, but few actually fight."

Savarkar interjected, "Back to the matter at hand. We need information on Gandhi's movements. We need to know where he goes. When he goes there. Who he goes with. Is there someplace he goes routinely? Somewhere we'll know he will be?"

Apte responded, "I was surveilling him before his hunger strike announcement. He's staying at the Balmiki Temple."

Pahwa asked, "The one near Gole Market in the north of the city?"

"Yes, he was holding regular prayer meetings there. That might work, but there are always a lot of people around. I'd rather not hurt innocent Hindus."

Nathuram nodded. "I agree." As soon as he said this, Shankar Kistayya, the rickshaw puller, interrupted.

"Uh, not anymore. I was there this morning. He isn't there anymore. The government requisitioned the temple to use as a shelter for refugees. He moved to Birla House."

Savarkar snorted, "Birla House! I've been there. It's a mansion. It's in the south, near the diplomatic section. Man of the people, huh?"

Kistayya shrugged. "He just lives in a couple of plain rooms attached to the main house."

Savarkar huffed, "Are you defending him now?"

"No, just stating the facts. Besides, that's good news for us. If he were living in a palace with guards and staff, it would be harder for us."

Nathuram Godse said, "Shankar is right. It would be hard if he were in the main house. Regardless, we need to confirm all this information. Who else is living with him? I assume his wife, but who else? Also, does he still lead prayers in the afternoon? If so, where? Being near the diplomatic section, I doubt many common people are around him. That'd be good."

Apte interjected, "Yeah, but being near the diplomatic section might mean more police or even soldiers to protect the foreigners."

"Well, that's what we need to find out. Shankar, go there tomorrow in your rickshaw. See what you can find out. Set up across the street and just watch."

"I can do that. If anyone tries to hire me, I'll tell them I'm being paid to wait for a wealthy client. It happens all the time. I'll take notes."

Nathuram smiled. "Good. We need someone to inquire about the prayer sessions."

Digambar Badge raised his hand. "I'll do it, but I need someone else with me. I will keep them talking while the other looks around."

Dattatraya volunteered. "I'll go. I can use my medical ID if we are questioned by the police. I will tell them I am there to drop off test results or something."

Nathuram stood. "Good. The rest of you go to the neighborhood. Talk to shopkeepers, gardeners, anyone you can find. Learn whatever you can. We'll meet back here tomorrow night at seven o'clock."

The next night, the conspirators met again. Savarkar started the meeting. "Okay, gentlemen. What did we learn?"

Kistayya spoke first. "I parked my rickshaw on Albuquerque Road, across from the mansion. There is an open courtyard in front of the house, but I never saw him out there. There is a road just southeast of the house that looks like it goes to the back. I didn't walk down it, though. I didn't want to leave my rickshaw unattended."

Digambar Badge chimed in. "We got down that road, Dattatraya and me. There were a lot of people using it to get to the gardens behind the house. That's where Gandhi holds his prayer meetings. The road provides access to a couple of the mansions back there, but it is wide open. There's no wall or fence between the road and the lawn behind Birla House."

Nathuram asked, "What about security? Any police or soldiers back there?"

"None that we observed. There were a few men back there who I think were part of his entourage. If they were security, they were doing a poor job. No one was searched or scrutinized in any way."

Savarkar smiled broadly. "Then that'll be our way in. We'll be waiting for him when he comes out of the house. Now, how to do it? We have a gun and the hand grenades. Digambar, can you get us more guns?"

He shrugged. "Sure. All I need is a day or two."

Nathuram Godse interjected. "Why wait? We had one pistol and the grenades. That should be sufficient to kill one feeble old man."

Savarkar shook his head. "No. I don't want to hurt innocent Hindus. Bad politics."

Nathuram replied, "Okay, I agree. How about this. One man throws his grenade away from the crowd. The explosion should cause a panic but no injuries. When the people run away, Gandhi will be alone. After his hunger strike, he'll be too weak to run very fast. We throw the second grenade straight at him."

Savarkar rubbed his chin. "That should work. And we then escape in the confusion." Looking to the group he asked, "Who is willing to throw the grenades?"

Madanlal Pahwa raised his hand. "I was in the British army. I know how to use them."

"Good. Thank you. Who else?"

The men looked at each other awkwardly. Nathuram said sheepishly, "Uh, I've never used one. Neither has my brother."

Digambar Badge stepped up. "I'll do it. I'm no soldier, but I'm familiar with weapons. That's my trade, after all."

Savarkar nodded. "All right then, we have our men. We may need a couple more people in the crowd, just in case. They can help Madanlal and Digambar escape by pointing out others as the attackers and sending the police in the wrong direction."

Vishnu Karkare raised his hand. "I'll do it."

Nathuram Godse said, "I'll go too."

"All right," Savarkar said, "We'll do it tomorrow. Apte, retrieve the grenades and give them to Madanlal and Digambar as soon as we leave."

* * *

On January 20, 1948, at four o'clock in the afternoon, the men made their way to Birla House. Blending in with the crowd of people who had come to listen to Gandhi, they made their way into the garden behind the house. There were a couple hundred people there—plenty to cover their escape. Gandhi moved onto a raised platform on the lawn and started his prayers. Madanlal Pahwa moved to the back of the crowd. Everyone was fixated on Gandhi.

Pahwa removed the grenade from his jacket and tucked it in next to his belly. After one last quick glance around, he pulled the pin and threw the grenade far behind him. A couple of seconds later, there was a large explosion. A cloud of white smoke rose, and dirt and grass rained down on the audience. People started screaming. Many ran for the Birla House, others toward the road to the south. As predicted, Gandhi was left alone on the speaker's platform.

Digambar Badge had worked his way to the front of the crowd. When Pahwa's grenade exploded, it startled him, but he didn't run. He kept his eyes fixed on Gandhi. The frail old man was surprised by the explosion, but rather than flee, he just stood there with a confused look on his face. Badge took his grenade from his jacket pocket, put his left index finger through the metal ring attached to the grenade pin, and . . . froze. He lost his nerve. His hands started shaking. He quickly removed his finger from the ring and stuffed the grenade back into his pocket.

Nathuram Godse was about fifteen meters away looking at Badge, waiting for him to act. He was shocked when Badge put the grenade in his pocket and followed the screaming crowd out of the yard at a run. He turned back to where Gandhi was standing. By now, security officers from inside the house had sprinted to him. They grabbed him by his arms and hustled him toward the safety of the house. Their opportunity had passed. Nathuram turned and followed the mass of people out toward Albuquerque Road.

Madanlal Pahwa did not run away. Inexplicably, he stayed where he stood when he threw the grenade. Someone pointed him out to a policeman, and he was arrested without incident.

* * *

The remaining conspirators fled the scene. They didn't want to risk being picked up by the local police. Later that evening, they met back at the apartment. Savarkar wasn't there. He'd returned to Bombay the day before the attack, confident his comrades would see it through. When Apte got there, he was furious. "What the hell happened? It's all over the radio that someone tried to kill Gandhi with an explosive. Tried and failed! What happened?"

Nathuram spoke, "I'm not sure. Madanlal threw his grenade toward the back of the lawn. No one was there, but it made a huge noise. People started screaming and running. As we expected, Gandhi was left on the speaker's dais all alone."

"So why is he still alive? Did Digambar's grenade fail to explode? Was it a dud?"

Nathuram replied, "He didn't throw it. I was watching him. He had it in his hand and was ready to pull the pin when he just put it back in his pocket and left."

"Left? What do you mean he just left?"

"I mean, he just left. I started to follow him, but I lost him in the crowd. I assumed he'd be here." The men looked around at each other. It was only then they realized Badge wasn't among them.

Apte then said, "Pahwa isn't here either. Where is he?"

Vishnu Karkare had been sitting quietly in the corner but now spoke up. "He got arrested."

"Arrested? How?"

"I was closest to him. Like Godse said, he threw his grenade, and it started a panic. He was at the back. I don't think anyone saw him do it, but he just stood there! He never ran away. Maybe he was waiting for Badge to act; for whatever reason, he just stood there. Someone pointed him out to the police, and they grabbed him. He didn't even put up a fight." As he said this, the door opened. It was Digambar Badge. All eyes were on him.

Badge said sheepishly, "Did everyone get out okay?"

Gopal Godse barked, "No. Pahwa was arrested. What happened? Why didn't you throw your grenade? You had the perfect opportunity."

Badge looked down at his feet. "I was going to. I had it out and ready but—"

"But what? My brother said you were right there."

"I . . . I was afraid I would injure some of the bystanders. Some were very close to Gandhi. You said we didn't want to hurt any innocent people, remember?"

Nathuram snapped, "That's bullshit. I was there. Gandhi was all alone. The only one near him was you! You were afraid, you coward."

"No! That's not true. I . . . I—" Gopal and Apte shut him up with just a look.

Nathuram took a deep breath. Tempers were flaring, and he didn't want his comrades distracted. "Gentlemen, we must take our friend at his word. Regardless, it is all water under the bridge now. We have a bigger problem. Pahwa is in the hands of the police. If he talked, the police might be on their way here as we speak. We must leave and never come back to this place. I also recommend those who can find different accommodations not return home. Savarkar is safely in Bombay, so he has an alibi. I have another apartment where we can meet. It's above a hardware store behind the railway station parcel office. There is no number, but it is on the second floor with a red door. If there's a newspaper sticking out from under the door, it means it is safe to enter. We will meet there in four days from tonight."

Vishnu asked, "And what then?"

"We'll need an alternative plan. We still must do what has to be done."

* * *

Over the ensuing couple of days, Nathuram and his brother Gopal had taken it upon themselves to return to Birla House. To their surprise, there was little in the way of increased security. There were two additional policemen posted out in front of the mansion, but the road leading back to the garden area was still unguarded. Just two days after the assassination attempt, crowds were again gathering to hear Gandhi speak as before. Could it really be that easy?"

On January 24, the conspirators—minus Madanlal Pahwa and Vinayak Savarkar—met to plan their next steps. The others were surprised when Godse told him what they had learned. "Only two extra policemen? Are you sure?" asked Apte.

"That's all we saw. We walked back to the garden with the pilgrims. We got right in."

"Did you see Gandhi?"

"No. We left before he came out. I was afraid I'd be recognized from the other day. I didn't want to risk it."

Apte mused, "They probably had guards in the crowd, mingling with the people. We need to find out for sure. That house is huge. They could be hiding a battalion of soldiers in there. We need to conduct a thorough reconnaissance. I can't believe they would be so lax in their security so soon after an attack."

Nathuram queried, "What do you recommend?"

"We watch the mansion. If they have increased security, they'll be working in shifts. We need to learn when they come, when they go, and how many there are. Policemen work regular schedules. If we observe the early morning and late afternoon, we should catch their shift change. That will tell us a lot."

"Narayan, that makes sense. I leave it to you to devise a schedule. How much time do you need?"

"Well, today is Saturday. The weekend shift might be different. If we surveil the house for say, four weekdays, we should have a good idea of the security situation by next Thursday."

Nathuram smiled. "Okay. That's the plan. You schedule the men. We'll meet again on Thursday evening, back here."

Gopal asked, "What about Pahwa? What if he talks?"

Nathuram replied, "This place is safe. Pahwa was never here. I don't believe he has talked. If he had, the police would have raided Savarkar's law offices by now. I spoke to him this morning. No raid has taken place. Regardless, everyone needs to lay low until we're done. We meet back here Thursday night. That's January 29."

* * *

The next Thursday, the men met again. When they compared notes, they didn't believe their good fortune. Despite their very public and very noisy failed assassination attempt, Gandhi's entourage had made no major changes to his security profile. There were a few more armed guards, but no fencing or barriers to control the crowds. People entering the area were not searched.

Apte beamed. "Well, they are foolish. We will take full advantage of that."

Nathuram Godse interrupted. "Pahwa was a brave soldier and believes in our mission but is certainly being interrogated. No one can hold out indefinitely. We need to strike immediately."

"Agreed. Any ideas?"

Nathuram replied, "Yes, Narayan. I take the Beretta, go to the Birla House, walk up to him, and shoot him."

"You'll have little chance of escape."

"I know. I'm prepared to sacrifice myself for this noble cause. The future of our country, of our people, requires sacrifice. The secularists must be defeated. India will never be a Hindu nation so long as the Mahatma lives."

"When will you do it?"

Godse replied, "Tomorrow."

* * *

On Friday, January 30, 1948, Nathuram Godse prepared himself. He got up, ate breakfast, and put on a pair of clean blue trousers, a white shirt, and a loose khaki jacket. He double-checked the Beretta. The gun was loaded with a round in the chamber. He placed it in his coat pocket. The gun was not large or particularly heavy, but to him it was like a brick. All there was to do now was wait.

He had mixed emotions about his mission. Like most Indians, he was always a great admirer of Gandhi. It was unlikely Great Britain would've given up the British Raj so peacefully or so soon had it not been for Gandhi's tireless efforts. His strict adherence to the principle of nonviolence cast the British colonialists in a terrible light when they responded to peaceful protests with batons and bullets. World opinion was squarely on Gandhi's side, and the British couldn't counter it. As invaluable as Gandhi was to Indian independence, he was now an impediment to the establishment of a Hindu Rashtra, a Hindu nation. Godse and his friends wanted India to return to that time when only Hindus ruled the subcontinent, the time before the Muslim invasion of 1206 and the establishment of the Delhi Sultanate. They were convinced the only person standing in their way was Gandhi.

A little before 5:00 p.m., Nathuram Godse arrived at Birla House. He walked down the small road southeast of the mansion toward the gardens in the back. Before entering, he scanned the area to identify any additional security. There were a few men with guns milling around—obviously armed security—but they were not particularly attentive, especially considering the assassination attempt only ten days earlier. He casually walked back into the garden amid the other people who'd come to attend the prayer meeting. There were fewer people this time, maybe because it was Friday, or maybe the hand grenade attack ten days earlier had frightened them away. He worked his way closer to the house. He checked his watch—4:55 p.m. The prayer meeting was scheduled to begin promptly at five o'clock.

Minutes ticked by and no Gandhi. He checked his watch again—5:05. Gandhi was late. Was the meeting canceled? Unbeknown to Godse, Gandhi was in the house meeting with Sardar Patel, the deputy prime minister. Their meeting ran late. As Gandhi left the meeting at 5:10, his secretary stopped him. "Mahatma, there are two leaders from Kathiawar who want to meet you."

Gandhi paused and said, "Tell them that if I remain alive, they can talk to me after the prayer on my walk." His little joke would prove prophetic.

As he walked toward the back of the house, he was joined by two young women—his great niece, Manuben Gandhi, on his right and his adopted daughter, Abhaben Chatterjee, on his left. He held onto them as if to steady himself as he walked. Walking up the stairs from the house to the garden, a man in the crowd said, "Gandhi, you are late." Gandhi turned and gave the man a look of irritation. As they reached the top of the steps, a solidly built man in khakis forced his way through the crowd and bowed in front of Gandhi with his hands folded. Manuben, who was carrying Gandhi's spittoon, notebook, and rosary, assumed the man wanted to touch Gandhi's feet. She pushed him out of the way and scolded, "Bapu is already ten minutes late, why do you embarrass him?" The man was Nathuram Godse.

Godse pushed the slight, eighteen-year-old girl aside with ease. She lost her balance, and the items fell from her hands. When she bent down to pick them up, there were four loud shots. Peering through a cloud of white smoke, she turned to her great uncle. He was on the ground lying in Abhaden's lap. He had been shot. Gandhi was struck three times in the abdomen and was bleeding profusely. Blood sprayed over the women's white clothes.

The crowd was standing in shock, and Godse made no attempt to flee. No one moved for several seconds until Herbert Reiner Jr., a young American diplomat and World War II navy veteran, grabbed Godse by his shoulders. When he did, the crowd was snapped back to reality. An Indian Air Force officer grabbled Godse's gun. A handful of people went to Gandhi, while others attacked Godse. Reiner shoved Godse toward some policemen who took him into custody.

Gandhi lay on the ground bleeding. His hands were folded across his torso. According to Manuben, he said, "Hey Ram . . . ! Hey Ram . . . !" He was scooped up and carried back to the house. There was no doctor present, so an aid called the local hospital, reaching no one. Someone drove to the nearest hospital in search of a doctor. Manuben, Abhaben, and others read the Gita over Gandhi's body until a military officer entered the room and pronounced him dead at 5:40 p.m. Mahatma Gandhi was dead.

* * *

Nathuram Godse was arrested. His coconspirators were arrested soon after; all were members of Hindu Mahasabha. Godse readily admitted killing Gandhi and explained his motives in a lengthy statement to the police. He believed the massacres of Hindus and Sikhs that occurred during the partition would have been avoided if Gandhi and the Indian government had acted more forcefully. He also claimed Gandhi believed only he had a monopoly on the truth, that he alone could judge what was right or wrong, and that the suffering of Hindus was not important to him. Gandhi exploited the tolerance of Hindus for the benefit of Muslims. Nathuram further claimed Gandhi's stance regarding the payments to Pakistan and the government's acquiescence to his wishes were proof that Gandhi wielded entirely too much influence over the government and its policies. Only killing Gandhi would free the government to pursue the true interests of the nation.

The trial started in late May 1948 and lasted eight months. The prosecution called 149 witnesses. The defense called none. The presiding judge, Justice Atma Charan, gave his verdict on February 10, 1949. Eight men were convicted in the murder conspiracy. Vinayak Savarkar, the oldest member of the cabal and the man many believed was the ringleader, was acquitted due to lack of evidence and released. Nathuram Godse and Narayan Apte were sentenced to death. The other six men were sentenced to life in prison.

All the men appealed their convictions except Nathuram Godse. He accepted his murder conviction and sentence. However, he did appeal his conspiracy conviction. He claimed there was no conspiracy and he acted alone. After their unsuccessful appeals, the death sentences for Godse and Apte were reaffirmed on November 8, 1949. Gandhi's two sons, Manilal and Ramdas, asked that the sentences be

The trial at the Special Court in Red Fort Delhi on May 27, 1948. Front row, left to right: Nathuram Godse, Narayan Apte, and Vishnu Karkare. Seated behind, left to right: Digambar Badge, Shankar Kistayya, Viniyak Savarkar, Gopal Godse and Dattatraya Parchure.

commuted in accordance with their father's belief in nonviolence, but their pleas were rejected by Prime Minister Nehru. They were hanged six days later. Apte died instantly. His neck snapped when he was dropped. Godse was not so fortunate. The hangman apparently miscalculated the drop. Godse's neck did not break, and it took him fifteen minutes to strangle to death.

Aftermath

The death of Mohandas Karamchand "Mahatma" Gandhi was mourned the world over by friends and foes alike. When he lived in South Africa from 1893 through 1914, he faced discrimination that steeled his desire to fight for civil rights. His opponent in that struggle was Field Marshall Jan Smuts, the former prime minister of South Africa. After Gandhi's death, Smuts said, "Gandhi was one of the great men of my time and my acquaintance with him over a period of more than thirty years has only deepened my high respect for him however much we differed in our views and methods. A prince among men has passed away and we grieve with India in her irreparable loss."

Nobel Prize winning scientist Albert Einstein wrote the following:

He died as the victim of his own principles, the principle of non-violence. He died because in time of disorder and general irritation in his country, he refused armed protection for himself. It was his unshakable belief that the use of force is an evil in itself, that therefore it must be avoided by those who are striving for supreme justice to his belief. With his belief in his heart and mind, he has led a great nation on to its liberation. He has demonstrated that a powerful human following can be assembled not only through the cunning game of the usual political maneuvers and trickery but through the cogent example of a morally superior conduct of life. The admiration for Mahatma Gandhi in all countries of the world rests on that recognition.

Over a million people joined the procession that took Gandhi's body from Birla House to Raj Ghat, the site of his cremation, and another million lined the streets as it passed. His body was placed on a converted weapons carrier modified with a high floor so the people might see him.

Gandhi's funeral procession

Out of respect, the vehicle was not driven, but pulled by four long ropes manned by fifty people each. It took five hours to make the four-mile trip.

For the Hindu nationalists, the assassination was a disaster. Prime Minister Jawaharlal Nehru was now the face of India. He used the incident to solidify public support behind the government, a government with the Congress Party in firm control. Nehru harnessed the outpouring of public grief and called on citizens of all religions to honor not only Gandhi's ideals but also his policies of secularism and inclusion.

The crackdown on Hindu nationalism was swift. Rastriya Swayamsevak Sangh, the RSS to which Godse belonged, was banned five days after the assassination, and many of its leaders were arrested. While the organization's active participation in the plot was never proven and its leaders acquitted of all charges, Deputy Prime Minister Patel noted, "RSS men expressed joy and distributed sweets after Gandhi's death." This type of behavior certainly did not win them many friends among Gandhi's millions of supporters. The ban was lifted a year and a half later, after the group's leader swore an oath to the Constitution of India.

All of the conspirators had been members of Hindu Mahasabha, a rival political party to Indian National Congress. Vinayak Savarkar had been the president of Hindu Mahasabha in the 1940s and opposed Gandhi's "Quit India" movement. Although the party is still in existence, it has never held more than four seats in the Lok Sabha, India's 543-seat lower house of parliament. It continues to espouse policies that can only be described as radical. In 2015 its vice president called for the forced sterilization of India's Muslims and Christians. That same year, its general secretary claimed it was not illegal to attack a church, describing churches as "conversion factories."

While the cause of Hindu nationalism was severely hindered by the assassination of Mahatma Gandhi, it was not irradicated. In 1998, fifty years after Gandhi's death, the Bharatiya Janata Party (BJP), became the ruling political party in India. The BJP traces its origins back to the RSS and is widely considered the political arm of the RSS. The BJP held the leadership position from 1998 to 2004, and again from 2014 to 2021, at the time of this writing.

No one can say definitively if Hindu nationalism would have taken hold sooner had Gandhi not died. At the time of his assassination, Gandhi was already seventy-eight years old, and it's unlikely he would have lived a great deal longer. Had he died of natural causes, the Congress Party wouldn't have had the opportunity to use his murder to solidify its political power, a power uncontested in India for fifty years. Nehru built a family dynasty, but one punctuated by tragedy. He served as prime minister from 1947 until his death in 1964. He was succeeded as prime minister by his daughter, Indira Gandhi, who served from 1966 to 1977, and again from 1980 until her assassination in 1984 by Sikh nationalists. She was succeeded by her son, Rajiv Gandhi, until his death by assassination in 1991.